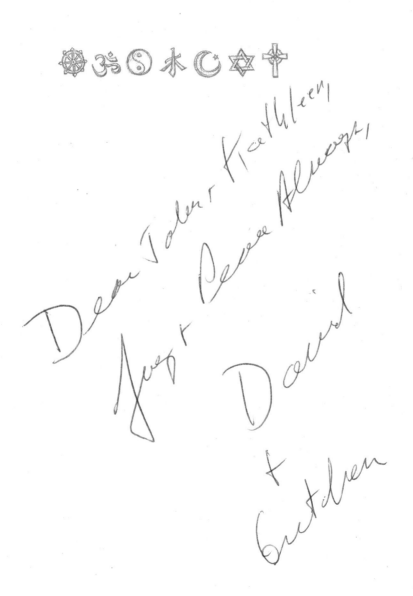

Dear John Kathleen

Just Peace Always,

David
& Gretchen

Acclaim for
What God Really Wants You to Know

"Lundberg presents inspirational principles from sacred texts in a wondrous and ingenious way. He gives greater meaning to what we think we already understand, further deepening and clarifying what we need most—a sense of oneness and promise and peace. Every place of worship would do well to have a copy of this book. Open it to any page and you will soon realize that the God of others and your God are one and the same. This book proves, whether you believe in God or not, that God believes in you."

— **Lewis M. Randa, Founder/Director, The Peace Abbey**

"Lundberg's work draws from all major religions the universal principles that transcend religious boundaries and expose our shared spiritual heritage. It is a rich compilation of fundamental truths that are applied to all areas of personal living and outline a path to peace and unity among all people. He brings our focus back to our true identity and our oneness as brothers and sisters in the one family of God."

— **Rev. Carl Showalter, Pastor, Spiritual Awareness Fellowship of Chicago; founder of Quantum Living Institute**

"*What God Really Wants You to Know* is a devastating refutation of those dark spirits who claim that world religions are hopelessly different. Differences there are--and they should be celebrated. But Lundberg here shows how close the world faiths are on the core issues of mercy, forgiveness, repentance, honesty, patience — in fact, all the great moral teachings of every religion are undeniably present in all the rest.
A splendid achievement."

— **Dr. Tim Winter, Faculty of Divinity, University of Cambridge**

"A gift to our fragmented world, this thoughtful reference guide for all spiritual leaders and seekers provides the incentives and the substance for reconciliation. Lundberg creates a bridge to higher consciousness by drawing forth universal spiritual principles and illuminating both our divine oneness and uniqueness. This book is a treasure to keep close at hand— a rich and inspiring resource in understanding our spiritual relationship to one another."

— Alberta Fredricksen, author of *Resumé of a Disciple — Stepping Up Spiritually,* Consultant, Certified Spiritual Life Coach, Minister, Educator

"David Lundberg distills the spiritual essence of seven major religions with examples from sacred and other writings that often reach exalted levels of literary expression. Despite historical, creedal, and philosophical differences, world religions do in fact bear remarkable similarities. The author's premise that varied religious traditions intuit the same knowledge of God should encourage devotees of every faith in their quest. The usefulness of this innovative book is enhanced by easy-to-follow presentation, extensive suggestions for further reading, and a detailed index. What a great resource for preachers and all seekers!"

— Ruth Hoppin, author of *Priscilla's Letter: Finding the Author of the Epistle to the Hebrews*

"I was fascinated by this thought-provoking, well-documented study of the world's major religions and their insights into universal truths. This captivating work provides a rich perspective of principles that support our spiritual journey and confirms that we are truly all one with each other. For all of us who are on a path that seeks understanding and diverse viewpoints, this book is invaluable."

— Cyndie Koopsen, RN, MBA, HN-BC, co-author of *Spirituality, Health, and Healing,* co-CEO of Allegra Learning Solutions, LLC

"Truly a wonderful gift to humanity! Mr. Lundberg has carefully researched and documented the truth of the perspective that I have intuitively felt: the various religions across the world all point to the same conclusion, which is even more relevant and important given that, in recent years, various groups with their own political agendas have promoted so much division among humans. This book is truly a breath of fresh air and a shining and loving light to illuminate the darkness. God bless you, Mr. Lundberg!"

— Dr. John A. Healy, Ph.D., Clinical Psychologist

"Religious polarization and intolerance threaten our peace and prosperity. David Lundberg identifies thirty-three basic values shared by seven world religions, giving us the opportunity to understand that all have the same common messages to mankind. It is up to us to try to bridge the gaps between cultures and religions, and this book will help us. It allows us to hope for and work toward a better world tomorrow than the one we live in today."

— Mobeen Khaja; President, Association of Progressive Muslims of Canada

"Lundberg highlights the universal themes behind all perennial wisdom teachings, gently reminding us that it is because of their very universality that these teachings have withstood the test of time. We have arrived in an era in which all faiths are enjoined to treat one another with harmony and respect. This is no longer a luxury but a necessity for global survival. Today we need heart-centered consciousness, which is unconditional love and acceptance of all faiths in their infinite diversity. We are the eyes and ears of a God who experiences itself through an infinite possibility of perspectives. By embodying the rules for loving living as the author suggests, we can rise to the call of being true custodians of divine love on the planet, as we honor it inside ourselves and embrace it within others. This book is based on love. It brings to the reader a sense of wellness and a light to the heart."

— Joy Leo, MA Buddhism, spiritual counselor, author, Buddhist-life coach

"That the world religions, while differing from one another, mediate the same truths about divinity and the human vocation is demonstrated in this book by the collection of beautiful quotations gathered from diverse religious traditions."

— Dr. Gregory Baum, Professor Emeritus, McGill University

"I am passionate about what David has set forth in this book. I believe that in our current global environment it is imperative that we focus on our commonalities rather than our differences."

— Andrew J. Blumenschein, International Event Facilitator and Lecturer

"Lundberg's research enlightens us to the reality that among the great religions of the world there is only disparity within the intricacy of the teachings, but little difference in the message. The magnanimity and sincerity he shows toward all the major religions will make this a most treasured addition to your library."

— Don Bergeron, BA Sociology, MS Community Health Administration

What **GOD** *Really* Wants **You** to Know

God's Universal Truths
Shared by All World Religions

C. David Lundberg

What GOD Really Wants You to Know
God's Universal Truths Shared by All World Religions
Copyright © 2009 by C. David Lundberg

HEAVENLIGHT PRESS
P. O. Box 8313
New Fairfield, CT 06812-8313

www.whatgodreallywants.com

Cover design: Cypress House / Mike Brechner
Cover concept: C. David Lundberg
Interior illustrations: David Martine

Excerpts from the Tanakh reprinted from
Tanakh: The Holy Scriptures, © 1985, published by
The Jewish Publication Society with the permission of the publisher.

Excerpts from *Tao Teh Ching* translated by
John C. H. Wu, © 1961 by St. John's University Press, New York.
Reprinted by arrangement with
Shambhala Publications, Inc., Boston, www.shambhala.com.

PUBLISHER'S CATALOGING-IN-PUBLICATION DATA

Lundberg, C. David.
What God really wants you to know : God's universal truths shared
by all world religions / C. David Lundberg. -- 1st ed. -- New Fairfield,
CT : Heavenlight Press, 2008.
p. ; cm.
ISBN: 978-0-9796308-0-4
Includes bibliographical references and index.
1. Spiritual life. 2. Truth--Religious aspects. 3. Religion and
ethics. I. Title.
BL624 .L86 2008
204.4--dc22 0803   2007940469

PRINTED IN CANADA
2 4 6 8 9 7 5 3 1

Dedication

This book is dedicated to God's One Divine Family living on Earth, in the hope that it will make a contribution to a greater understanding of ultimate reality and our divinity in the Family of God. Let God's Light, Love, Wisdom, and Power flow through every reader of these universal truths, creating a higher level of consciousness of God's many wonderful blessings.

Acknowledgments

What God Really Wants You to Know benefited from a terrific team of helpers. Special thanks go to the following for their efforts:

Linda Czaplinski, Kevin Javillonar, David Martine, Cynthia Frank, Joe Shaw, Sal Glynn, Peter Bowerman, Patricia Spadaro, Nigel Yorwerth, Susan Colleen Browne, Joel Whitsell, Lou Ann Nelson, Christine Barrere, Laren Bright, Ellen Reid, John Kremer, Penny Sansevieri, Robin Bartlett, William Star, and Jeanne Glynn. Each of your unique contributions helped to produce a significantly better work.

Eric, Joan, Ted, and Nancy Lundberg also provided additional encouragement and editorial feedback which is greatly appreciated. This work certainly would not exist without the help of my "angel" wife, Gretchen, who acted as the overall project assistant and provided excellent editorial suggestions.

Finally, I am grateful to God for the inspiration to gather these universal Divine Truths together, and for His guidance to show how fulfilling and loving life can be.

Our Divine Identity

THERE IS ONE UNDERLYING CAUSE for the sufferings of mankind through the ages — the majority of men and women have suffered from an identity crisis. We have forgotten who we really are.

Every world religion says that God is within you and that you have unlimited potential to be fully conscious of God and experience God's unlimited love, wisdom, and power. You are a child of God, a unique spiritual aspect of awareness. You are spirit, temporarily inhabiting a physical form.

This book is for active seekers of spiritual truth. It contains thirty-three universal truths comprising a code, or philosophy, shared by all major religions.

The truth of your divinity is simple and powerful. What is important is that you accept what rings true in your heart. Contemplate these teachings, apply what you feel and know is right, and grow in divine love, wisdom, and power.

Contents

Author's Prayer

In 2004, at the beginning stages of this project, I felt it was important to write this prayer, which was given at regular intervals during the creation of the book.

Beloved Father,

Help me to gather up my years of research and experiences and bring them together into a work that is acceptable to Thee and mankind. Let truth prevail. Let our hearts and minds be opened to Thy sacred keys for right living. Let all see these universal simple rules for right living, to simplify life and enjoy our divine nature as Your sons and daughters. Let us find our inner peace and fulfillment as co-creators with Thee.

Let this book raise the level of understanding among us. Let its truths be so self-evident that no one will ever again consider that their religion is the only "right" one. Let the quarreling and unnecessary suffering fade away. Let us establish a higher foundation of understanding that can make possible the creation of a new Golden Age of peace, prosperity, and divine attunement.

Guide me, Father, every step of the way. Let this book appeal to the hearts of all who have ever sensed how foolish and how wrong it is for men to fight each other in Thy Name. Let this book clearly demonstrate our oneness, our brotherhood, and our mutual love of Thy great self in each one. Let peace, blessings, and illumination radiate from every page of this text. May Thy Light expose the darkness. May the simple way common in all sacred texts shine forth.

Thank you and I accept it done in this hour.

Amen

What **GOD** *Really* Wants **You** to Know

Introduction

It is only natural that God would give to us simple universal prin-
ciples for living life, which if followed, would lead to peace, fulfill-
ment, and joy.

It is only natural that these laws could be found commonly held
within the sacred texts of the world's major religions.

It is only natural that a simple philosophy of love holds these prin-
ciples together.

It is only natural that we should embrace these truths and enjoy
their supreme, eternal benefits.

IN 2004, A SURVEY CONDUCTED by Harris Interactive revealed
that 69 percent of American adults believe that religious differences are the biggest roadblock to the attainment of world peace.
Mankind has been focusing on the *differences* of the various religions far more than on *what they have in common.* This effectively
blocks the powerful realization of divine truth that can yield divine
love, wisdom, and power for personal and planetary freedom.

Over thousands of years, countless cultures have developed
around the world, formed by their various situations, needs, and
experiences. Different beliefs, priorities, ways of thinking, and religions emerged from each culture. Yet the differences in our religions were never meant to fuel hatred and wars, and breed discord

1

and violence. The differences in religions only make life, love, and God easier for each culture to understand and assimilate.

Ramakrishna (1836-1886), an Indian holy man, said the following:

God has made different religions to suit different aspirations, times, and countries. All doctrines are only so many paths; but a path is by no means God Himself. Indeed, one can reach God if one follows any of the paths with whole-hearted devotion. One may eat a cake with icing either straight or sidewise. It will taste sweet either way....

As one can ascend to the top of a house by means of a ladder or a bamboo or a staircase or a rope, so diverse are the ways and means to approach God, and every religion in the world shows one of these ways....

People in ignorance say, "My religion is the only one, my religion is the best." But when a heart is illumined by true knowledge, it knows that above all these wars of sects and sectarians presides the one indivisible, eternal, all-knowing bliss.

As a mother, in nursing her sick children, gives rice and curry to one, and sago arrowroot to another, and bread and butter to a third, so the Lord has laid out different paths for different people suitable for their natures.

The Sayings of Sri Ramakrishna

While seeming differences exist among the world's great traditions, their most important principles are, in fact, universal. They can be found within every one of the great religions. This book presents the simple and positive principles of life shared by *all* the world's major religions. These truths can bring us together instead of driving us apart. They comprise a foundation of knowledge that God has consistently given to us. By focusing on this set of comprehensive and guiding truths rather than our far-less-important differences, we can transcend the hatred, ignorance, and greed that have caused so much of our past destruction.

The first goal of this book is to identify and extract those universal principles that are common to all seven major religions and found in their scriptures. I have organized over 800 quotations from their sacred texts into thirty-three such principles. The book's second goal is to reveal the simple philosophy that takes shape from those principles, the philosophy that can lead us to a path of wisdom, love, and unity.

To travel that path, we need to embrace the true understanding of life's purpose, who we really are, and who and what is God (addressed in part I, which presents the first eleven principles). We also need to understand and apply the essential responsibilities required for living a joyous, peaceful, and loving life (addressed in part II, which presents the remaining twenty-two principles). Finally, we can benefit from a simple philosophy that ties our understanding and essential responsibilities together (part III).

Sometimes it can be surprising to remember that we are spiritual beings, temporarily inhabiting a physical form. We are, in reality, spirit, and spirit is *mystical.* Webster's Dictionary defines "mystical" as:

1a: having a spiritual meaning or reality that is neither apparent to the senses nor obvious to the intelligence. b: involving or having the nature of an individual's direct subjective communion with God or ultimate reality.
— Webster's Ninth New Collegiate Dictionary

Each of the seven world religions covered in this book have an inner mystical aspect as well as a more traditional aspect. *Christianity* has its Gnostic works, including teachings dating back to and before the time of Jesus. *Islam* has Sufism. (Another beautiful religion, Sikhism, is based in part on Islam and Hinduism).

Judaism has the Kabbalah. *Buddhism* has Zen and other offshoots of the original Buddhism. *Hinduism* has a huge volume and range of teachings that cover all aspects of mystical as well as more traditional concepts. *Taoism* and *Confucianism* each have several aspects that incorporate teachings from other traditional and mystical disciplines. It is a joy to study these and the many other beautiful religions of the world. They all contain at least some aspect of every principle presented in this work.

Because of the common perception that the religions are so different from one another, I felt that it was important, and long overdue, to see the common truths located and emphasized within the more orthodox interpretations of these religions. So I have chosen the more traditional sacred texts of seven of the world's religions to illustrate and confirm the universality of these principles (a complete source listing and source notes are included at the end of the book). For many of the religions, it would have been easier to document these truths using the texts of their inner mystical teachings cited above. I felt, however, that locating quotations within the traditional texts confirming these principles would contribute far more to reversing the misperception about religions being so different. I wanted to demonstrate that even the orthodox/traditional teachings of each religion contain the truth of our mystical divine Oneness.

The importance of the powerful universal truths comprising *What God Really Wants You to Know* has been significantly hidden within the sacred texts by a vast amount of information of secondary importance. The secondary issues within the various texts certainly have value in providing important background information, including biographical and historical facts. They also contain ritual practices and laws designed for a particular culture. The universal principles have also been hidden by mistranslations and even occasional purposeful distortions to fit less-than-divine personal agendas of those in power during the translations and selections for the sacred texts. Excessive or unnecessarily complex language can also add to the confusion. Nevertheless, the truths are there in all their liberating power.

I have always felt the need to search for the answers to the fundamental questions of life. What influenced me, in part, was being raised in a family that runs a successful inspirational publishing company (still going strong for over sixty-five years), focusing on the power of prayer and faith. During grade school summers I worked at the publishing company as well as for several years after graduating college.

As a youth I regularly attended a Christian church, and was an acolyte and a choir member for many years. I have always loved Jesus. Approximately forty years ago, however, while in my teens, I realized that my many unanswered questions could only be answered if I searched beyond the traditional teachings of Christianity. Today, I consider myself a Christian — yet also to a large extent a Hindu, Buddhist, Muslim — really a friend and fellow member of *all* religions. Like a growing number of people, I see myself as a trans-religious seeker, an aspect of spirit who seeks and loves spiritual truth wherever it is found.

My search has included research into Christian texts that were excluded from the Bible as well as the traditional and esoteric texts of other world religions, memberships and study within several spiritual and religious organizations, training in and practicing spiritual counseling, meditation and prayer on the principles God has given to us within the world's religions, and travel to more fully experience other religious and spiritual practices. I've also had many powerful spiritual experiences, including the strong guidance to write and compile this book. These promptings have been so strong that there seemed absolutely no choice in the matter — I *had* to write this book. I do not believe that the world can have true peace until the common universal principles have been firmly established.

We stand at a crucial time in human history. Our planet continues to experience large-scale suffering, including starvation, disease, terrorism, war, and hatred. Now, in the twenty-first century, we also have the technological ability to destroy life and civilization as we know it. We have reached an important fork in our evolutionary road. Which path will we choose: our divine evolution or much needless suffering?

When applied, the wisdom and eternal truth of the concepts outlined in this book will enable you to:

* Have more love, fulfillment, and meaning in your life.
* Enjoy new levels of joy and peace.
* Take command and control of your life.
* Improve your relationships.
* Rediscover a zest for living.
* Improve your ability to succeed in any area of life.

Whether you follow a recognized religion, participate in a less traditional spiritual practice, or pursue the spirit of your own heart, I believe this beautiful collection of spiritual teachings can empower you to choose the path of peace and live with greater inspiration, strength, and wisdom.

About the Book

There are thirty-three chapters in the first two parts of the book, one chapter being devoted to each principle. At least two quotations from a sacred text of each religion are presented to illustrate the principle, for an absolute minimum of fourteen quotations in each chapter. For several of the more important or complex principles, I have included more than two quotations from each religion to provide additional understanding or emphasis.

My focus has been to allow the hundreds of quotations from the scriptures to speak directly and strongly to the reader through the meaning behind the words and between the lines. To that end, I have kept my commentary to a minimum within the chapters, locating it instead in the other sections of the book. It was necessary, however, to have a greater amount of commentary in the first five chapters, especially chapters 4 and 5, because of the diversity of views over our true identity.

I start each chapter of the book with Christian quotations to illustrate that chapter's principle, because Christianity has been the primary religion of the United States and other English-speaking countries. Islam, one of the three "Western/Abrahamic religions" that consist of Judaism, Christianity, and Islam, and the youngest religion of the seven, is presented next. It is presented after Christianity for ease of comparison of the two and because of the current state of tensions between Christian and Muslim nations and groups. Of course, these conflicts also involve Judaism, which is presented next. Hinduism, the oldest religion, follows. Next are Buddhist quotations, allowing for easy comparison to Hinduism. Taoism and Confucianism round out the seven world religions.

Some of the selected quotations incorporate concepts that go beyond the principle being illustrated. There is a significant degree of overlap between some of the varying principles. Also, because certain key quotations illustrate more than one point, a few quotations have been used a second time in different chapters.

Although my primary source for the Jewish quotations was the Tanakh translation of the *Jewish Study Bible*, I did take the liberty of using some quotations from the Old Testament of the *King James Bible* instead, as that translation better illustrated certain principles.

The principles are organized to facilitate understanding as well as to illustrate their relationship to the other principles and how they fit into a general philosophy of life. The first two parts of the book are broken down into the following sections:

Part I: The Understanding

The first eleven chapters present the first eleven principles.

Section I: The Meaning and Purpose of Life
The three principles that form part of the overall simple philosophy of life that God has given us. Chapter 3, about our responsibilities in life, refers to the twenty-two essentials for loving living that comprise part II of the book.

Section II: Who We Really Are
The two principles about our true identity.

Section III: Who and What God Is
The six principles about God. These principles are also additional qualities about the potential within each one of us.

Part II: Essentials for Loving Living

Lists twenty-two essential responsibilities given to us by God that help us live up to our potential of an eternal, divine life.

Section I: Love God
The four essential responsibilities that help us to keep God intimately close in our minds and hearts.

Section II: Love Your Divine Self (Love God within you)
The six essential responsibilities that enable us to transcend the challenges in this world that would hold us back from our divine evolution. These enable us to eliminate self-centeredness, and to focus on loving God, others, and our work.

Section III: Love Others (Love God within others)
The eight essential responsibilities that enable us to more easily love one another and transcend the sense of separation so often felt between people.

Section IV: Love What You Do (Love God within your work)
The four essential responsibilities that help us to achieve success in every endeavor that is aligned with the will of God. God always guides us to that which results in the greatest goodness and joy, if we focus on divine attunement with Him.

Part III summarizes the most important points of the thirty-three principles presented in Parts I and II. (Appendix A offers another, more concise listing of the principles).

Part IV includes my comments and conclusions along with a few helpful affirmations. My sincere wish is that you will find the principles and passages within of significant value to you in realizing and experiencing a greater connection with God and our true nature.

— *C. David Lundberg*

Experience the Reality Beyond the Words

Words are symbols, a step away from reality. The word "God" is not really God. The word "love" is not really love. Find the meaning and spirit beyond the words. *Experience* the reality of the meaning the words point to. Only accept what rings true in your heart.

Study the linked words, no doubt, but look
Behind them to the thought they indicate,

And having found it, throw the words away
As chaff when you have sifted out the grain.
   The Upanishads

PART I

The Understanding

ONE WAY TO LOOK AT WHAT GOD has consistently been telling His children is that we need the understanding and essentials to get back home — to get back to Heaven. This book contains essential information needed for an understanding of how to make Earth more heaven-like, and ensure that when our life in human form is over, we have the very best chance to get back home to Heaven, where our souls yearn to be.

In part I, you will learn what the world's sacred texts have to say about the *Meaning and Purpose of Life* (section I, principles 1-3); *Who We Really Are* (section II, principles 4-5); and *Who and What Is God* (section III, principles 6-11). The quotations from the various world religions add depth and confirmation to an understanding of this essential knowledge. Once we have this understanding, it is easier to accept our essential responsibilities given in part II, for they will be seen as joyous experiences on our road back home.

Section I

The Meaning and Purpose of Life

Chapter 1: Life, with God, is Good

Chapter 2: Love Creates Joyous Living

Chapter 3: We Are Responsible

IT CAN BE DIFFICULT FOR THOSE who have suffered loss and hardships, or for those who watch the evening news, to believe in the fundamental goodness of life. Yet the world's traditions tell us that the knowledge of this goodness should never be lost, no matter what is going on around us. That is why the first principle found throughout the world's scriptures is "Life, with God, is Good."

These varied traditions also tell us that life is ultimately about love, and so the second principle is "Love Creates Joyous Living." God's love for his children is evident within every principle in this book.

The third and final principle in this section, "We Are Responsible," confirms the necessity of taking on life's many responsibilities to be a part of such goodness and love. Our essential responsibilities are easier to embrace when seen in the overall context of life's fundamental goodness and love.

Chapter 1

Life, with God, is Good

THE FIRST PRINCIPLE IS KEY to our understanding of life and its meaning and purpose:

Life is good, joyful, meaningful, and positive — with God.

With the suffering in the world, many have forgotten this important truth. Even when we are being strengthened through tests, challenges, and difficulties we cannot forget that life, despite its trials, is good. All dark times are followed by the dawn of new life and new goodness when we include God in our consciousness.

The world religions tell us that life's purpose is to live with joy in an intimate relationship with God. This is revealed step-by-step through the other principles and responsibilities in this book.

The fruits of life and goodness are: happiness, peace, and the successful completion of worthwhile goals. As we understand and apply the following principles we can create heaven on earth, one person at a time.

 Christianity Affirms Life, with God, is Good

For the kingdom of God is not meat and drink; but righteousness, and peace, and joy in the Holy Ghost [Spirit].
Romans 14:19

If ye keep my commandments, ye shall abide in my love; even as I have kept my Father's commandments, and abide in his love.
These things have I spoken unto you, that my joy might remain in you, and that your joy might be full.
　　John 15:10-11

But the fruit of the Spirit is love, joy, peace, long-suffering, gentleness, goodness, faith, meekness, temperance: against such there is no law.
　　Galatians 5:22-23

The dictionary definitions of three of the lesser-known words used above are:

LONG-SUFFERING: "Long and patient endurance of offense."
MEEK[NESS]: "Enduring injury with patience and without resentment."
TEMPERANCE: "Habitual moderation in the indulgence of the appetites or passions."
　　(*Webster's Ninth New Collegiate Dictionary*)

Or what man is there of you, whom if his son ask bread, will he give him a stone?
Or if he ask a fish, will he give him a serpent?
If ye then, being evil, know how to give good gifts unto your children, how much more shall your Father which is in heaven give good things to them that ask him?
Therefore all things whatsoever ye would that men should do to you, do ye even so to them: for this is the law and the prophets.
　　Matthew 7:9-12

If we choose to use our free will to live a good life, with God, we are promised an even better life after this lifetime is over:

In my Father's house are many mansions: if it were not so, I would have told you. I go to prepare a place for you.
John 14:2

 ## Islam Affirms Life, with God, is Good

Abraham is the common denominator in the Western religions also known as the Abrahamic religions. Judaism, Christianity, and Islam each consider the Old Testament of the Bible as a sacred text, and give Abraham a special place in their belief systems. What do God, Abraham, Muhammad (author of the Holy Qur'an), and Jesus think about the violence, hatred, and wars that have been fought in their names? By looking at the common truths shared by the belief systems within our religions, we can raise our understanding to higher levels that transcend the man-made divisions installed within them.

Surely Allah [God] wrongs not the weight of an atom; and if it is a good deed, He multiplies it and gives from Himself a great reward.
Qur'an 4:40

And Allah's is whatever is in the heavens and whatever is in the earth, that He may reward those who do evil for that which they do, and reward those who do good with goodness.
Qur'an 53:31

Whoever brings a good deed will have tenfold like it, and whoever bring an evil deed, will be recompensed only with the like of it, and they shall not be wronged.
Qur'an 6:160

Whoever does evil will be requited for it and will not find for himself besides Allah a friend or a helper.
And whoever does good deeds, whether male or female, and he (or she) is a believer — these will enter the Garden (Spiritual Bliss), and they will not be dealt with a whit unjustly.
And who is better in religion than he who submits himself entirely to Allah while doing good (to others) and follows the faith of Abraham, the upright one? And Allah took Abraham for a friend.
     Qur'an 4:123-125

And it is said to those who guard against evil: What has your Lord revealed? They say, Good. For those who do good in this world is good. And certainly the abode of the Hereafter is better. And excellent indeed is the abode of those who keep their duty.
Gardens of perpetuity which they enter, wherein flow rivers: they have therein what they please. Thus does Allah reward those who keep their duty.
     Qur'an 16:30-31

 ## Judaism Affirms Life, with God, is Good

From the first book and first chapter of the Old Testament, we have:

God said, "Let there be light;" and there was light.
God saw that the light was good, and God separated the light from the darkness.
     (Tanakh) Genesis 1:3-4

As various aspects of the world are created, in Genesis 1:10, 12, 18, 21, 25 the verse ends:
     "...and God saw that this was good."

And God created man in His image, in the image of God He created him; male and female He created them.

God blessed them and God said to them, "Be fertile and increase; fill the earth and master it; and rule the fish of the sea, the birds of the sky, and all the living things that creep on earth."

And God saw all that He had made, and found it very good.

(Tanakh) Genesis 1:27-28,31

Happy is the man that finds wisdom, the man that attains understanding.

Her value in trade is better than silver, her yield, greater than gold.

She [understanding] is more precious than rubies; all of your goods cannot equal her.

In her right hand is length of days, in her left, riches and honor.

Her ways are pleasant ways, and all her paths, peaceful.

She is a tree of life to those who grasp her, and whoever holds on to her is happy.

(Tanakh) Proverbs 3:13-18

Thus I realized that the only worthwhile thing there is for them [men] is to enjoy themselves and do what is good in their lifetime; also, that whenever a man does eat and drink and get enjoyment out of all his wealth, it is a gift of God.

(Tanakh) Ecclesiastes 3:12-13

 ## Hinduism Affirms Life, with God, is Good

He whose mind is not attached to external objects of sense, obtaineth that happiness which is in self; and by concentrating his mind on the contemplation of Brahma [God], he enjoyeth a happiness that is imperishable.

The Mahabharata, book 6, section 29

*For I am the Home of the Spirit, the continual Source of
immortality, of eternal Righteousness and of infinite Joy.*
     The Bhagavad Gita, chapter 14

*Having abandoned selfishness, power, arrogance, anger and
desire, possessing nothing of his own and having attained
peace, he is fit to join the Eternal Spirit.*
*And when he becomes one with the Eternal, and his soul
knows the bliss that belongs to the Self, he feels no desire and
no regret, he regards all beings equally and enjoys the blessing
of supreme devotion to Me. [Krishna/God]*
     The Bhagavad Gita, chapter 18

*Devoid of desire and possessed of a tranquil mind, the person in Yoga
[Union with God] is never shaken by pain and sorrow and fear, the
terrible effects that flow from attachment and affection. Weapons
never pierce him; death does not exist for him. Nowhere in the world
can be seen any one that is happier than he.*
     The Mahabharata, book 14, section 19

*I will now reveal to thee, since thou doubtest not, that profound
mysticism, which when followed by experience, shall liberate thee
from sin.*
*This is the Premier Science, the Sovereign Secret, the Purest and
Best; intuitional, righteous; and to him who practiseth it pleasant
beyond measure.*
     The Bhagavad Gita, chapter 9

Buddhism Affirms Life, with God, is Good

Let us live happily then, not hating those who hate us! Among men who hate us let us dwell free from hatred!
Let us live happily then, free from ailments among the ailing! Among men who are ailing let us dwell free from ailments!
Let us live happily then, free from greed among the greedy! Among men who are greedy let us dwell free from greed!
Let us live happily then, though we call nothing our own! We shall be like the bright gods, feeding on happiness!

   The Dhammapada, chapter 15

A disciplined man is free; being free, he is joyous, he is calm and happy.

   The Majjhima-Nikaya

The bliss of the religious life is attainable by every one who walks in the noble eightfold path. He that cleaves to wealth had better cast it away than allow his heart to be poisoned by it; but he who does not cleave to wealth, and possessing riches, uses them rightly, will be a blessing unto his fellows.
It is not life and wealth and power that enslave men, but the cleaving to life and wealth and power....
The Dharma of the Tathagata [the Buddha mind-nature hidden within every being] requires each man to free himself from the illusion of self, to cleanse his heart, to give up his thirst for pleasure, and to lead a life of righteousness....
If they [men] are like the lotus, which, although it grows in the water, yet remains untouched by the water, if they struggle in life without cherishing envy or hatred, if they live in the world not a life of self but a life of truth, then surely joy, peace, and bliss will dwell in their minds.

   Buddha, The Gospel: Anathapindika, The Man of Wealth

The concept of material possessions is mentioned often in the Buddhist philosophy of peace and happiness, as reflected in the previous quotation. It is believed that Buddha said:

The feeling of possession is measured not by objects but by thoughts. One may have objects and still not be a possessor.
Gautama Buddha

Thus according to Buddhism, what matters is not that we have possessions, but how we think and feel about possessions and power. Have we allowed our possessions to be the object of our focus, displacing our focus on God? Have we allowed money, celebrities, "success", sports, or any other thing to become our idols, the object of our primary attention instead of God? Or, do we acknowledge our power in this world as coming from God?

 Taoism Affirms Life, with God, is Good

The Way of Heaven has no private affections,
But always accords with the good.
Tao Teh Ching, chapter 79

The Sage is always good at saving men,
And therefore nobody is abandoned;
Always good at saving things,
And therefore nothing is wasted.
This is called "following the guidance of the Inner Light."
Hence, good men are teachers of bad men,
While bad men are the charge of good men.
Tao Teh Ching, chapter 27

Confucianism Affirms Life, with God, is Good

Let the states of equilibrium and harmony exist in perfection, and a happy order will prevail throughout heaven and earth, and all things will be nourished and flourish.

The Doctrine of the Mean

All things are nourished together without their injuring one another. The courses of the seasons, and of the sun and moon, are pursued without any collision among them. The smaller energies are like river currents; the greater energies are seen in mighty transformations. It is this which makes heaven and earth so great.

The Doctrine of the Mean

To seek gladness through righteous persistence is the way to accord with heaven and to respond to men.

I Ching 58

We can see that our divine, loving, heavenly Father (or, the One/ Beingness/Absolute/Ultimate Reality) wants us to be happy and enjoy life, and to include Him in our experience. Despite the suffering on earth caused by ignorance and greed, each of us can contribute to establishing Heaven on earth by knowing and applying the truth.

Let us now look at the greatest, most dynamic, and wonderful key to life: Love.

Chapter 2

Love Creates Joyous Living: We Are to Love and Be Loved

WHY DID GOD DIVIDE HIMSELF to create other beings from His Essence? The answer may be as simple as "So He would have someone to love." Just as children enrich the lives of couples in love, we bring joy to God. When we consciously share our lives, intimately, with God, family, and friends, we enrich life to the fullest. Life with God and love is joyous.

Love is the permeating principle and energy that runs through all the principles taken from the sacred texts. Being in the "One Universal Circuit" of flowing divine love is the goal of every soul, whether realized or not. Part II will focus on this by establishing essentials for loving God. This includes loving God in ourselves, God in others, and loving God in the work that we do.

Love is essential for joyous living. Every moment we receive the flow of energy from God, and we qualify or charge it by our thoughts, feelings, and actions into varying degrees of positivity or negativity. This flow of energy through us gives us life. Love is the ultimate and highest form of qualifying God's continuous flow of divine energy.

There is a simple way to vastly improve the joy that each day can bring: Visualize this energy radiating out from your heart to love everything that comes into your world.

The continual outpouring of a feeling of Peace and Divine Love to every person and everything unconditionally, no matter whether you think it be deserved or not, is the Magic Key that unlocks the door and releases instantly this tremendous "Inner God-Power." Fortunate indeed is he who has learned this "Law" for he then seeks to BE all Peace and Love. Without it humanity has nothing good, and with it they have all things "Perfect." Harmony is the Keynote, the "one Great Law of Life." Upon it rests all Perfect Manifestation and without it all form disintegrates and returns into the Great Sea of Universal Light."
  Unveiled Mysteries, Godfre Ray King

We are much more loved than we realize. In addition to the love of families and friends, we are loved by God, Jesus, Gautama Buddha, other spiritual masters, and multitudes of angels, as well as loved ones who have passed on.

Love is the ultimate fulfillment and purpose of life. It is the source of the greatest joy, bliss, and ecstasy. Believing in the power of love and using that power raises us all, and the entire planet.

Love also has a serious side. Love contains duty, discipline, and drive as well as devotion. It moves us to defend children, the innocent, the downtrodden, the weak, and the helpless. If the reason is strong enough, love can inspire souls to give their life for family, friends, or country.

Love is also the antidote to fear, which is the common denominator of all negative emotions and is the cause of much of man's suffering. As such, love empowers courage (*coeur* in French means "heart"). The root of courage lies within our hearts.

The challenge is in learning to love those who have caused us to suffer. Acceptance of and forgiveness for being wronged is essential before we can return to the natural flow of love. It is impossible to be truly free without forgiving and even loving those who have caused us harm. We may find forgiveness less difficult if we can understand why a harmful act has been committed. (Chapter 27 addresses forgiveness and mercy).

Love is crucial to the process of evolving. Love is the most joyful, positive, meaningful, and fulfilling action in life. The sensation of the flow of love through one's consciousness and body feels divine.

Beauty is a product of love. The beauty God has created on earth, and the beauty artists and musicians create is fueled by the fire of love. God's Loving Spirit manifests beauty for our enjoyment.

 ## Christianity Affirms the Power of Love

Two great commandments from Jesus hold the promise of God's greatest gifts:

Jesus said unto him, Thou shalt love the Lord thy God with all thy heart, and with all thy soul, and with all thy mind.
This is the first and great commandment.
And the second is like unto it, Thou shalt love thy neighbour as thyself.
On these two commandments hang all the law and the prophets.
    Matthew 22:37-40

For this cause I bow my knees unto the Father of our Lord Jesus Christ,
Of whom the whole family in heaven and earth is named,
That he would grant you, according to the riches of his glory, to be strengthened with might by his Spirit in the inner man;
That Christ may dwell in your hearts by faith; that ye, being rooted and grounded in love,
May be able to comprehend with all saints what is the breadth, and length, and depth, and height;

*And to know the love of Christ, which passeth knowledge, that ye
might be filled with all the fullness of God.*
Ephesians 3:14-19

As you read the following excerpt substitute "love" for charity. Charity originally meant "love," coupled with understanding,
gentleness, and compassion.

*Though I speak with the tongues of men and of angels, and have not
charity, I am become as sounding brass, or a tinkling cymbal.*
*And though I have the gift of prophecy, and understand all myster-
ies, and all knowledge; and though I have all faith, so that I could
remove mountains, and have not charity, I am nothing.*
*And though I bestow all my goods to feed the poor, and though I
give my body to be burned, and have not charity, it profiteth me
nothing.*
*Charity suffereth long, and is kind; charity envieth not; charity vaun-
teth not itself, is not puffed up,*
*Doth not behave itself unseemly, seeketh not her own, is not easily
provoked, thinketh no evil;*
Rejoiceth not in iniquity, but rejoiceth in the truth;
*Beareth all things, believeth all things, hopeth all things, endureth
all things.*
*Charity never faileth: but whether there be prophecies, they shall fail;
whether there be tongues, they shall cease; whether there be knowledge, it shall vanish away.*
For we know in part, and we prophesy in part.
*But when that which is perfect is come, then that which is in part
shall be done away....*
*And now abideth faith, hope, charity, these three; but the greatest
of these is charity.*
1 Corinthians 13:1-10, 13

Islam Affirms the Power of Love

Islamic tradition emphasizes that God loves his obedient servants and that righteous men love God. It also includes much emphasis on doing good works for others, which is love in action.

Yet there are some men who take for themselves objects of worship besides Allah, whom they love as they should love Allah. And those who believe are stronger in (their) love for Allah.
   Qur'an 2:165

On those who believe and do good there is no blame...when they keep their duty and believe and do good deeds, then keep their duty and do good (to others). And Allah loves the doers of good.
   Qur'an 5:93

Heaven and earth contain me not, but the heart of my faithful servant contains me.
   The Hadith of Suhrawardi

Surely Allah loves those who trust (in Him).
   Qur'an 3:159

Whoso seeketh to approach Me one span, I approach him one cubit; and whoso seeketh to approach Me one cubit, I approach him two fathoms; and whoever walks towards Me, I run towards him.
   Hadith

Judaism Affirms the Power of Love

You shall not hate your kinsfolk in your heart. Reprove your kinsman but incur no guilt because of him. You shall not take vengeance or bear a grudge against your countrymen. Love your fellow as yourself: I am the Lord.
    (Tanakh) Leviticus 19:17-18

You shall love the Lord your God with all your heart and with all your soul and with all your might.
Take to heart these instructions with which I charge you this day. Impress them upon your children. Recite them when you stay at home and when you are away, when you lie down and when you get up.
    (Tanakh) Deuteronomy 6:5-7

Those who love me I love,
And those who seek me will find me.
I endow those who love me with substance;
I will fill their treasuries
    (Tanakh) Proverbs 8:17, 21

 ## Hinduism Affirms the Power of Love

As the radiant sun shines upon all regions above, below, and across, so does this glorious one God of love protect and guide all creatures.
    Svetasvatara Upanishad 5.4

That one I love who is incapable of ill will, who is friendly and compassionate.
    The Bhagavad Gita, chapter 12

The infinite joy of touching the Godhead is easily attained by those who are free from the burden of evil and established within themselves. They see the Self in every creature and all creation in the Self. With consciousness unified through meditation, they see everything with an equal eye.

I am ever present unto those who have realized me in every creature. Seeing all life as my manifestation, they are never separated from me. They worship me in the hearts of all, and all their actions proceed from me. Wherever they may live, they abide in me.

When a person responds to the joys and sorrows of others as if they were his own, he has attained the highest state of spiritual union.

The Bhagavad Gita, chapter 6

In the fifteenth century, a poet named Kabir was a disciple of the Hindu ascetic Ramananda. One of the poet's lovely *Songs of Kabir* follows. It expresses beautiful and powerful devotion to the God Vishnu, who represents the personal aspect of the Divine Nature. This long quotation is too beautiful to shorten. It is well worth reading from beginning to end.

The light of the sun, the moon, and the stars shines bright:
The melody of love swells forth, and the rhythm of love's detachment beats the time.
Day and night, the chorus of music fills the heavens; and Kabîr says
"My Beloved One gleams like the lightning flash in the sky."
Do you know how the moments perform their adoration?
Waving its row of lamps, the universe sings in worship day and night,
There are the hidden banner and the secret canopy:
There the sound of the unseen bells is heard.
Kabîr says: "There adoration never ceases; there the Lord of the Universe sitteth on His throne."

The whole world does its works and commits its errors: but few are the lovers who know the Beloved.

The devout seeker is he who mingles in his heart the double currents of love and detachment, like the mingling of the streams of Ganges and Jumna;

In his heart the sacred water flows day and night; and thus the round of births and deaths is brought to an end.

Behold what wonderful rest is in the Supreme Spirit! and he enjoys it, who makes himself meet for it.

Held by the cords of love, the swing of the Ocean of Joy sways to and fro; and a mighty sound breaks forth in song.

See what a lotus blooms there without water! and Kabîr says "My heart's bee drinks its nectar."

What a wonderful lotus it is, that blooms at the heart of the spinning wheel of the universe! Only a few pure souls know of its true delight.

Music is all around it, and there the heart partakes of the joy of the Infinite Sea.

Kabîr says: "Dive thou into that Ocean of sweetness: thus let all errors of life and of death flee away."

Behold how the thirst of the five senses is quenched there! And the three forms of misery are no more!

Kabîr says: "It is the sport of the Unattainable One: look within, and behold how the moon-beams of that Hidden One shine in you."

There falls the rhythmic beat of life and death:

Rapture wells forth, and all space is radiant with light.

There the Unstruck Music is sounded; it is the music of the love of the three worlds.

There millions of lamps of sun and of moon are burning;

There the drum beats, and the lover swings in play.

There love-songs resound, and light rains in showers; and the worshipper is entranced in the taste of the heavenly nectar.

Look upon life and death; there is no separation between them,

The right hand and the left hand are one and the same.
Kabîr says: "There the wise man is speechless; for this truth may never be found in Vedas or in books."
I have had my Seat on the Self-poised One,
I have drunk of the Cup of the Ineffable,
I have found the Key of the Mystery,
I have reached the Root of Union.
Traveling by no track, I have come to the Sorrowless Land: very easily has the mercy of the great Lord come upon me.
They have sung of Him as infinite and unattainable: but I in my meditations have seen Him without sight.
That is indeed the sorrowless land, and none know the path that leads there:
Only he who is on that path has surely transcended all sorrow.
Wonderful is that land of rest, to which no merit can win;
It is the wise who has seen it, it is the wise who has sung of it.
This is the Ultimate Word: but can any express its marvelous savour?
He who has savoured it once, he knows what joy it can give.
Kabîr says: "Knowing it, the ignorant man becomes wise, and the wise man becomes speechless and silent,
The worshipper is utterly inebriated,
His wisdom and his detachment are made perfect;
He drinks from the cup of the inbreathings and the outbreathings of love."
There the whole sky is filled with sound, and there that music is made without fingers and without strings;
There the game of pleasure and pain does not cease.
Kabîr says: "If you merge your life in the Ocean of Life, you will find your life in the Supreme Land of Bliss."
What a frenzy of ecstasy there is in every hour! And the worshipper is pressing out and drinking the essence of the hours: he lives in the life of Brahma.

I speak truth, for I have accepted truth in life; I am now attached to truth, I have swept all tinsel away.
Kabîr says: "Thus is the worshipper set free from fear; thus have all errors of life and of death left him."
There the sky is filled with music:
There it rains nectar:
There the harp-strings jingle, and there the drums beat.
What a secret splendour is there, in the mansion of the sky!
There no mention is made of the rising and the setting of the sun;
In the ocean of manifestation, which is the light of love, day and night are felt to be one.
Joy for ever, no sorrow, — no struggle!
There have I seen joy filled to the brim, perfection of joy;
No place for error is there.
Kabîr says: "There have I witnessed the sport of One Bliss!"
I have known in my body the sport of the universe: I have escaped from the error of this world.
The inward and the outward are become as one sky, the Infinite and the finite are united: I am drunken with the sight of this All!
This Light of Thine fulfils the universe: the lamp of love that burns on the salver of knowledge.
Kabîr says: "There error cannot enter, and the conflict of life and death is felt no more."

      Songs of Kabir, chapter 17 (II.61)

 ## Buddhism Affirms the Power of Love

Gautama Buddha had this to say about love:

However men may speak concerning you, whether appropriately or inappropriately, whether courteously or rudely, whether wisely or foolishly, whether kindly or maliciously, thus, my disciples, must you train yourselves. Our minds should remain unsullied; neither should evil word escape our lips. Kind and compassionate will we ever remain, loving of heart, not harboring secret hate. And we will bathe them with the unfailing stream of loving thought. And proceeding further, we will embrace and flood the whole wide world with constant thoughts of loving kindness, wide, ample, expanding, immeasurable as the world, free from enmity, free from ill will. Thus, disciples, must you train yourselves.

Majjhima-Nikaya

Full of love for all things in the world, practicing virtue in order to benefit others, this man alone is happy.

The Dhammapada

Just as a mother would protect her only child at the risk of her own life, even so, let him cultivate a boundless heart towards all beings. Let his thoughts of boundless love pervade the whole world.

Sutta Nipata 149, Metta Sutta

The following quotation is from a wonderful book on Buddhism. It is, however, not considered a sacred text of that religion.

The love that his [Buddha's] disciples had to cultivate was the boundless stream of kindness radiating to all four quarters of space, above and below, in all places the wide world over.

According to the Teaching these waves of kindness, compassion, or joy sent into space reach a mind afflicted with sorrow and grief, which suddenly feels within itself a welling-up of peace and serenity.

Thought is energy and as such acts in full conformity with its intensity and the impetus given to it.

Love, as taught by the Blessed One, being the deliverance of mind, was at the root of everything really great.

"The greatest of all is the loving heart."

Foundations of Buddhism, Helena Roerich

Taoism Affirms the Power of Love

The Supreme loves and nourishes all things.
    Tao Teh Ching, chapter 34

In keeping the spirit and the vital soul together,
Are you able to maintain their perfect harmony?...
In loving your people and governing your state,
Are you able to dispense with cleverness?
    Tao Teh Ching, chapter 10

If we have no body, what calamities can we have?
Hence, only he who is willing to give his body for the sake of the world
is fit to be entrusted with the world.
Only he who can do it with love is worthy of being the steward of
the world.
    Tao Teh Ching, chapter 13

 Confucianism Affirms the Power of Love

Better than the one who knows what is right is he who loves what
is right.
    Confucian Analects, chapter 6

Fan Ch'ih asked about benevolence.
The Master said, "It is to love all men."
    Confucian Analects, chapter 12

The world's Holy Scriptures show how wonderful and essential
it is to love God, and to love others and ourselves as God loves
us — fully and powerfully. Love often comes in the form of good

works. In addition to thinking and feeling love, love is taking loving action in the service of others.

When we love God, our Creator and divine parent, and when we have sufficient wisdom to use that power for good, we then attune to divine power. Love is the magic key that unlocks the flow of Holy Spirit. The Holy Spirit is the energy and light of the universe. Let us radiate love to all in our world.

It is not sufficient not to hate, not to dislike, not to retaliate to hurts. These can be inactive, even negative conditions under some circumstances. Love must be sent out with power, knowingly and with direct purpose. It must be sent out as a musician sends out his melody. Just because one refrains from inharmony does not make him a musician. To be a musician one must send out melody; and to be a master of music requires hours of practice. So to be a master of the divine gift of love one must practice, and he is both the instrument and the musician, for upon his own being is the divine melody played, first within himself, then within the hearts of others. And love is the theme song of the universe. Sing that song and you can never be out of tune. It is the melody of heaven.

Ye Are Gods, Annalee Skarin

Chapter 3

We Are Responsible: For All We Create and Certain Disciplines

THE FIRST TWO PRINCIPLES SHOW that life is supposed to be good and filled with love, despite many appearances to the contrary. In addition to perceiving and receiving this goodness and love, we need to give or *radiate* it outward to all in our world. Because we have free will, we are responsible for all we create. And, to live a life in close communion with God, we are responsible for applying the twenty-two responsibilities, or disciplines, for loving living contained in Part II. The wonderful blessings of life won't happen unless we contribute to their creation.

We can use our God-given free will for good or ill. Life does not tell us what we have to think about. In a large measure, we live in a mental world — our thoughts precede our words or actions.

Why did God grant us free will? It's natural for any parent to want his children to have freedom. Would any parent prefer that his children love him because they *have* to, or because they *choose* to? Is it more helpful for a parent to simply hand achievements to a child, or to allow the child to strive for him or herself and assist if necessary? Is it not a joy to behold children maturing?

We are indeed co-creators with God. Every moment, we co-create using God's supply of energy/light from which all matter is made. This energy flows through us every moment. Every one of our creations falls somewhere on a scale that ranges from excellent all the way down to horrific. In other words, every moment, we are using divine light for positive or negative results. The free will that we have is a huge responsibility.

A record is kept of our every thought, word, and deed in the "Akasha," (which in Sanskrit means "primary substance," that out of which all things are formed). How we have used our energy is our karma. Karma has been called the law of cause and effect. We are responsible and accountable for all that we create. We are forgiven as we forgive. God's grace can transmute our (negative) karma as we acknowledge and understand our past errors. In order for us to understand the consequences of certain things we have done, sometimes it is necessary to physically experience for ourselves what we have done to others. At other times, it is only necessary to do this mentally with an empathetic consciousness. Either way, it is necessary for us to experience similar circumstances and actions that we have caused others.

Everything that we say, think, and do that is good is God in action — our divine reality. Everything that we say, think, and do that is not worthy to be called God/goodness still utilizes God's divine energy. But these negative actions are not God's will in action, and these actions do not contribute to raising ourselves higher and closer to eternal reality, but take us in the other direction.

What we create for others we create for ourselves. As we continuously qualify God's energy each moment for good or ill, what we send out eventually returns to us. When we radiate positive and loving feelings and thoughts, we receive the many benefits, rewards, and blessings of joy, love, abundance, and more.

Fortunately, God's grace does not always require us to suffer as much as we have, in our ignorance or purposeful harming of others, caused others to suffer. We are responsible, however, for learning from these experiences, and transmuting some portion of the energy that we have misqualified.

Trust in divine justice. Even if justice is not witnessed on earth, know that it is always eventually served.

Each person is also responsible for manifesting a divine plan — one or more projects that only that particular individual can do to be of service to God and to our brothers and sisters. The time that each one spends on his or her divine plan (also known as a life plan) is a joy, for it involves doing something that inspires us. In addition, part of our plan includes experiencing one or more lessons about life. More information about divine plans is in chapter 30 of Part II, "Essential Responsibilities for Loving Living."

 Christianity Affirms We Are Responsible

Be not deceived; God is not mocked: for whatsoever a man soweth, that shall he also reap.
Galatians 6:7

If we confess our sins, he is faithful and just to forgive us our sins, and to cleanse us from all unrighteousness.
1 John 1:9

Let your light so shine before men, that they may see your good works, and glorify your Father which is in heaven.
Matthew 5:16

He shall reward every man according to his works.
Matthew 16:27

Blessed are the dead which die in the Lord from henceforth: Yea saith the Spirit, that they may rest from their labours; and their works do follow them.
Revelation 14:13

Islam Affirms We Are Responsible

And We have made every man's action to cling to his neck, and We shall bring forth to him on the day of Resurrection a book which he will find wide open.
Read thy book. Thine own soul is sufficient as a reckoner against thee this day.
Whoever goes aright, for his own soul does he go aright; and whoever goes astray, to its detriment only does he go astray. And no bearer of a burden can bear the burden of another.
    Qur'an 17:13-15

And surely there are keepers over you,
Honourable recorders,
They know what you do.
    Qur'an 82:10-12

When the earth is shaken with her shaking,
And the earth brings forth her burdens,
And man says: What has befallen her?
On that day she will tell her news,
As if thy Lord had revealed to her.
On that day men will come forth in sundry bodies that they may be shown their works.
So he who does an atom's weight of good will see it.
And he who does an atom's weight of evil will see it.
    Qur'an 99:1-8

Whoever does good, it is for his own soul; and whoever does evil, it is against it. And thy Lord is not in the least unjust to the servants.
    Qur'an 41:46

Judaism Affirms We Are Responsible

If you say, "We knew nothing of it,"
Surely He who fathoms hearts will discern (the truth),
He who watches over your life will know it,
And He will pay each man as he deserves.
   (Tanakh) Proverbs 24:12

The person who sins, he alone shall die. A child shall not share the
burden of a parent's guilt, nor shall a parent share the burden of
child's guilt; the righteousness of the righteous shall be accounted
to him alone, and the wickedness of the wicked shall be accounted
to him alone.
Moreover, if the wicked one repents of all the sins that he commit-
ted and keeps all My laws and does what is just and right, he shall
live; he shall not die. None of the transgressions he committed shall
be remembered against him; because of the righteousness he has
practiced, he shall live. Is it my desire that a wicked person shall
die? — says the Lord God. It is rather that he shall turn back from
his ways and live.
   (Tanakh) Ezekiel 18:20-21

One thing God has spoken;
two things have I heard:
that might belongs to God,
and faithfulness is Yours, O Lord,
to reward each man according to his deeds.
   (Tanakh) Psalms 62:12-13

Better is a poor man who lives blamelessly
Than a rich man whose ways are crooked.
   (Tanakh) Proverbs 28:6

Hinduism Affirms We Are Responsible

Single is each being born; single it dies; single it enjoys the reward of its virtue; single it suffers the punishment of its sin.
The Laws of Manu 4:240

Godly qualities lead to liberation; godless to bondage.
The Bhagavad Gita, chapter 16

The sinner, the ignorant, the vile, deprived of spiritual perception by the glamour of Illusion, and he who pursues godless life — none of them shall find Me.
The Bhagavad Gita, chapter 7

The fruit of good action is said to be good and untainted.
The fruit, however of passion, is misery;
(and) the fruit of darkness is ignorance.
From goodness is produced knowledge;
From passion, avarice;
(and) from darkness are error, delusion and also ignorance.
They that dwell in goodness go on high;
They that are addicted to passion dwell in the middle;
(while) they that are of darkness, being addicted to the lowest quality, go down.
The Mahabharata, book 6, section 38

 ## Buddhism Affirms We Are Responsible

Make haste in doing good; check your mind from evil; for the mind of him who is slow in doing meritorious actions delights in evil. Should a person commit evil, he should not do it again and again; he

should not find pleasure therein: painful is the accumulation of evil.
Should a person perform a meritorious action, he should do it again
and again; he should find pleasure therein: blissful is the accumu-
lation of merit.

The Dhammapada, 116-118

Said the king, "Bhanta Nagasena, what is the reason that men are
not all alike, but some long-lived and some short-lived, some healthy
and some sickly, some handsome and some ugly, some powerful and
some weak, some rich and some poor, some of high degree and some
of low degree, some wise and some foolish?"
Said the elder, "Your majesty, why are not trees all alike, but some
sour, some salt, some bitter, some pungent, some astringent, some
sweet?"
"I suppose, bhante, because of a difference in the seed."
"In exactly the same way, your majesty, it is through a difference
in their karma that men are not all alike, but some long-lived and
some short-lived, some healthy and some sickly, some handsome
and some ugly, some powerful and some weak, some rich and some
poor, some of high degree and some of low degree, some wise and
some foolish. Moreover, your majesty, The Blessed One has said as
follows: 'All beings...have karma as their portion; they are heirs of
their karma; they are sprung from their karma; their karma is their
kinsman; their karma is their refuge; karma allots beings to mean-
ness or greatness.'"

The Milindapanha 65

But every deed a man performs,
With body, or with voice, or mind,
'T is this that he can call his own,
This with him take as he goes hence.
This is what follows after him,
And like a shadow ne'er departs.

Let all, then, noble deeds perform,
A treasure-store for future weal;
For merit gained this life within,
Will yield a blessing in the next.
        The Samyutta-Nikaya 42

 Taoism Affirms We Are Responsible

What helps to make life so wonderful is that all of our responsibilities, established in Part II, can be described as virtuous and noble. They are part of our divine nature and simply feel right to do.

Tao gives them life,
Virtue nurses them,
Matter shapes them,
Environment perfects them.
Therefore all things without exception worship Tao and do homage to Virtue.
They have not been commanded to worship Tao and do homage to Virtue,
But they always do so spontaneously.
It is Tao that gives them life:
It is Virtue that nurses them, grows them, fosters them, shelters them, comforts them, nourishes them, and covers them under her wings.
        Tao Teh Ching, chapter 51

Cultivate Virtue in your own person,
And it becomes a genuine part of you.
Cultivate it in the family,
And it will abide.
Cultivate it in the community,
And it will live and grow.

Cultivate it in the state,
And it will flourish abundantly.
Cultivate it in the world,
And it will become universal.
Tao Teh Ching, chapter 54

 Confucianism Affirms We Are Responsible

The Master said, "Shan, my doctrine is that of an all-pervading
unity." The disciple Tsang replied, "Yes."
The Master went out, and the other disciples asked, saying, "What
do his words mean?" Tsang said, "The doctrine of our master is to
be true to the principles — of our nature and the benevolent exercise
of them to others — this and nothing more."
Confucian Analects, book 4

Only by perfect virtue can the perfect path, in all its courses, be
made a fact.
The Doctrine of the Mean

The Master said, "What the superior man seeks is in himself; what
the mean man seeks is in others."
Confucian Analects, book 15

In summary, we should engrain into our hearts and minds the
first three principles:

1. **Life, with God, is good.** In other words, *Life is meant to be*
   good, especially when we share it with God. Despite outward
   appearances of negativity and suffering in the world, it is
   essential to remember that with God comes goodness.

2. **Love Creates Joyous Living.** Therefore, *Love is the ultimate goal.* This must be known and demonstrated for the conscious increase of love on earth — despite all appearances and situations.

3. **We are Responsible.** *We are responsible for what we do as well as what we were supposed to do but failed to do (acts of commission and omission).* A record is kept of our every thought, word, and deed. We are accountable for this record. God wants us to live in a very loving way, as delineated in Part II's responsibilities.

We will make many errors along the way, and receive much forgiveness and grace for our errors to the degree we offer it to others who wrong us.

Section II

Who We Really Are

THERE IS ONE UNDERLYING CAUSE for the needless tragedy, suffering, fighting, and lack in the world. It is simply this: *mankind has an identity crisis.*

Because we have forgotten that we are truly spirit, just temporarily inhabiting a physical form, we are vulnerable to all kinds of fears, stress, misunderstandings, jealousies, and a host of other negatives.

The importance of knowing our true identity cannot be overemphasized. When we forget that we are ultimately One with God, and with our fellow man, we get into trouble. We need to remember that divinity lies in everyone (though in some its Light has been totally eclipsed), and we need to practice *seeing* and *knowing* that divinity.

The self-image that we each have of ourselves is crucial to how we treat ourselves, others, and God. One of the most universal concepts in the many modalities of psychological treatment is the understanding of how essential a positive self-image is for happiness and mental balance. Life can be heaven or hell depending on our closeness with spirit and how well we forgive ourselves and others for errors. Each of us needs to discover, remember, and apply the truth of our divinity, elevating our self-image to a level of perfection and purity (chapter 18). This enables us to experience perfection in our self-talk and in all our life experiences.

Because this subject is so important, several different quotations from each religion will be given in the next two chapters. They are most illuminating on different aspects of our divine reality.

The question of "who we really are" is answered only partially within the next two chapters. Because we are a part of God, the answers to who we are *becoming*—our divine potential—continues beyond this section through the next section entitled "Who and What is God."

Chapter 4

Our Divinity: We Are a Part of God, Sons and Daughters of God

WE ARE A PART OF GOD. We are spirit, temporarily inhabiting a physical body (temple). We are not only a part of God, we are children of God, as many of the following quotations affirm.

Some may think, "That sounds terrific. But why am I not happier, and why is there so much suffering in this world?"

That's because God gave us free will. God has free will, and if we are aspects of God, then we must also have free will. God gave us free will because He loves his children. He wants His Divine Family to co-create with Him in ever more glorious goodness, beauty, and joy.

Just as a child makes a lot of mistakes while learning to walk, we also make mistakes as we learn to perfect ourselves in all areas of life. And when errors occur, suffering occurs. This is simply the reality of life. What is forgotten or misinterpreted by certain belief systems is that it is possible to perfect ourselves.

We might then ask "How can that be?" when reflecting on numerous past sins or errors. After all, God is perfect, but how can we be?

It is important to understand that the *real you* is perfect. The *real you* was created by God, and God can only create perfection. And God has qualities that would make it impossible for Him to be separate from the *real you*. Among God's aspects are omnipresence, omniscience, and omnipotence. Thus it would be impossible for God to not be within the *real you*.

Each one of us is a being of awareness/consciousness that can be 100 percent attuned to God and His many blessings. The pure, good, and true aspect of every person is a part of God — a son or daughter of God. This is the part that is the *real you*. We can also choose to ignore God, or be poorly attuned with God. We can hold many false beliefs and even feel a great sense of separateness from God, others, or even ourselves.

We may call the perfect, divine, and eternal part of ourselves our Higher or Divine Self. We may call the imperfect non-eternal part of ourselves our unreal or not-self. The imperfect, human aspects of us are not divine, not perfect, and not eternal.

When we create negatives such as hatred, greed, or jealousy, we are still using God's energy (which all energy is), but not in accordance with God's will for good. We are removed from God to the degree that we have chosen to think, act, and feel in ways that are not of God.

The unreal self is the product of misusing our free will. We are not our unreal self with its imperfections. Our imperfections are baggage that weighs us down. This weight can be lightened and eliminated. As we gradually change the negative aspects contained in our unreal selves, we become more "real" and we can attune more readily to Divine Wisdom and Divine Love, which then allow access to more Divine Power/Light/Energy.

God's will is always perfect. Doing God's will makes one happy and content — if not immediately, eventually. As we focus on the many positive God qualities in our lives (such as peace, love, kindness, mercy, forgiveness, and wisdom) we become more of our True/Divine Self. Focusing on God/Light helps us to shed more of the unreal aspects of self that consist of ego, illusion, and negativity. We are co-creators *with* God every moment we qualify His energy for good. We are creators, but not with God's blessing or will, every moment we qualify His energy unwisely.

We are God incarnate, in the sense that we can co-create using God's energy. For many people, ignorance caused by our unreal self blocks the awareness of this. Each one of us needs to discover, remember, and apply the truth of our divinity, anchoring our Higher Self into our self-image.

It is important to regularly monitor our thoughts. We need to recognize when our negative/separate/unreal self is operating. Our ability to distinguish right from wrong resides within, in the still small voice of our conscience, an aspect of our Divine Self. The ability to attune to and hear our conscience can be blocked by our past or present focus on negatives. As we focus on positive goodness by applying God's Universal Truths, our Higher Self can clearly communicate with us.

Every moment that we think and act for the good, we allow another portion of our unreal self to fade away. At the same time, we re-attune to and strengthen our bond to the Divine Light within.

Our Higher/True/Divine Selves are made in the image and likeness of God. Our true appearance is a dazzling sphere of Light! God lives in us. His true form is Light. Our true form is also Light. We are pure, radiant, and eternal Light. We are spirit, temporarily inhabiting a physical form. We come from a spiritual world and will return to a spiritual world after this embodiment is over.

Our consciousness is who we really are. It is not dependent on a physical body. When our current physical form is no more, we will be less encumbered in our ability to see our real, spiritual world.

But as many as received him, to them gave he power to become the sons of God, even to them that believe on his name:
Which were born, not of blood, nor of the will of the flesh, nor of the will of man, but of God.
John 1:12-13

Christianity Affirms We Are Children of God

First, let's look at what Christianity has to say about who we are. Starting in the very first book and first chapter of the Bible, we find:

And God said, Let us make man in our image, after our likeness: and let them have dominion over the fish of the sea, and over the fowl of the air, and over the cattle, and over all the earth, and over every creeping thing that creepeth upon the earth.
So God created man in his own image, in the image of God created he him; male and female created he them.
   Genesis 1:26-27

Because the Bible says this, some people believe that God looks like man, often depicted as an old man with a long flowing white beard. What it really means is that we look like Him, not that He looks like us. We are pure spirit, temporarily inhabiting a physical form. And that spirit is in the form of Light. For in the beginning, God said "Let there be Light" (Genesis 1:3). God wanted to create, expand, and abide in many forms. We are really pure Light, pure spirit, pure energy.

For as many as are led by the Spirit of God, they are the sons of God.
The Spirit itself beareth witness with our spirit, that we are the children of God:
And if children, then heirs; heirs of God, and joint-heirs with Christ.
   Romans 8:14, 16-17

Know ye not that ye are the temple of God, and that the Spirit of God dwelleth in you?
1 Corinthians 3:16

Our Father, who art in Heaven....
Matthew 6:9

Because God gave each of us free will, we can choose to be led by Spirit, or be distracted by all kinds of things. So, although we are truly God's children, if we choose to focus our attention on other things to the point of *forgetting or disbelieving who we really are*, then we will wallow in the world of doubt, fear, lack, confusion, and other negative limitations and sufferings.

And ye have forgotten the exhortation which speaketh unto you as unto children, My son, despise not thou the chastening of the Lord, nor faint when thou art rebuked of him:
For whom the Lord loveth he chasteneth, and scourgeth every son whom he receiveth.
If ye endure chastening, God dealeth with you as with sons; for what son is he whom the father chasteneth not?
But if ye be without chastisement, whereof all are partakers, then are ye bastards, and not sons.
Furthermore we have had fathers of our flesh which corrected us, and we gave them reverence: shall we not much rather be in subjection unto the Father of spirits, and live?
Hebrews 12:5-9

Here we are reminded of the blessings of wise parental corrections. On this planet, we need all the guidance we can receive. Our real Father is spirit, as we are truly spirit. To receive our Divine Father's spiritual guidance and correction is a great blessing.

The Orthodox Christian's Belief that Jesus Was the Only Son of God

The view of the traditional Christian church is that Jesus was the only son of God. Early church leaders decided that a number of texts including the Gospel of Thomas, the Gospel of Mary, and the Secret Book of James were not to be included in the New Testament, despite the fact that they were popular in the first and second centuries. Many of those texts that were excluded assert that any individual can attain mystical union with God, just as Jesus did. The church's stand was not only that Jesus was the only son of God, but that others could not communicate directly with God. It's likely that this interpretation of scripture was to make individuals dependent on the church as a necessary go-between from man to God.

Our elder brother, the Master Jesus Christ, strived to show us the direct way for man and God to communicate at a more intimate level. Jesus also taught and demonstrated the power of Love. He never claimed to be the *only* son of God, and he did not desire to be worshiped.

And Jesus said unto him,
Why callest thou me good?
There is none good but one, that is, God.
    Mark 10:18

On the subject of our potential, Jesus tells us:

Verily, verily, I say unto you, He that believeth on me, the works that I do shall he do also; and greater works than these shall he do; because I go unto my Father.
    John 14:12

Have faith in God.
For verily I say unto you, that whosoever shall say unto this moun-
tain, Be thou removed, and be thou cast into the sea; and shall not
doubt in his heart, but shall believe that those things which he saith
shall come to pass; he shall have whatsoever he saith.
Therefore I say unto you, What things soever ye desire, when ye pray,
believe that ye receive them, and ye shall have them.
  Mark 11:22-24

This is the true message of Jesus. If we do as Jesus did, having great faith, keeping a close relationship with God, radiating love, speaking truth, and practicing the other essentials for loving living, we have the potential to achieve as much or more than he did. This interpretation, unfortunately, is considered blasphemy by many orthodox Christians.

The interpretation that Jesus was the only son of God hides from us the truth of our birthright, our divine potential. It is easy for this concept to be misunderstood. What Jesus did was to become One with the only Son of God, the Christ.

What is "the Christ?" *The Universal Christ is the universal con-*
sciousness of God that went forth as the Word, the Logos that God
used to fire the pattern of his Divine Identity in his sons and daugh-
ters and to write his laws in their inward parts. The individual Christ
is the fulfillment of this Word, this Logos, in the individed duality.
Each individualization of the Universal Christ is unique, because
each individual was ordained by God to reflect in all of its glory a
particular facet of the Universal Christ.
  Climb the Highest Mountain, Mark and Elizabeth Clare Prophet

The Christ contains the potential of the personification of God, the Universal One, within each one of us. It is the Christ Consciousness that Jesus and other saints and masters attained through constant attunement with God, focusing attention on God, resulting in absorption into the Godhead while still retaining individuality.

Why make the effort to discipline ourselves, to become perfect, when we are taught that we are worthless sinners, incapable of perfecting ourselves? We are not supposed to dwell on our mistakes, but rather to learn from them and not repeat them. If the goal of perfection is thought to be unattainable, it will not be pursued.

Some Christians believe that they will receive an automatic ticket to heaven solely by asking to be forgiven for their sins. Unfortunately, this is not the case. We must consciously strive to improve ourselves. Studying the sacred texts of the world's religions is one helpful area of concentration. It is good to attune to Spirit, keeping in mind one's true identity as a child of God. Over time, God will remove the layers of illusion and reveal divine reality. The illusions of unreal and unnecessary limitation are obstacles holding back our development.

I and my Father are one.
Then the Jews took up stones again to stone him.
Jesus answered them, Many good works have I shewed you from my Father: for which of those works do ye stone me?
The Jews answered him, saying, For a good work we stone thee not; but for blasphemy; and because that thou, being a man, makest thyself God.
Jesus answered them, Is it not written in your law, I said, Ye are gods?
If he called them gods, unto whom the word of God came, and the scripture cannot be broken;
Say ye of him, whom the Father hath sanctified, and sent into the world, Thou blasphemest; because I said, I am the Son of God?
If I do not the works of my Father believe me not.

But if I do, though ye believe not me, believe the works: that ye may know, and believe, that the Father is in me, and I in him.
John 10:30-38

Jesus the Christ had reached a perfect level of attainment, and he operated from a level of perfect attunement and Oneness with God. Jesus came as an example of the perfection any one of us can attain — complete attunement with the Christ, the One Son of God. This is accomplished when our effort earns the divine grace of Christhood.

And call no man your father upon the earth: for one is your Father, which is in heaven.
Neither be ye called masters: for one is your Master, even Christ.
Matthew 23:9-10

In the above quotation, Jesus is referring to the Christ, not to himself exclusively, but to the Christ that is the One Mediator between God and man.

For as many as are led by the Spirit of God, they are the sons of God.
For ye have not received the spirit of bondage again to fear; but ye have received the Spirit of adoption, whereby we cry, Abba, Father.
The Spirit itself beareth witness with our spirit, that we are the children of God:
And if children, then heirs; heirs of God, and joint-heirs with Christ.
Romans 8:14-17

When we are with Christ, the One Son, then we are joint heirs of God.

For those readers who are fundamentalist Christians, please keep in mind that although this interpretation of the Bible may be different from yours, it does not take anything away from Jesus. It simply removes the unnecessary limitations upon the rest of us, and upon God, revealing the truth about our identity, and our potential.

God cannot be limited. When we believe that we are not a part of God, we limit ourselves. How can God be everywhere in His Omnipresence and *not* Be within us?

Jesus never said that he was the only son of God. He was, instead, fully and completely at One with the One son, the Christ. His perfect Higher Self, just like ours, operates at the level of the Christ — the intermediary between God and man that is part of every one of us. The mission of Jesus was to show us the way, to bring us new teachings about love and forgiveness, and demonstrate the Power of God to defy death.

The traditional Christian view of Jesus deifies him, making him either God incarnate or the only son of God. Either way, this interpretation precludes the potential of everyone else. This interpretation is inconsistent with many other early Christian teachings that were not chosen to be included in the New Testament, and keeps us in earthly bondage.

In truth, however, Jesus taught us to live in the same loving way as he did. To view Jesus as our elder brother and mentor in this way takes away none of our love, respect, gratitude, and honor for him. He never wanted us to worship him, only to worship God our Father. He *did* want and expect, however, respect for the office he had attained, the mantle of the Christ.

The Book of John is one of the most mystical books in the Bible. Mysticism refers to a direct communion with God. This can be a frightening concept for those afraid of losing their unique individuality, but the beautiful aspect of Oneness with God is that each of us can retain our individuality at the same time as we are attuned in Oneness.

At that day ye shall know that I am in my Father, and ye in me, and I in you.
John 14:20

This is a very concise confirmation of our ability to achieve Oneness with the Divine, yet retain our individuality. This powerful quotation also confirms that Jesus is not claiming to be the sole son of God.

Jesus answered and said unto him, If a man love me, he will keep my words: and my Father will love him, and we will come unto him, and make our abode with him.
John 14:23

Thus, we can evolve into full awareness of our One Divine Family, with all of the good and positive aspects of our unique individuality remaining.

Islam Affirms We Are Children of God

While orthodox Christianity has a problem with others besides Jesus being children of God, the Holy Qur'an contains a few statements denying that God had any children. This is probably due to those statements referring to the lower self of man, rather than the Higher/Christ Self. Also, the Qur'an contains many statements that *affirm* that we are children of God. This apparent contradiction is examined more fully in Appendix B. The Hadith also contains statements that affirm that we are children of God.

Then He made his progeny [child] of an extract, of worthless water
Then He made him complete and breathed into him His spirit, and
gave you ears and eyes and hearts; little it is that you give thanks!
Qur'an 32: 8-9

Maulana Muhammad Ali, the Muslim translator of the Qur'an, added a footnote to the above, stating in part:

This verse shows that the spirit of God is breathed into every man.
This points to a mystical relation between human nature and Divine
nature.... It is due to this spirit Divine that he [man] rules the creation
and it is due to the same Divine spirit in him that he receives a new
life after death — a life in which he lives in God and with God.
Qur'an 32:8-9 footnote by translator.

Anas and Abdullah reported God's Messenger [the prophet Muham-
mad] as saying, "All [human] creatures are God's children, and those
dearest to God are the ones who treat His children kindly."
Hadith of Baihaqi

On God's own nature has been molded man's.
Hadith

The Prophet declared, "We have returned from the lesser holy war
(al jihad al-asghar) to the greater holy war (al jihad al-akbar)." They
asked, "O Prophet of God, which is the greater war?" He replied,
"Struggle against the lower self."
Hadith

This statement is an acknowledgement by the Prophet Muhammad of the Higher Self's existence distinct from the lower self.

Other Islamic quotations affirming that we are God's children include:

Allah is He Who made the earth a resting-place for you and the heaven a structure, and He formed you, then made goodly your forms, and he provided you with goodly things. That is Allah, your Lord — so blessed is Allah, the Lord of the worlds.
He it is Who created you from dust, then from a small life-germ, then from a clot, then He brings you forth as a child, then that you may attain your maturity, then that you may be old.

    Qur'an 40:64, 67

Does man think that he will be left aimless?
Was he not a small life-germ in sperm emitted?
Then he was a clot; so He created (him), then made (him) perfect.
Then He made of him two kinds, the male and the female.

    Qur'an 75:36-39

This last quote states that God made us perfect. This refers to our Higher or Divine Self.

And when thy Lord said to the angels: I am going to create a mortal of sounding clay, of black mud fashioned into shape.
So when I have made him complete and breathed into him of My Spirit, fall down making obeisance to him.
So the angels made obeisance, all of them together —

    Qur'an 15:28-30

Why would angels make obeisance to us "mortals?" It is because we contain God's Spirit and are part of the One Divine Family.

Certainly We created man in the best make.
Then We render him the lowest of the low,
Except those who believe and do good; so theirs is a reward never to be cut off.

    Qur'an 95:4-6

Here are a few of the several references in the Qur'an to God's omnipresence and omniscience in relation to man's Oneness with God.

And certainly We created man, and We know what his mind suggests to him — and We are nearer to him than his life-vein.
Qur'an 50:16

...and He is with you wherever you are. And Allah is Seer of what you do.
Qur'an 57:4

Surely Allah is the Knower of the unseen in the heavens and the earth. Surely He is Knower of what is in the hearts.
Qur'an 35:38

The other religions also affirm that we are sons and daughters of God, but each religion expresses this in its own way.

Judaism Affirms We Are Children of God

You are children of the Lord your God.
(Tanakh) Deuteronomy 14:1

As a mother comforts her son
So I will comfort you;
(Tanakh) Isaiah 66:13

Have we not all one Father? Did not one God create us?
(Tanakh) Malachi 2:10

And God created man in His image, in the image of God He created him; male and female He created them.
   (Tanakh) Genesis 1:27

A son should honor his father, and a slave his master. Now if I am a father, where is the honor due Me? And if I am a master, where is the reverence due Me? — said the Lord of Hosts to you, O priests who scorn My name.
   (Tanakh) Malachi 1:6

 ## Hinduism Affirms We Are Children of God

Hinduism offers many beautiful teachings affirming that we are a part of God. Here are just a few:

He who is devoted to Me knows; and assuredly he will enter into Me. Know thou further that Nature and God have no beginning; and that differences of character and quality have their origin in Nature only.
Nature is the Law which generates cause and effect; God is the source of the enjoyment of all pleasure and pain.
God dwelling in the heart of Nature experiences the Qualities which Nature brings forth; and His affinity towards the Qualities is the reason for His living in a good or evil body.
Thus in the body of man dwells the Supreme God; He who sees and permits, upholds and enjoys, the Highest God and the Highest Self. He who understands God and Nature along with her Qualities, whatever be his condition in life, he comes not again to earth.
   The Bhagavad Gita, chapter 13

The Person not larger than a thumb, the inner Self, is always settled in the heart of men. Let a man draw that Self forth from his body with steadiness, as one draws the pith from a reed. Let him know that Self as the Bright, as the Immortal; yes, as the Bright, as the Immortal.
Katha Upanishad, II, 6

Lord Shri Krishna said: I will now reveal to thee, since thou doubtest not, that profound mysticism, which when followed by experience, shall liberate thee from sin.
This is the Premier Science, the Sovereign Secret, the Purest and Best; intuitional, righteous; and to him who practiseth it pleasant beyond measure.
They who have no faith in this teaching cannot find Me, but remain lost in the purlieus [outlying districts] of this perishable world.
The whole world is pervaded by Me, yet My form is not seen. All living things have their being in Me, yet I am not limited by them.
Nevertheless, they do not consciously abide in Me. Such is My Divine Sovereignty that though I, the Supreme Self, am the cause and upholder of all, yet I remain outside.
As the mighty wind, though moving everywhere, has no resting place but space, so have all these beings no home but Me.
The Bhagavad Gita, chapter 9

Man should discover his own reality and not thwart himself.
For he has his self as his only friend, or as his only enemy.
A person has the self as friend when he has conquered himself, but if he rejects his own reality, the self will war against him.
The Bhagavad Gita, chapter 6

Now man is a creature of will. According to what his will is in this world, so will he be when he has departed this life. Let him therefore have this will and belief:
The intelligent, whose body is spirit, whose form is light, whose

thoughts are true, whose nature is like ether, omnipresent and invisible, from whom all works, all desires, all sweet odours and tests proceed; he who embraces all this, who never speaks, and is never surprised, he is my self within the heart, smaller than corn of rice, smaller than a corn of barley, smaller than a mustard seed, smaller than a canary seed or the kernel of a canary seed. He also is my self within the heart, greater than the earth, greater than the sky, greater than heaven, greater than all these worlds.

He from whom all works, all desires, all sweet odours and tests proceed, who embraces all this, who never speaks and who is never surprised, he, my self within the heart, is that Brahman. When I shall have departed hence, I shall obtain him (that Self). He who has this faith has no doubt; thus said Sandilya, yea, thus he said.

Khandogya Upanishad, III, 14

In the beginning...this was Self alone, in the shape of a person. He looking round saw nothing but his Self. He feared, and therefore any one who is lonely fears. He thought, "As there is nothing but myself, why should I fear?" Thence his fear passed away. For what should he have feared? Verily fear arises from a second only.

But he felt no delight. He wished for a second. He was so large as man and wife together. He then made that his Self to fall in two, and thence arose husband and wife....

He knew, "I indeed am this creation, for I created all this...."

And when they say, "Sacrifice to this or sacrifice to that god," each god is but his manifestation, for he is all gods....

He [Brahman or the Self] cannot be seen, for, in part only, when breathing he is breath by name; when speaking, speech by name; when seeing, eye by name; when hearing, ear by name; when thinking, mind by name. All these are but the names of his acts. And he who worships (regards) him as the one or the other, does not know him, for he is apart from this when qualified by the one or the other. Let men worship him as Self, for in the Self all these are one. This

Self is the footstep of everything, for through it one knows everything. And as one can find again by footsteps what was lost, thus he who knows this finds glory and praise.

This, which is nearer to us than anything, this Self, is dearer than a son, dearer than wealth, dearer than all else.

And if one were to say to one who declares another than the Self dear, that he will lose what is dear to him, very likely it would be so. Let him worship the Self alone as dear. He who worships the Self alone as dear, the object of his love will never perish.

Now if a man worships another deity, thinking the deity is one and he another, he does not know.

Brihadaranyaka Upanishad I, 4

I will speak to thee now of that great Truth which man ought to know, since by its means he will win immortal bliss — that which is without beginning, the Eternal Spirit which dwells in Me, neither with form, nor yet without it.

Everywhere are Its hands and Its feet, everywhere It has eyes that see, heads that think and mouths that speak; everywhere It listens; It dwells in all the worlds; it envelops them all.

Beyond the senses, It yet shines through every sense perception. Bound to nothing, It yet sustains everything. Unaffected by the Qualities, It still enjoys them all.

It is within all beings, yet outside; motionless yet moving; too subtle to be perceived, far away yet always near.

In all beings undivided, yet living in division, It is the upholder of all, Creator and Destroyer alike;

It is the Light of lights, beyond the reach of darkness; the Wisdom, the only thing that is worth knowing or that wisdom can teach; the Presence in the hearts of all.

Thus have I told thee in brief what Matter is, and the Self worth realizing and what is Wisdom. He who is devoted to Me knows; and assuredly he will enter into Me.

The Bhagavad Gita, chapter 13

What is then the light of man?
Yajnavalkya said: "The Self indeed is his light; for, having the Self alone
as his light, man sits, moves about, does his work, and returns."
Janaka Vaideha said: "Who is that Self?"
Yajnavalkya replied: "He who is within the heart, surrounded by the pra-
nas (senses), the person of light, consisting of knowledge.... And there
are two states for that person, the one here in this world, the other in
the other world, and as a third an intermediate state, the state of sleep.
When in that intermediate state, he sees both those states together, the
one here in this world, and the other in the other world....
"If a man clearly beholds this Self as God, and as the lord of all that
is and will be, then he is no more afraid.... This eternal being that
can never be proved, is to be perceived in one way only; it is spotless,
beyond the ether, the unborn Self, great and eternal. Let a wise Brah-
mana, after he has discovered him, practise wisdom. Let him not
seek after many words, for that is mere weariness of the tongue."
    Brihadaranyaka Upanishad IV, 3-4

 ## Buddhism Affirms We Are Children of God

Buddhism does not deny God, but doesn't use the term "God."
Instead, it uses other terms. The *Tathagata* is "the mind of clear
and pure reflection" or "the Buddha mind-nature hidden within
every being." Sometimes Gautama Buddha used this term to refer
to himself.

Nothing can ever destroy the Buddha nature. The nature of self is
nothing but the undisclosed storehouse of the Tathagata. Such a
storehouse can never be broken, put to fire or plundered. Though it
is not possible to destroy or see it, one can know it when one attains
the unsurpassed enlightenment.
    Mahaparinirvana Sutra 220

You men are all my children,
And I am your Father.
For age upon age, you have been scorched by multitudinous woes,
And I have saved you all.
     Lotus Sutra 3

This is Gautama Buddha speaking to a disciple, likening him-self to a father who has aided his children "for age upon age." At this point, Buddha was so unified with his Divine Self, God — that this was really God speaking to his children.

Every being has the Buddha Nature. This is the self. Such a self is,
since the very beginning, under cover of innumerable illusions. That
is why a man cannot see it.
     Mahaparinirvana Sutra 214

When appearances and names are put away and all discrimina-
tion ceases, that which remains is the true and essential nature of
things and, as nothing can be predicated as to the nature of essence,
it is called the "Suchness" of Reality. This universal, undifferenti-
ated, inscrutable Suchness is the only Reality, but it is variously
characterized as Truth, Mind-Essence, Transcendental Intelli-
gence, Perfection of Wisdom, etc. This Dharma [Universal Law] of
the imagelessness of the Essence-nature of Ultimate Reality is the
Dharma which has been proclaimed by all the Buddhas, and when
all things are understood in full agreement with it, one is in posses-
sion of Perfect Knowledge.
     Lankavatara Sutra, chapter 4

Today I indeed know that I am really a son of Buddha, born from
the mouth of Buddha, evolved from the Law, and have obtained a
place in the Buddha-law.
     Lotus Sutra 3

For him who...knows his own mind and sees intuitively his own nature, he is a Hero, a Teacher of gods and men, a Buddha.
Sutra of Hui Neng 1

 ## Taoism Affirms We Are Children of God

The Tao is like an empty bowl,
Which in being used can never be filled up.
Fathomless, it seems to be the origin of all things....
It unites the world into one whole.
Hidden in the deeps,
Yet it seems to exist forever.
I do not know whose child it is;
It seems to be the common ancestor of all, the father of things.
Tao Teh Ching, chapter 4

The Supreme gives man His expression, and gives him His form.
Kwang Tze 5

The Valley Spirit never dies.
It is named the Mysterious Female.
And the Doorway of the Mysterious Female
Is the base from which Heaven and Earth sprang.
It is there within us all the while;
Draw upon it as you will, it never runs dry.
Tao Teh Ching, chapter 6

Confucianism Affirms We Are Children of God

It is characteristic of the most entire sincerity to be able to foreknow....
When calamity or happiness is about to come, the good shall cer-
tainly be foreknown by him, and the evil also. Therefore the individ-
ual possessed of the most complete sincerity is like a spirit.
    The Doctrine of the Mean

The Master said, "Heaven produced the virtue that is in me."
    Confucian Analects, book 7

Chapter 5

Our Destiny: Our Divine Potential

WE COME FROM HIGHER, SPIRITUAL REALMS and if we act well on Earth we will return there. Each of us has the potential to become more godlike. How quickly we do this is dependent on our free will.

Our planet needs each of us to develop our attunement with the divine as quickly as possible. Otherwise there will be far greater suffering due to the lower nature of mankind, coupled with today's technological advances that are designed for war.

God guides and corrects us the most when we are consciously including Him in our life.

But without faith it is impossible to please Him: for he that cometh to God must believe that He is, and that He is a rewarder of them that diligently seek Him.
Hebrews 11:6

God is within us, and has the most intimate relationship with every one of us. We are unique yet at the same time One with God and all of life. Only the aspect of our consciousness that is divine mind can fully comprehend this apparent contradiction.

As we grow in achieving greater Divine Love and Divine Wisdom, God releases to us greater Power/Light/Energy. Love × Wisdom = Power. Love without Wisdom, or Wisdom without Love is less powerful and effective.

As we practice the twenty-two essential responsibilities in part II, we attune with God and do good works. As we do this, we grow in our Oneness with God, in our spiritual nature, and we transmute what is not of God within us into what is good and divine.

There are many levels of attainment both on Earth and in the heavenly realms. In the spiritual world, many souls are on each level, forming a Divine Hierarchy. This hierarchy includes angels. It also includes those who have attained mastery — men and women who are adepts or masters.

And we all, with unveiled face, beholding the glory of the Lord, are being changed into his likeness from one degree to another; for this comes from the Lord who is the Spirit.
2 Corinthians 3:18

Behold, what manner of love the Father hath bestowed upon us, that we should be called the sons of God: therefore the world knoweth us not, because it knew him not.
Beloved, now are we the sons of God, and it doth not yet appear what we shall be: but we know that, when he shall appear, we shall be like him.
1 John 3:1-2

We have divine potential — to grow into greater attunement and Oneness with God. This is our divine destiny.

Christianity Affirms Our Divine Potential

Consider what Jesus had to say about those he prayed for:

Neither pray I for these alone, but for them also which shall believe on me through their word;
That they all may be one; as thou, Father, are in me, and I in thee, that they also may be one in us: that the world may believe that thou hast sent me.
And the glory which thou gavest me I have given them; that they may be one, even as we are one:
I in them and thou in me, that they may be made perfect in one; and that the world may know that thou hast sent me, and hast loved them, as thou hast loved me.
And I have declared unto them thy name, and will declare it: that the love wherewith thou hast loved me may be in them, and I in them.
     John 17:20-23, 26

The truth is simple, yet awesome at the same time. We are really one big family. Because of our varying degrees of sense of separation, caused by false beliefs and residual energies of our unreal self, most people don't fully feel or know this yet.

And no man hath ascended up to heaven, but he that came down from heaven, even the Son of man which is in heaven.
     John 3:13

Jesus makes the point that all of us came from God, from heaven, in the first place — an excellent confirmation of our spiritual nature. Before we were born on Earth, we lived in Heaven.

It's important to know not only who we are, but also the

wonderful joyous future that awaits us as we grow in greater attunement and Oneness with our true reality.

And when he was demanded of the Pharisees, when the kingdom of God should come, he answered them and said, The kingdom of God cometh not with observation:
Neither shall they say, Lo here! or lo there! for behold, the kingdom of God is within you.
>   Luke 17:20-21

My little children, of whom I travail in birth again until Christ be formed in you.
>   Galatians 4:19

God's only son, the Christ, manifests within us as we purify ourselves, focus on our divinity, acquire the freedom of discipline, accomplish our mission on earth, and learn our lessons. Our efforts result in clearing the debris from our past errors to clarify our vision and to empower our Christ presence.

Let this mind be in you, which was also in Christ Jesus:
Who, being in the form of God, thought it not robbery to be equal with God.
>   Philippians 2:5-6

The Son can do nothing of himself, but what he seeth the Father do: for what things soever he doeth, these also doeth the Son likewise. For the Father loveth the Son, and sheweth him all things that himself doeth: and he will shew him greater works than these, that ye may marvel.
>   John 5:19-20

For I know that this shall turn to my salvation through your prayer, and the supply of the Spirit of Jesus Christ.

According to my earnest expectation and my hope, that in nothing I shall be ashamed, but that with all boldness, as always so now also Christ shall be magnified in my body, whether it be by life, or by death.

Philippians 1:19-20

Having set the proper context to allow a greater opportunity for a truer interpretation, let us look at what this tells us:

Let not your heart be troubled: ye believe in God, believe also in me.

In my Father's house are many mansions: if it were not so, I would have told you. I go to prepare a place for you.

And if I go and prepare a place for you, I will come again, and receive you unto myself; that where I am, there ye may be also.

And whither I go ye know, and the way ye know.

Thomas saith unto him, Lord, we know not whither thou goest; and how can we know the way?

Jesus saith unto him, I am the way, the truth, and the life: no man cometh unto the Father, but by me.

John 14:1-6

Traditional Christians believe this means that every person must have Jesus Christ as their Lord and Savior. Others, however, must have the chance to attain salvation who have never had the opportunity to hear of Jesus. Jesus was referring to the One Son, the Christ. No one can come unto the Father except through the same general methods of purification, perfection, peace, and other work that Jesus practiced (Part II).

If ye had known me, ye should have known my Father also: and from henceforth ye know him, and have seen him.
Philip saith unto him, Lord, shew us the Father, and it sufficeth us.
Jesus saith unto him, Have I been so long time with you, and yet hast thou not known me, Philip? He that hath seen me hath seen the Father; and how sayest thou then, Shew us the Father?
    John 14:7-9

Contemplate what it was like for Jesus to be at One with God. God, being pure spirit, manifests Himself on earth through those who purify themselves as Jesus did. The western mind has difficulty understanding this concept — that other individuals besides Jesus can strive for and achieve perfection. Only when we comprehend this mystical concept do we cease from limiting God in our lives.

Believest thou not that I am in the Father; and the Father in me? The words that I speak unto you I speak not of myself: but the Father that dwelleth in me, he doeth the works.
Believe me that I am in the Father, and the Father in me: or else believe me for the very works' sake.
Verily, verily, I say unto you, He that believeth on me, the works that I do shall he do also; and greater works that these shall he do; because I go unto my Father.
And whatsoever ye shall ask in my name, that will I do, that the Father may be glorified in the Son.
If ye shall ask any thing in my name, I will do it.
    John 14:10-14

In their Oneness, what is the difference between Jesus and God, our Father, in their instruction that we can ask anything in their name, and receive it? Jesus asked in his Father's name. We can also ask in the name of the One Son, the Christ.

He shall reward every man according to his works.
Matthew 16:27

Jesus attuned with God through the One Son, the Christ that is the mediator between God and men. The crucial point evident in the preceding quotations is that God and Jesus are not separate from us in their divinity. Jesus is not the only son of God. We are God's sons and daughters too, and with desire and focus we can achieve the fullness of our potential, just as Jesus did.

Jesus demonstrated a state of consciousness which each one of us has the potential to achieve. Because of his Oneness with God the Father, God was able to speak to us directly through Jesus. Jesus was able to retain his individuality and be fully attuned to his Father at the same time. This is the mystical teaching of Jesus — that we can achieve this same unlimited life of freedom, love, wisdom, and power.

I can do all things through Christ which strengtheneth me.
Philippians 4:13

Jesus did not have exclusive sonship. Not everyone needs to go through Jesus to reach their divine potential. We do, however, have to go through the Christ, the Mediator between God and man.

This interpretation does not limit God, and it does not deprive us of our divine potential. It also does not discourage our pursuit of perfection — we must remember that God looks for the degree of perfection in our heart's intention.

Islam Affirms Our Divine Potential

O soul that art at rest,
Return to thy Lord, well-pleased, well-pleasing.
     Qur'an 89:27-28

He indeed is successful who purifies himself.
And remembers the name of his Lord, then prays.
     Qur'an 87:14-15

O man, thou must strive a hard striving (to attain) to thy Lord, until
thou meet Him.
     Qur'an 84:6

I, Allah, am the best Knower.
Do men think that they will be left alone on saying We believe, and
will not be tried?
And indeed We tried those before them, so Allah will certainly know
those who are true and he will know the liars.
Or do they who work evil think that they will escape Us? Evil is it
that they judge!
Whoever hopes to meet with Allah, the term of Allah is then surely
coming. And He is the Hearing, the Knowing.
And whoever strives hard, strives for himself. Surely Allah is Self-
sufficient, above (need of) (His) creatures.
And those who believe and do good, We shall certainly do away with
their afflictions and reward them for the best of what they did.
     Qur'an 29:1-7

The heart of him who knows, and so believes with full assurance, is
the throne of God.
     Khalifa Ali

Heaven and earth contain me not, but the heart of my faithful servant contains me.
Hadith of Suhrawardi

I saw my Lord with the eye of the Heart.
I said: "Who are you?"
He answered: "You."
Al-Hallaj (A Sufi text)

 ## Judaism Affirms Our Divine Potential

For I the Lord am your God:
You shall sanctify yourselves and be holy,
For I am holy....
You shall be holy, for I am holy.
(Tanakh) Leviticus 11:44-45

I will put My Teaching into their inmost being and inscribe it upon their hearts. Then I will be their God, and they shall be My people. No longer will they need to teach one another and say to one another, "Heed the Lord;" for all of them, from the least of them to the greatest, shall heed Me — declares the Lord.
For I will forgive their iniquities and remember their sins no more.
(Tanakh) Jeremiah 31:33-34

Oh that men would praise the Lord for his goodness, and for his wonderful works to the children of men!
For he satisfieth the longing soul, and filleth the hungry soul with goodness.
(King James Bible) Psalms 107:8-9

The spirit of the Lord will grip you, and you will speak in ecstasy along with them [prophets]; you will become another man.
   (Tanakh) 1 Samuel 10:6

What we can look forward to is a new level of knowledge and experience far beyond what we have known, a wonderfully improved state of consciousness. This level is far beyond mere intellectual experience. It is the joyful state of higher consciousness.

Study of Torah leads to precision, precision to zeal, zeal to cleanliness, cleanliness to restraint, restraint to purity, purity to holiness, holiness to meekness, meekness to fear of sin, fear of sin to saintliness, saintliness to the holy spirit, and the holy spirit to life eternal.
   (Talmud) Aboda Zara 20b

 Hinduism Affirms Our Divine Potential

Hinduism contains many beautiful teachings about becoming One with God.

Fix thy mind on Me, devote thyself to Me, sacrifice for Me, surrender to Me, make Me the object of thy aspirations, and thou shalt assuredly become one with Me, Who am thine own Self.
   The Bhagavad Gita, chapter 9

As the one fire, after it has entered the world, though one, becomes different according to whatever it burns, thus the one Self within all things becomes different, according to whatever it enters, and exists also without. As the one air, after it has entered the world, though one, becomes different according to whatever it enters, thus the one Self within all things becomes different, according to whatever it enters, and exists also without. As the sun, the eye of the whole world, is not contaminated by the external impurities seen by the eyes, thus the one Self within all things is never contaminated by the misery of the world, being himself without.

There is one ruler, the Self within all things, who makes the one form manifold. The wise who perceive him within their Self, to them belongs eternal happiness, not to others. There is one eternal thinker, thinking non-eternal thoughts, who, though one, fulfils the desires of many. The wise who perceive him within their Self, to them belongs eternal peace, not to others.

Katha Upanishad II, 5

I am the source of all; from Me everything flows. Therefore the wise worship Me with unchanging devotion.

With minds concentrated on Me, with lives absorbed in Me, and enlightening each other, they ever feel content and happy.

To those who are always devout and who worship Me with love, I give the power of discrimination, which leads them to Me.

By My grace, I live in their hearts; and I dispel the darkness of ignorance by the shining light of wisdom.

The Bhagavad Gita, chapter 10

As long as the individual soul does not free itself from Nescience [ignorance] in the form of duality — which Nescience may be compared to the mistake of him who in the twilight mistakes a post for a man — and does not rise to the knowledge of the Self, whose nature is unchangeable, eternal Cognition — which expresses itself in the form 'I am Brahman' — so long it remains the individual soul.

But when, discarding the aggregate of body, sense-organs and mind, it arrives, by means of Scripture, at the knowledge that it is not itself that aggregate, that it does not form part of transmigratory existence, but is the True, the Real, the Self, whose nature is pure intelligence; then knowing itself to be of the nature of unchangeable eternal Cognition, it lifts itself above the vain conceit of being one with this body, and itself becomes the Self, whose nature is unchanging, eternal Cognition.

As is declared in such scriptural passages as 'He who knows the highest Brahman becomes even Brahman' (Mu. Up. III, 2, 9). And this is the real nature of the individual soul by means of which it arises from the body and appears in its own form.

Vedanta Sutra I, 3, 19

I am the same to all beings. I favor none, and I hate none. But those who worship Me devotedly, they live in Me, and I in them.

The Bhagavad Gita, chapter 9

 ## Buddhism Affirms Our Divine Potential

Within Buddhism the mystical attunement with God is strongly linked to Mind.

A Bhikshu [a mendicant or member of a religious order who owns little] who has entered his empty house, and whose mind is tranquil, feels a more than human delight when he sees the law clearly.

As soon as he has considered the origin and destruction of the elements of the body, he finds happiness and joy which belong to those who know the immortal (Nirvana).

And this is the beginning here for a wise Bhikshu: watchfulness over the senses, contentedness, restraint under the law; keep noble friends whose life is pure, and who are not slothful.

Let him live in charity, let him be perfect in his duties; then in the fullness of delight he will make an end of suffering.

The Dhammapada, chapter 25

Know that Buddha and mind
Are in essence inexhaustible.
If people know the actions of mind
Create all the worlds,
They will see the Buddha
And understand Buddha's true nature....
If people want to really know
All Buddhas of all times,
They should contemplate the nature of the cosmos:
All is but mental construction.
       Garland Sutra 20

Since all Dharmas [truths] are immanent in our mind there is no
reason why we should not realize intuitively the real nature of Such-
ness [Mind-essence]. The Bodhisattva Sila Sutra says, "Our Essence
of Mind is intrinsically pure, and if we know our mind and realized
what our nature is, all of us would attain Buddhahood."
       Sutra of Hui Neng 2

You are the source
Of all purity and all impurity.
No one purifies another.
       The Dhammapada, chapter 12

Supported by the sustaining power of the Buddhas, the Bodhisatt-
vas at this stage enter into the bliss of the Samadhi of perfect tran-
quillisation. Owing to their original vows [made for the salvation
of beings, saying, "So long as they do not attain Nirvana, I will not
attain it myself"] they are transported by emotions of love and com-
passion as they become aware of the part they are to perform in the
carrying out of their vows for the emancipation of all beings. Thus
they do not enter into Nirvana, but, in truth, they too are already in
Nirvana because in their emotions of love and compassion there is

no rising of discrimination; henceforth, with them, discrimination no more takes place.... This is called the Bodhisattva's Nirvana — the losing oneself in the bliss of perfect self-yielding.
Lankavatara Sutra, chapter 11

You have no name and no form.
Why miss what you do not have?
The Dhammapada, chapter 25

In essence, we are pure spirit/consciousness. We are not really our name or physical body. Why worry about losing what eventually we do not need?

Him I call indeed a Brahmana [an Arhat, or Buddhist who has attained enlightenment] who...knows the end of his suffering, has put down his burden, and is unshackled.
Him I all indeed a Brahmana whose knowledge is deep, who possesses wisdom, who knows the right way and the wrong, and has attained the highest end....
Him I call indeed a Brahmana who finds no fault with other beings, whether feeble or strong, and does not kill nor cause slaughter.
Him I call indeed a Brahmana who is tolerant with the intolerant, mild with fault-finders, and free from passion among the passionate.
Him I call indeed a Brahmana from whom anger and hatred, pride and envy have dropt like a mustard seed from the point of a needle.
Him I call indeed a Brahmana who utters true speech, instructive and free from harshness, so that he offend no one....
Him I call indeed a Brahmana who in this world is above good and evil, above the bondage of both, free from grief from sin, and from impurity....

Him I call indeed a Brahmana, the manly, the noble, the hero, the great sage, the conqueror, the impassible, the accomplished, the awakened.

Him I call indeed a Brahmana who knows his former abodes, who sees heaven and hell, has reached the end of births, is perfect in knowledge, a sage, and whose perfections are all perfect.

The Dhammapada, chapter 26

 ## Taoism Affirms Our Divine Potential

Between Heaven and Earth,
There seems to be a Bellows:
It is empty, and yet it is inexhaustible;
The more it works, the more comes out of it.
No amount of words can fathom it:
Better look for it within you.

Tao Teh Ching, chapter 5

It lies in the nature of Grand Virtue
To follow the Tao and the Tao alone.
Now what is the Tao?
It is Something elusive and evasive.
Evasive and elusive!
And yet It contains within Itself a Form.
Elusive and evasive!
And yet It contains within Itself a Substance.
Shadowy and dim!
And yet It contains within Itself a Core of Vitality.
The Core of Vitality is very real,
It contains within Itself an unfailing Sincerity.
Throughout the ages Its Name has been preserved
In order to recall the Beginning of all things.

How do I know the ways of all things at the Beginning?
By what is within me.
    Tao Teh Ching, chapter 21

 ## Confucianism Affirms Our Divine Potential

He who is greatly virtuous will be sure to receive the appointment
of Heaven.
    The Doctrine of the Mean

It is only he who is possessed of the most complete sincerity that can
exist under heaven, who can give its full development to his nature.
Able to give its full development to his own nature, he can do the
same to the nature of other men. Able to give its full development
to the nature of other men, he can give their full development to the
nature of creatures and things, he can assist the transforming and
nourishing powers of Heaven and Earth. Able to assist the trans-
forming and nourishing powers of the Heaven and Earth, he may
with Heaven and Earth form a ternion [a set of three].
    The Doctrine of the Mean

It is only he, possessed of all sagely qualities that can exist under
heaven, who shows himself quick in apprehension, clear in knowl-
edge, fitted to exercise rule....
All-embracing is he and vast, deep and active as a fountain, send-
ing forth in their due season his virtues.
All-embracing and vast, he is like Heaven.
    The Doctrine of the Mean

Section III

Who and What God Is

THERE ARE MANY WONDERFUL and exciting perspectives about Who and What God Is. This section contains six aspects of God that are common to the sacred texts.

This section is also an extension of the last section that discussed who we are. Since we have the divine potential to become more like God, attune with God, and unite with God, these six qualities also express our potential.

Many people have experienced "mystical glimpses" — moments of experiencing all of life as one — of having a strong sense of omnipresence and omniscience. There have also been a number of NDE's (near death experiences) in which this type of experience lasted for some time.

The only thing that can limit us is the act of accepting the outer world of appearances as the sum total of reality and ignoring the active presence of God in our world.

God's Kingdom is a state of being. To enter, we need to focus on God within. Each one of us needs to seek our own progressive revelation as we experience the results of focusing on the divine inner light.

Let your present awareness of your state of consciousness motivate you to discover and be more a part of God's consciousness. From each new level a new awareness of the next level will be made known to you. Each new level will consist of what will appeal to your heart. Part II, "Essential Responsibilities for Loving Living" contains much information on how to do this.

Ask God to come into your being so that you may experience more of Him in consciousness. The Law of Free Will requires that you ask. This is important to self-mastery, self-discipline, and freedom, because one is then in conscious cooperation and co-creation with God.

In addition to the six qualities of God in these six chapters, it is also important to remember:

God is Love. Love is an important aspect of every principle in life.

And we have known and believed the love that God hath to us. God is love; and he that dwelleth in love dwelleth in God, and God in him.
1 John 4:16

Every moment we receive divine energy. It flows through us and gives us life. And every moment we qualify that energy in some positive or negative way, such as in peace and patience, or fear and anger. The best way to qualify your divine energy every moment is with love — for God, for others, your work, and yourself (God in you) — because love contains every other positive divine quality such as forgiveness, peace, patience, compassion, and generosity.

"Good" is what describes the intent and the flow of Love.

Goodness and love are the meaning and purpose of life (along with our essential responsibilities required to enjoy goodness and love). Therefore, God is, in addition to the six qualities in this section, also the meaning and purpose of Life. God is also Love, and God is Good.

As a loving creator and caregiver, God is also our Divine Father and Mother.

There are aspects of God that are incomprehensible. The experience of God can be quite awesome and magnificent, and beyond our intellectual understanding.

In addition to the six qualities of God established in the following chapters, remember that other qualities of God include:

God is Love.
God is Good and Goodness.
God is the Meaning and Purpose of Life.
God is our Divine Father and Mother.
God is beyond our total intellectual comprehension.

Chapter 6

Unity: There is Only One God

HOW CAN MEN FIGHT ONE ANOTHER in God's name, when we all have the same God? The answer lies in mankind's having forgotten the purpose of life — the love, the goodness, and our responsibilities. We have forgotten who we really are, and how close we can be to God, and to each other, in peace.

A far greater feeling of unity with one another is needed. We need to comprehend and put into action the most unifying interpretations of the truth from our respective religions — the truth common to all world religions.

The oneness of God can include us as well. Here is a sample of what the sacred texts say about there being only one God.

 Christianity Affirms There is Only One God

There is one body, and one Spirit, even as ye are called in one hope of your calling;
One Lord, one faith, one baptism,
One God and Father of all, who is above all, and through all, and in you all.

Ephesians 4:4-6

And Jesus answered him, The first of all the commandments is, Hear,
O Israel; The Lord our God is one Lord.
And the scribe said unto him, Well, Master, thou hast said the truth:
for there is one God; and there is none other but He.

  Mark 12:29, 32

...and that there is none other God but one.
For though there be that are called gods, whether in heaven or in
earth, (as there be gods many, and lords many,)
But to us there is but one God, the Father, of whom are all things,
and we in him....

  1 Corinthians 8:4-6

Is he the God of the Jews only? Is he not also of the Gentiles? Yes, of
the Gentiles also:
Seeing it is one God, which shall justify the circumcision by faith,
and the uncircumcision through faith.

  Romans 3:29-30

 ## Islam Affirms There is Only One God

The fact that there is only One God is one of the fundamental
tenets of Islam. It is mentioned throughout the Qur'an.

And your God is one God; there is no God but He! He is the Benefi-
cent, the Merciful.

  Qur'an 2:163

Your God is one God, so those who believe not in the Hereafter, their
hearts refuse to know and they are proud.

  Qur'an 16:22

So your God is One God, therefore to Him should you submit. And give good news to the humble.
Qur'an 22:34

 ## Judaism Affirms There is Only One God

Judaism, the oldest of the Abrahamic religions, contains many references to God as being One.

The Lord is our God, the Lord alone.
(Tanakh) Deuteronomy 6:4

I am the Lord and there is none else;
Beside Me, there is no god.
I engird you, though you have not known Me,
So that they may know, from east to west,
That there is none but Me.
I am the Lord and there is none else.
(Tanakh) Isaiah 45:5-6

For the Lord your God is God supreme and Lord supreme.
(Tanakh) Deuteronomy 10:17

 ## Hinduism Affirms There is Only One God

Hinduism has a reputation for having hundreds of gods, but behind the different gods has been a steadfast belief in one Supreme God.

There was a man who worshipped Shiva but hated all other deities. One day Shiva appeared to him and said, "I shall never be pleased with you so long as you hate the other gods." But the man was inexorable. After a few days Shiva again appeared to him and said, "I shall never be pleased with you so long as you hate." The man kept silent. After a few moments Shiva again appeared. This time one side of his body was that of Shiva, and the other side that of Vishnu. The man was half pleased and half displeased. He laid his offerings on the side representing Shiva, and did not offer anything to the side representing Vishnu. Then Shiva said, "Your bigotry is unconquerable. I, by assuming this dual aspect, tried to convince you that all gods and goddesses are but various aspects of the one Absolute Brahman."

The Sayings of Sri Ramakrishna

He is the one God, hidden in all beings, all-pervading, the self within all beings, watching over all works, dwelling in all beings, the witness, the perceiver, the only one…. He is the one ruler of many who seem to act, but really do not act; he makes the one seed manifold. The wise who perceive him within their self, to them belongs eternal happiness, not to others.

Svetasvatara Upanishad, VI

And when they say, "Sacrifice to this or sacrifice to that god," each god is but his manifestation, for he is all gods.

Brihabaranyaka Upanishad, I, 4

Lord Shri Krishna said: Now, O Prince! Listen to My supreme advice, which I give thee for the sake of thy welfare, for thou art My beloved.

Neither the professors of divinity nor the great ascetics know My origin, for I am the source of them all. He who knows Me as the unborn, without beginning, the Lord of the universe, he, stripped of his delusions, becomes free from all conceivable sin.

Intelligence, wisdom, non-illusion, forgiveness, truth, self-control,

calmness, pleasure, pain, birth, death, fear and fearlessness;
Harmlessness, equanimity, contentment, austerity, beneficence,
fame and failure, all these, the characteristics of beings, spring
from Me only.
The seven Great Seers, the Progenitors of mankind, the Ancient Four,
and the Lawgivers were born of My Will and came forth direct from
Me. The race of mankind has sprung from them.
He who rightly understands My manifested glory and My Creative
Power, beyond doubt attains perfect Peace.
I am the source of all; from Me everything flows. Therefore the wise
worship Me with unchanging devotion.
With minds concentrated on Me, with lives absorbed in Me, and
enlightening each other, they ever feel content and happy.
To those who are always devout and who worship Me with love, I
give the power of discrimination, which leads them to Me.
By My grace, I live in their hearts; and I dispel the darkness of igno-
rance by the shining light of wisdom.

The Bhagavad Gita, chapter 10

The concept of "God" is somewhat different in Buddhism, Taoism, and Confucianism. Instead, other terms and concepts are used. The concepts of Unity, Oneness, and Wholeness are used to allude to God, known as the Source or Cause.

Buddhism Affirms There is Only One God

The concept of God is addressed in Buddhism as "Self," "Suchness," "Truth," "Mind-Essence" and similar concepts. It is clear within Buddhist texts that these terms don't represent multiple, separate realities, but One Reality.

*When appearances and names are put away and all discrimination
ceases, that which remains is the true and essential nature of things
and, as nothing can be predicated as to the nature of essence, it is
called the "Suchness" of Reality. This universal, undifferentiated,
inscrutable Suchness is the only Reality, but it is variously characterized as Truth, Mind-Essence, Transcendental Intelligence, Perfection
of Wisdom, etc. This Dharma [Universal Law] of the imagelessness of
the Essence-nature of Ultimate Reality is the Dharma which has been
proclaimed by all the Buddhas, and when all things are understood
in full agreement with it, one is in possession of Perfect Knowledge.*
    Lankavatara Sutra, chapter 4

*There is, O monks, an Unborn, neither become nor created nor
formed.... Were there not, there would be no deliverance from the
formed, the made, the compounded.*
    Gautama Buddha

 ## Taoism Affirms There is Only One God

*From of old there are not lacking things that have attained
Oneness.*
The sky attained Oneness and became clear;
The earth attained Oneness and became calm;
*The spirits attained Oneness and became charged with mystical
powers;*
The fountains attained Oneness and became full;
*The ten thousand creatures attained Oneness and became
reproductive;*
*Barons and princes attained Oneness and became sovereign rul-
ers of the world.*
All of them are what they are by virtue of Oneness.
    Tao Teh Ching, chapter 39

The Tao is to the world what a great river or an ocean is to the streams and brooks.

Tao Teh Ching, chapter 32

Unite the world into one whole!
This is called the Mystical Whole,
Which you cannot court after nor shun,
Benefit nor harm, honour nor humble.
Therefore, it is the Highest of the world.

Tao Teh Ching, chapter 56

 ## Confucianism Affirms There is Only One God

The Master said, "Shan, my doctrine is that of an all-pervading unity." The disciple Tsang replied, "Yes."
The Master went out, and the other disciples asked, saying, "What do his words mean?" Tsang said, "The doctrine of our master is to be true to the principles — of our nature and the benevolent exercise of them to others...."

The Confucian Analects, book 4

The Master said, "Ts'ze, you think, I suppose, that I am one who learns many things and keeps them in memory?"
Tsze-kung replied, "Yes, but perhaps it is not so?"
"No," was the answer; "I seek a unity all pervading."

The Confucian Analects, book 15

Chapter 7

The Creator: God is the Creator of All Good Things

GOD IS THE SOURCE AND CREATOR of all good things, including us. All positive and good qualities are God/Divine qualities. Some of the wonderful qualities of God are love, perfection, intelligence, creativity, beauty, and truth. If you go through the dictionary, you can find hundreds of words that represent the many positive, beautiful, and meaningful aspects of God.

This principle of God as the creator of all good ties right in to the first principle of "Life, with God, is Good." For God creates and sustains our life, and a person taking action for good is "God in action."

We, as individuals, can become the fullness of the meaning of these God qualities. We can increase our focus on God and His all-positive qualities. As a result of doing so, we can become the living manifestation of all good things.

God individuated Himself in you so that love and joyful life experience could expand throughout the universe. To be able to fully participate in the physical world, God exists within every positive aspect of life. Love and joyful interaction abound between people attuned with God's good will.

God loves his children and wants his divine family to co-create with Him in ever more goodness, beauty, and joy.

We can aim to attain the level of God self-awareness: an

awareness and love of good. We can desire to always love taking action for the good. Working with all thirty-three principles ensures the growth of our love of good.

Christianity Affirms God is the Creator of All Good Things

In the first chapter, we looked at several quotations from Genesis about God creating the world. In addition, the Bible contains other quotations about God in the act of creating.

For, behold, I create new heavens and a new earth: and the former shall not be remembered, nor come into mind.
But be ye glad and rejoice for ever in that which I create.
   Isaiah 65:17-18

Thou art worthy, O Lord, to receive glory and honour and power: for thou hast created all things, and for thy pleasure they are and were created.
   Revelation 4:11

Mankind needs to attain the level of spiritual self-awareness as the Christ, which is a total awareness and love of good. From that level, we will best co-create good works with God.

Finally, brethren, whatsoever things are true, whatsoever things are honest, whatsoever things are just, whatsoever things are pure, whatsoever things are lovely, whatsoever things are of good report; if there be any virtue, and if there be any praise, think on these things.
   Philippians 4:8

But the fruit of the Spirit is love, joy, peace, longsuffering [patience], gentleness, goodness, faith, meekness, temperance: against such there is no law.

Galatians 5:22-23

Make every effort to supplement your faith with virtue, and virtue with knowledge, and knowledge with self-control, and self-control with steadfastness, and steadfastness with godliness, and godliness with brotherly affection, and brotherly affection with love. For if these things are yours and abound, they keep you from being ineffective or unfruitful in the knowledge of our Lord Jesus Christ.

2 Peter 1:5-8

 ## Islam Affirms God is the Creator of All Good Things

Allah is the Creator of all things, and He is the One, the Supreme.

Qur'an 13:16

Praise be to Allah, Who created the heavens and the earth, and made darkness and light. Yet those who disbelieve set up equals to their Lord.

Qur'an 6:1

We are able to co-create goodness with God — thanks to His Will.

Allah is He Who created the heavens and the earth and sent down water from the clouds, then brought forth with it fruits as a sustenance for you, and He has made the ships subservient to you to run their course in the sea by His command, and He has made the river subservient to you.

And He has made subservient to you the sun and the moon, pursuing their courses; and He has made subservient to you the night and the day.
And He gives you of all you ask of Him. And if you count Allah's favours, you will not be able to number them.

Qur'an 14:32-34

See you not that Allah has made subservient to you whatever is in the heavens and whatever is in the earth, and granted to you His favours complete outwardly and inwardly?

Qur'an 31:20

If thou derive pleasure from the good which thou hast done, and be grieved for the evil which thou hast committed, thou art a true believer.

Hadith

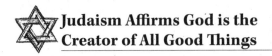

Judaism Affirms God is the Creator of All Good Things

And God created man in His image, in the image of God He created him; male and female He created them.
God blessed them and God said to them, "Be fertile and increase, fill the earth and master it; and rule the fish of the sea, the birds of the sky, and all the living things that creep on earth."
And God saw all that He had made, and found it very good.

(Tanakh) Genesis 1:27-28, 31

The heavens declare the glory of God,
the sky proclaims His handiwork.

(Tanakh) Psalms 19:2

All who are linked to My name,
Whom I have created,
Formed, and made for My glory —
  (Tanakh) Isaiah 43:7

The Lord is gracious and compassionate,
slow to anger and abounding in kindness.
The Lord is good to all,
and His mercy is upon all His works.
All your works shall praise You, O Lord,
and Your faithful ones shall bless You.
They shall talk of the majesty of Your kingship,
and speak of Your might,
to make His mighty acts known among men
and the majestic glory of His kingship.
  (Tanakh) Psalms 145:8-12

ॐ Hinduism Affirms God is the Creator of All Good Things

Neither the professors of divinity nor the great ascetics know My origin, for I am the source of them all.
He who knows Me as the unborn, without beginning, the Lord of the universe, he, stripped of his delusions, becomes free from all conceivable sin....
He who rightly understands My manifested glory and My Creative Power, beyond doubt attains perfect Peace.
I am the source of all; from Me everything flows.
  The Bhagavad Gita, chapter 10

O Arjuna! The aspects of My divine life are endless. I have mentioned but a few by way of illustration.
Whatever is glorious, excellent, beautiful and mighty, be assured that it comes from a fragment of My splendour.
But what is the use of all these details to thee? O Arjuna!
I sustain this universe with only a small part of Myself.
    The Bhagavad Gita, chapter 10

The supreme Brahma, the supreme soul, the substance of the world, the lord of all creatures, the universal soul, the supreme ruler...of his own will having entered into matter and spirit, agitated the mutable and immutable principles, the season of creation being arrived....
    Vishnu Purana, book 1, chapter 2

Next, we have a list of God qualities that lead to creating freedom.

Lord Shri Krishna continued: Fearlessness, clean living, unceasing concentration on wisdom, readiness to give, self-control, a spirit of sacrifice, regular study of the scriptures, austerities, candour,
Harmlessness, truth, absence of wrath, renunciation, contentment, straightforwardness, compassion towards all, uncovetousness, courtesy, modesty, constancy,
Valour, forgiveness, fortitude, purity, freedom from hate and vanity; these are his who possesses the Godly Qualities....
Godly qualities lead to liberation; godless to bondage.
    The Bhagavad Gita, chapter 16

Buddhism Affirms God is the Creator of All Good Things

"Thus," replied the Buddha,
"the Tathagata knows the straight path that leads to a union with
Brahma.
He knows it as one who has entered the world of Brahma and has
been born in it.
There can be no doubt in the Tathagata.
    Buddha, The Gospel: The Two Brahmans

In the above quote the term "Tathagata" refers to "the mind of clear and pure reflection" or "'the Buddha' mind-nature hidden within every being." "Brahma" refers to the creative force of Brahman (God). God's three attributes were personalized and were called "Brahma, Vishnu and Shiva." [The Creator, Preserver and Destroyer/transmuter].

There is, O monks, an unborn, unoriginated, uncreated, unformed.
Were there not, O monks, this unborn, unoriginated, uncreated,
unformed, there would be no escape from the world of the born, origi-
nated, created, formed. Since, O monks, there is an unborn, unorigi-
nated, uncreated, and unformed, therefore is there an escape from
the born, originated, created, formed.
    Buddha, The Gospel: The Three Characteristics and the Uncreated

The above reference to the "unborn, unoriginated, uncreated, and unformed" is an acknowledgement of God our Creator.
    Buddhism also encourages man's creation of good works.

Even ornamented royal chariots wear out. So too the body reaches
old age. But the Dhamma [Teaching, or Mind] of the Good grows
not old. Thus do the Good reveal it among the Good.
    The Dhammapada (Thera) 151

The Great Compassionate Heart is the essence of Buddhahood.
　　Gandavyuha Sutra

O good man! Compassion is the Buddha nature of all beings.
Such a Buddha nature is long overshadowed by illusion.
That is why being cannot see.
The Buddha nature is Compassion.
Compassion is the Tathagata.
　　Mahaparinirvana Sutra 259

 ## Taoism Affirms God is the Creator of All Good Things

In Taoism, the Eternal Tao is God the Creator.

Tao can be talked about, but not the Eternal Tao.
Names can be named, but not the Eternal Name.
As the origin of heaven-and-earth, it is nameless:
As "the Mother" of all things, it is nameable.
So, as ever hidden, we should look at its inner essence:
As always manifest, we should look at its outer aspects.
These two flow from the same source, though differently named;
And both are called mysteries.
The Mystery of mysteries is the Door of all essence.
　　Tao Teh Ching, chapter 1

The Tao is like an empty bowl,
Which in being used can never be filled up.
Fathomless, it seems to be the origin of all things....
I do not know whose child it is;
It seems to be the common ancestor all, the father of things.
　　Tao Teh Ching, chapter 4

Although these quotations do not describe a God Who creates only good, the *Tao Teh Ching* is filled with teachings on living a virtuous life. Living a life of good is emphasized so that the individual may be in the natural flow of the Tao. When in that flow, we can easily co-create goodness with the Eternal Tao [God].

Confucianism Affirms God is the Creator of All Good Things

The Master said, "I would prefer not speaking."
Tsze-kung said, "If you, Master, do not speak, what shall we, your disciples, have to record?"
The Master said, "Does Heaven speak? The four seasons pursue their courses, and all things are continually being produced, but does Heaven say anything?"
The Confucian Analects, book 17

The above quotation indirectly states that Heaven is the cause of all things being continually produced.

On the subject of mankind being co-creators with God, we have:

It is only he who is possessed of the most complete sincerity that can exist under heaven, who can give its full development to his nature. Able to give its full development to his own nature, he can do the same to the nature of other men. Able to give its full development to the nature of other men, he can give their full development to the nature of creatures and things, he can assist the transforming and nourishing powers of Heaven and Earth. Able to assist the transforming and nourishing powers of the Heaven and Earth, he may with Heaven and Earth form a ternion [a set of three].
Next to the above is he who cultivates to the utmost the shoots of

*goodness in him. From those he can attain to the possession of
sincerity. This sincerity becomes apparent. From being apparent,
it becomes manifest. From being manifest, it becomes brilliant.
Brilliant, it affects others. Affecting others, they are changed by it.
Changed by it, they are transformed. It is only he who is possessed
of the most complete sincerity that can exist under heaven, who can
transform.*

The Doctrine of the Mean

*What Heaven has conferred is called the Nature....
Let the states of equilibrium and harmony exist in perfection, and
a happy order will prevail throughout heaven and earth, and all
things will be nourished and flourish.*

The Doctrine of the Mean

Each religion has given to us a definite acknowledgement of
God as creator. In this and other chapters, each religion also discusses divine qualities that mankind can utilize to be co-creators
with God. When individual souls use God's energy in a positive
way to create good, we are a part of God in action. God is then
working through us.

Chapter 8

Omnipotence: God is All-Powerful

THE NEXT THREE CHAPTERS are about the three "omni's." The term "omni" means "all" or "universally." In this chapter we look at the omnipotence of God, keeping in mind that as we grow in our attunement with God our power increases.

God is all-powerful. The highest and best use of God's energy is to qualify it with love. The energy qualified by God into creation is love energy. Divine energy/Light *is* Love. All we need to do is respond in kind.

All matter is energy/frequency/vibration — this is now an accepted fact of science. Despite how solid our bodies feel, or even how solid a rock feels, every bit of matter is simply a pattern of energy waves — frequencies/vibrations.

One reason that you are a part of God and have the potential to grow in divinity is because there is one God and God's energy is everywhere. God's energy is Divine Light. The real "you" is composed of Divine Light.

 Christianity Affirms God is All-Powerful

Christianity and Judaism share many wonderful descriptions of God's power in creating the universe in Genesis, the first book of the Old Testament. Other landmark Bible stories such as the parting of the Red Sea and the destruction of Sodom and Gomorrah demonstrate the power of God in the Old Testament. The New Testament also contains many stories of the power of God.

And I heard as it were the voice of a great multitude, and as the voice of many waters, and as the voice of mighty thunderings, saying, Alleluia: for the Lord God omnipotent reigneth.
Revelation 19:6

In the beginning was the Word, and the Word was with God, and the Word was God.
The same was in the beginning with God.
All things were made by him; and without him was not any thing made that was made.
In him was life; and the life was the light of men.
And the light shineth in darkness; and the darkness comprehended it not.
There was a man sent from God whose name was John.
The same came for a witness, to bear witness of the Light, that all men through him might believe.
He was not that Light, but was sent to bear witness of that Light.
That was the true Light, which lighteth every man that cometh into the world.
John 1:1-9

In the above quotation, the "Word" is energy, vibration, or light. God and all creation are composed of this life and light. In line 7, the "Light" that John came to bear witness of can be understood as being the Light of God through Jesus. It also refers to the divine truth that Jesus Christ spoke. Jesus, so perfectly attuned with our Divine Father, radiated the pure Light of God. His message included new teachings on love and forgiveness. Also, Jesus wanted to share with us divine, mystical truth about his oneness of perfect attunement with God and our potential oneness.

In truth, we are already one, but do not fully realize or believe this. Our errors, which are misqualifications of light, have blocked our full realization of this and caused a sense of separateness, particularly when viewed as sin accompanied by a sense of guilt. Divine light/energy and truth gives everyone life.

Then spake Jesus again unto them, saying, I am the light of the world: he that followeth me shall not walk in darkness, but shall have the light of life.
John 8:12

Jesus is telling us that if we follow in his footsteps, we can become re-attuned perfectly and be in the full flow of light, life, divine power, wisdom, and love.

And Jesus came and spake unto them, saying, All power is given unto me in heaven and in earth.
Matthew 28:18

Jesus is unafraid to proclaim that due to his perfect attunement and oneness with God, he is fully connected to all power.

And Jesus looking upon them saith, With men it is impossible [to be saved], but not with God: for with God all things are possible.
Mark 10:27

When we think we are only human — when we close our personal belief system to the possibility of our true divine identity, it is difficult to realize it. How can we receive something that we do not believe in, that we don't see as real? With God, however, all things are possible. Therefore, we do indeed have that potential, to be re-united with God. Remember, God's energy/Light is everywhere, including within and around you.

Islam Affirms God is All-Powerful

The Qur'an has many references to the power of God. Here are just a few.

And if Allah had pleased, He would have taken away their hearing and their sight. Surely Allah is Possessor of power over all things.
      Qur'an 2:20

O you who believe, turn to Allah with sincere repentance. It may be your Lord will remove from you your evil and cause you to enter Gardens wherein flow rivers, on the day on which Allah will not abase the Prophet and those who believe with him. Their light will gleam before them and on their right hands — they will say: Our Lord, make perfect for us our light, and grant us protection; surely Thou art Possessor of power over all things.
      Qur'an 66:8

If we sincerely regret our sins, God will remove them from us so that we can be in the full flow of divine light.

Allah is the light of the heavens and the earth.
      Qur'an 24:35

 Judaism Affirms God is All-Powerful

Besides the many descriptions of God's power within Genesis, here are a few more:

God is my strength and power.
      (King James) 2 Samuel 22:33

Above the expanse over their heads was the semblance of a throne,
in appearance like sapphire; and on top, upon this semblance of
a throne, there was the semblance of a human form. From what
appeared as his loins up, I saw a gleam as of amber — what looked
like fire encased in a frame; and from what appeared as his loins
down, I saw what looked like fire. There was a radiance all about
him. Like the appearance of the bow which shines in the clouds on a
day of rain, such was the appearance of the surrounding radiance.
That was the appearance of the semblance of the Presence of the
Lord. When I beheld it, I flung myself down on my face.
    (Tanakh) Ezekiel 1:26-28

The appearance of God was overwhelming in its light and
power.

The Lord will reign for ever and ever.
    (Tanakh) Exodus 15:18

God has the power forever.

Hinduism Affirms God is All-Powerful

Hinduism has many profound and mystical passages about this
principle. No effort will be made to explain every aspect of these
lines. Let them speak to you directly and encourage further
contemplation.

As the one fire, after it has entered the world, though one, becomes
different according to whatever it burns, thus the one Self within all
things becomes different, according to whatever it enters, and exists
also without. As the one air, after it has entered the world, though one,
becomes different according to whatever it enters, thus the one Self

within all things becomes different, according to whatever it enters, and exists also without. As the sun, the eye of the whole world, is not contaminated by the external impurities seen by the eyes, thus the one Self within all things is never contaminated by the misery of the world, being himself without.

There is one ruler, the Self within all things, who makes the one form manifold. The wise who perceive him within their Self, to them belongs eternal happiness, not to others. There is one eternal thinker, thinking non-eternal thoughts, who, though one, fulfils the desires of many. The wise who perceive him within their Self, to them belongs eternal peace, not to others.

Katha Upanishad II, 5

Some wise men, deluded, speak of nature, and others of time as the cause of everything; but it is the greatness of God by which this Brahma-wheel is made to turn. It is at the command of him who always covers this world, the knower, the time of time, who assumes qualities and all knowledge, it is at his command that this work, creation, unfolds itself, which is called earth, water, fire, air, and ether; he who, after he has done that work and rested again, and after he has brought together one essence (the self) with the other (matter), with one, two, three, or eight, with time also and with the subtle qualities of the mind, who, after starting the works endowed with the three qualities, can order all things, yet when, in the absence of all these, he has caused the destruction of the work, goes on, being in truth different from all that he has produced; he is the beginning, producing the causes which unite the soul with the body, and being above the three kinds of time, past, present, future, he is seen as without parts, after we have first worshipped that adorable god, who has many forms, and who is the true source of all things, as dwelling in our own mind.

Svatasvatara Upanishad, VI

Remember that the Light which, proceeding from the sun, illumines the whole world, and the Light which is in the moon, and That which is in the fire also, all are born of Me.

I enter this world and animate all My creatures with My vitality; and by My cool moonbeams I nourish the plants.

Becoming the fire of life, I pass into their bodies and, uniting with the vital streams of Prana and Apana, I digest the various kinds of food.

I am enthroned in the hearts of all; memory, wisdom and discrimination owe their origin to Me. I am He Who is to be realised in the scriptures; I inspire their wisdom and I know their truth.

There are two aspects in Nature: the perishable and the imperishable. All life in this world belongs to the former, the unchanging element belongs to the latter.

But higher than all am I, the Supreme God, the Absolute Self, the Eternal Lord, Who pervades the worlds and upholds them all.

Beyond comparison of the Eternal with the non-eternal am I, Who am called by scriptures and sages the Supreme Personality, the Highest God.

He who with unclouded vision sees Me as the Lord-God, knows all there is to be known, and always shall worship Me with his whole heart.

Thus, O Sinless One [Arjuna], I have revealed to thee this most mystic knowledge. He who understands gains wisdom and attains the consummation of life.

The Bhagavad Gita, chapter 15

Could a thousand suns blaze forth together it would be but a faint reflection of the radiance of the Lord-God....

Without beginning, without middle and without end, infinite in power, Thine arms all-embracing, the sun and moon Thine eyes, Thy face beaming with the fire of sacrifice, flooding the whole universe with light.

The Bhagavad Gita, chapter 11

Buddhism Affirms God is All-Powerful

*Then the Buddha, wishing to enable all the enlightening beings
to realize the spiritual power...of the Enlightened One, emitted a
light from between his brows. It...caused all networks of worlds to
tremble.*

    Garland Sutra 2

*Just as a great conflagration can burn up all things,
So does Buddha's field of blessings burn up all fabrication.*

    Garland Sutra 10

 Taoism Affirms God is All-Powerful

*The Great Tao is universal like a flood.
How can it be turned to the right or to the left?
All creatures depend on it,
And it denies nothing to anyone.
It does its work,
But it makes no claims for itself.
It clothes and feeds all,
But it does not lord it over them:
Thus, it may be called "the Little."
All things return to it as to their home,
But it does not lord it over them:
Thus, it may be called "the Great."
It is just because it does not wish to be great
That its greatness is fully realized.*

    Tao Teh Ching, chapter 34

There was Something undefined and yet complete in itself,
Born before Heaven-and-Earth.
Silent and boundless,
Standing alone without change,
Yet pervading all without fail,
It may be regarded as the Mother of the world.
I do not know its name;
I style it "Tao;"
And, in the absence of a better word, call it "The Great."
Tao Teh Ching, chapter 25

 ## Confucianism Affirms God is All-Powerful

Part of the same quotation used in the last chapter about God the Creator is also relevant to the omnipotence of God.

It is only he who is possessed of the most complete sincerity that can exist under heaven, who can give its full development to his nature. Able to give its full development to his own nature, he can do the same to the nature of other men. Able to give its full development to the nature of other men, he can give their full development to the nature of creatures and things, he can assist the transforming and nourishing powers of Heaven and Earth. Able to assist the transforming and nourishing powers of the Heaven and Earth, he may with Heaven and Earth form a ternion [a set of three].
The Doctrine of the Mean

Despite a reference to spiritual beings in the next quote, Confucianism does not worship an array of gods, but rather refers to all things coming from "Heaven."

The Master said, "How abundantly do spiritual beings display the powers that belong to them!
"We look for them, but do not see them; we listen to, but do not hear them; yet they enter into all things, and there is nothing without them."
The Doctrine of the Mean

This is in reference to souls who are filled with the spirit of God by their attunement with God. The all-power of God flows through whoever has purified themselves and attained great virtue.

Chapter 9

Omniscience:
God is All-Knowing and Wise

ONE THING WE KNOW FOR SURE is that consciousness exists. If it exists for us, it most certainly exists even more so for God, our Creator.

God is aware of all our thoughts and actions. Thank God that He is so forgiving! This is a powerful motivator for true believers to monitor their thoughts and to raise them up. God's omnipotence must have the wisdom of His divine direction. His omniscience goes hand in hand with His omnipotence and omnipresence.

Every religion readily affirms God's total awareness and wisdom. We cannot hide anything from Him. God is aware of everything. As we grow in our attunement with God, we too will increase our awareness and wisdom regarding whatever is going on in our field of focus.

Therefore, it is wise to occasionally spend time contemplating what subjects we want to focus on, and what subjects we no longer want to focus on. As we purify our consciousness, it will expand in its capacity and wisdom.

Let us now look at some quotations that affirm God's omniscience, and our potential to expand our individual consciousness in that direction.

**Christianity Affirms God is
All-Knowing and Wise**

*O the depth of the riches both of the wisdom and knowledge of God!
How unsearchable are his judgments and his ways past finding
out!
For who hath known the mind of the Lord? Or who hath been his
counselor?
Or who hath first given to him, and it shall be recompensed unto
him again?
For of him, and through him, and to him, are all things: to whom be
glory for ever. Amen*
        Romans 11:33-36

*Now are we sure that thou knowest all things, and needest not that
any man should ask thee: by this we believe that thou camest forth
from God.*
        John 16:30

This is referring to Jesus the Christ, who had succeeded in purifying his consciousness and attuning with God to the point where
his awareness was great. Keep in mind, however, that even Jesus,
at times, felt separate from God (*O my Father, if it be possible, let
this cup pass from me.* Matthew 26:39).

*If any of you lack wisdom, let him ask of God, that giveth to all men
liberally, and upbraideth not; and it shall be given him.*
        James 1:5

God is the source of wisdom and awareness, and will bless us
with more as we ask for and earn it.

For the word of God is quick, and powerful, and sharper than any two-edged sword, piercing even to the dividing asunder of soul and spirit, and of the joints and marrow, and is a discerner of the thoughts and intents of the heart.

Neither is there any creature that is not manifest in his sight: but all things are naked and opened unto the eyes of him with whom we have to do.

Hebrews 4:12-13

 ## Islam Affirms God is All-Knowing and Wise

There is no question that Islam also affirms God's omniscience.

Our Lord, surely Thou knowest what we hide and what we proclaim. And nothing is hidden from Allah, either in the earth, or in the heaven.

Qur'an 14:38

Surely Allah is He with Whom is the knowledge of the Hour and He sends down the rain, and He knows what is in the wombs. And no one knows what he will earn on the morrow. And no one knows in what land he will die. Surely Allah is Knowing, Aware.

Qur'an 31:34

Allah is the light of the heavens and the earth. A likeness of His light is as a pillar on which is a lamp — the lamp is in a glass, the glass is as it were a brightly shining star — lit from a blessed olive-tree, neither eastern nor western, the oil whereof gives light, though fire touch it not — light upon light. Allah guides to His light whom He pleases. And Allah sets forth parables for men, and Allah is Knower of all things.

Qur'an 24:35

Judaism Affirms God is All-Knowing and Wise

O lord, You have examined me and know me.
When I sit down or stand up You know it;
You discern my thoughts from afar.
You observe my walking and reclining,
and are familiar with all my ways.
There is not a word on my tongue
but that You, O Lord, know it well.
You hedge me before and behind;
You lay Your hand upon me.
It is beyond my knowledge;
it is a mystery; I cannot fathom it.
    (Tanakh) Psalms 139:1-6

He made the earth by His might,
Established the world by His wisdom,
And by His understanding stretched out the skies.
    (Tanakh) Jeremiah 10:12

And my lord is wise, according to the wisdom of an angel of God, to
know all things that are in the earth.
    (King James) 2 Samuel 14:20

 ## Hinduism Affirms God is All-Knowing and Wise

O Arjuna! The body of man is the playground of the Self; and That
which knows the activities of Matter, sages call the Self.
I am the Omniscient Self that abides in the playground of Matter;
knowledge of Matter and of the all-knowing Self is wisdom.
    The Bhagavad Gita, chapter 13

He makes all, he knows all, the self-caused, the knower, the time of time, who assumes the qualities and knows everything, the master of nature and of man.

Svetasvatara Upanishad, VI

The world appears real, as an oyster-shell appears to be silver; but only so long as the Brahman remains unknown, he who is above all, and indivisible. That Being, true, intelligent, comprehends within itself every variety of being, penetrating and permeating all as a thread which strings together beads.

Sankaracharya's Atma Bodha

 Buddhism Affirms God is All-Knowing and Wise

I am the Tathagata, O ye gods and men! The Arhat, the perfectly enlightened one; having reached the shore myself, I carry others to the shore; being free, I make free; being comforted, I comfort; being perfectly at rest, I lead others to rest. By my perfect wisdom I know both this world and the next, such as they really are. I am all-knowing, all-seeing. Come to me, ye gods and men! Hear the law. I am he who indicates the path; who shows the path, as knowing the path, being acquainted with the path.

Saddharma-Pundarika, chapter 5

All the great congregation, gratefully attentive to the words of Buddha Tathagata...obtained illumination; this great assembly perceived that each one's mind was coextensive with the universe....
[Buddha now speaks] "This unity alone in the world is boundless in its reality, and being boundless is yet one...it is one with Divine Knowledge; it is manifested as the effulgent Nature of the Divine Intelligence of Tathagata...."

The Surangama Sutra

Taoism Affirms God is All-Knowing and Wise

To return to the root is to find peace.
To find peace is to fulfill one's destiny.
To fulfill one's destiny is to be constant.
To know the Constant is called Insight.
If one does not know the Constant,
One runs blindly into disasters.
If one knows the Constant,
One can understand and embrace all.
  Tao Teh Ching, chapter 16

The preceding quotation affirms how we can, through find-ing peace, be attuned to the "Constant," which places us in the Tao. Then we would "understand and embrace all." This is omni-science.

The following discusses one's ability to attune to divine omni-science through purification and open-ness through "heaven's gate" and non-attachment.

In washing and clearing your inner vision,
Have you purified it of all dross?
...In the opening and shutting of heaven's gate,
Are you able to play the feminine part?
Enlightened and seeing far into all directions,
Can you at the same time remain detached and non-active?
  Tao Teh Ching, chapter 10

He who cultivates the Tao is one with the Tao;
He who practices Virtue is one with Virtue....
To be one with the Tao is to be a welcome accession to the Tao;
To be one with Virtue is to be a welcome accession to Virtue.
  Tao Teh Ching, chapter 23

Confucianism Affirms God is All-Knowing and Wise

Tsze-kung said, "What do you mean by thus saying — that no one knows you?"
The Master replied, "I do not murmur against Heaven. I do not grumble against men. My studies lie low, and my penetration rises high. But there is Heaven — that knows me!"
The Confucian Analects, book 14

Referring to "man in his ideal," we have:

He may be compared to heaven and Earth in their supporting and containing, their overshadowing and curtaining, all things....
It is only he, possessed of all sagely qualities that can exist under heaven....
All-embracing is he and vast, deep and active as a fountain, sending forth in their due season his virtues.
All-embracing and vast, he is like heaven. Deep and active as a fountain, he is like the abyss. He is seen, and the people all reverence him; he speaks, and the people all believe him; he acts, and the people all are pleased with him.
The Doctrine of the Mean

The world religions affirm God's "All-knowing-ness." They also affirm that we are a product of our thought. We will benefit from regularly reviewing the subject matter of our consciousness, with the goal of only having positive and virtuous categories of thought that we contemplate.

Chapter 10

Omnipresence: God is Everywhere

GOD IS ALWAYS WITH US, as God is in all energy which makes up all matter. Energy is everywhere. God is everywhere, including in our hearts and minds now and every moment, whether we believe it and focus on that fact or not. He is with us even more when we focus on Him.

The omnipresence of God goes hand in hand with His omnipotence and omniscience. God cannot have power and awareness everywhere without *being* everywhere. Naturally there is a significant overlap in these three divine qualities.

When the stresses of life's situations seem overwhelming, go for a walk in a park or somewhere in nature. Being with nature makes it easier to hand over our problems to God. The beauty of nature is a reminder of God's hand in everything, everywhere. Never forget that God is within you, right now.

 Christianity Affirms God is Everywhere

God that made the world and all things therein, seeing that he is Lord of heaven and earth...
He giveth to all life, and breath, and all things;
And hath made of one blood all nations of men for to dwell on all the face of the earth, and hath determined the times before appointed, and the bounds of their habitation;

*That they should seek the Lord, if haply they might feel after him,
and find him though he be not far from every one of us:
For in him we live, and move, and have our being; as certain also of
your own poets have said, For we are also his offspring.*
Acts 17:24-28

*For thus saith the high and lofty One that inhabiteth eternity, whose
name is Holy; I dwell in the high and holy place, with him also that
is of a contrite and humble spirit, to revive the spirit of the humble,
and to revive the heart of the contrite ones.*
Isaiah 57:15

 ## Islam Affirms God is Everywhere

*And to Allah belongs whatever is in the heavens and whatever is in
the earth. And Allah ever encompasses all things.*
Qur'an 4:126

*He is the First and the Last and the manifest and the Hidden, and
He is Knower of all things.
He it is Who created the heavens and the earth in six periods, and
He is established on the Throne of Power. He knows that which goes
down into the earth and that which comes forth out of it, and that
which comes down from heaven and that which goes up to it. And
He is with you wherever you are.*
Qur'an 57:3-4

Judaism Affirms God is Everywhere

Where can I escape from Your spirit?
Where can I flee from Your presence?
If I ascend to heaven, You are there;
If I descend to Sheol, You are there too.
If I take wing with the dawn
to come to rest on the western horizon,
even there Your hand will be guiding me,
Your right hand will be holding me fast.
If I say, "Surely darkness will conceal me,
night will provide me with cover,"
darkness is not dark for You;
night is as light as day;
darkness and light are the same.
My frame was not concealed from You
when I was shaped in a hidden place,
knit together in the recesses of the earth.
Your eyes saw my unformed limbs;
they were all recorded in Your book;
in due time they were formed,
to the very last one of them.
How weighty Your thoughts seem to me, O God,
how great their number!
I count them — they exceed the grains of sand;
I end — but am still with You.
    (Tanakh) Psalms 139:7-18

The eyes of the Lord are everywhere,
Observing the bad and the good.
    (Tanakh) Proverbs 15:3

Hinduism Affirms God is Everywhere

I will speak to thee now of that great Truth which man ought to know, since by its means he will win immortal bliss — that which is without beginning, the Eternal Spirit which dwells in Me, neither with form, nor yet without it.

Everywhere are Its hands and Its feet, everywhere It has eyes that see, heads that think and mouths that speak; everywhere It listens; It dwells in all the worlds; It envelops them all.

Beyond the senses, It yet shines through every sense perception. Bound to nothing, It yet sustains everything. Unaffected by the Qualities, It still enjoys them all.

It is within all beings, yet outside; motionless yet moving; too subtle to be perceived; far away yet always near.

The Bhagavad Gita, chapter 13

The whole world is pervaded by Me, yet My form is not seen. All living things have their being in Me, yet I am not limited by them.

Nevertheless, they do not consciously abide in Me. Such is My Divine Sovereignty that though I, the Supreme Self, am the cause and upholder of all, yet I remain outside.

As the mighty wind, though moving everywhere, has not resting place but space, so have all these beings no home but Me.

The Bhagavad Gita, chapter 9

The Lord Shri Krishna, the Almighty Prince of Wisdom, showed to Arjuna the Supreme Form of the Great God.

There were countless eyes and mouths, and mystic forms innumerable, with shining ornaments and flaming celestial weapons.

Crowned with heavenly garlands, clothed in shining garments, anointed with divine unctions, He showed Himself as the Resplendent One, Marvelous, Boundless, Omnipresent.

The Bhagavad Gita, chapter 11

Buddhism Affirms God is Everywhere

How should enlightening beings see the body of Buddha?...Buddha is omnipresent, in all places, in all beings, in all things, in all lands.
Garland Sutra 37

Let us bear in mind, O brethren, that Gotama Siddhattha has revealed the truth to us. He was the Holy One and Perfect One and the Blessed One, because the eternal truth had taken abode in him. The Tathagata taught us that the truth existed before he was born into this world, and will exist after he has entered into Nirvana. The Tathagata said: 'The truth is omnipresent and eternal, endowed with excellencies innumerable, above all human nature, and ineffable in its holiness.'
Buddha, The Gospel: Conclusion

 Taoism Affirms God is Everywhere

There was Something undefined and yet complete in itself,
Born before heaven-and-Earth.
Silent and boundless,
Standing alone without change,
Yet pervading all without fail,
It may be regarded as the Mother of the world.
Tao Teh Ching, chapter 25

The Cosmic Spirit (Tao) embraces Heaven and supports Earth. It stretched the four quarters of the Universe and generated the eight points of the firmament. There is no limit to its height, and its depth is unfathomable. It constituted Heaven and Earth and endowed them with the primary elements, when as yet they were without form. Flowing like a fountain, bubbling like a spring, impalpable, its energies bubbled forth in the void and filled space. Continuing to effervesce, it transformed the murky air of chaos into crystal clearness. Hence it filled Heaven and Earth and stretched to the uttermost parts of the sea.

The Huai Nan Tzu, The Cosmic Spirit

Confucianism Affirms God is Everywhere

Confucianism likens God to certain qualities, one of which is sincerity.

Sincerity is the end and beginning of things; without sincerity there would be nothing....
Evidencing itself, it reaches far. Reaching far, it becomes large and substantial. Large and substantial, it becomes high and brilliant. Large and substantial; this is how it contains all things. High and brilliant; this is how it overspreads all things. Reaching far and continuing long; this is how it perfects all things.

The Doctrine of the Mean

Spiritual beings have the attributes of God:

The Master said, "How abundantly do spiritual beings display the powers that belong to them!
"We look for them, but do not see them; we listen to, but do no hear them; yet they enter into all things, and there is nothing without them."

The Doctrine of the Mean

We can find an acknowledgement of God's omnipresence within all religions. He is always with us. Life is enhanced when we focus on God and share our life with Him.

Chapter 11

Forever: God is Eternal

GOD INCORPORATES AN ETERNAL unchanging aspect as well as a constantly changing aspect. God's pure consciousness changes as His divine awareness of the worlds of form change. Because we are God's children, we also are composed of an eternal unchanging aspect as well as a constantly changing one.

Science has demonstrated that everything is ultimately energy. It has also concluded that energy cannot be destroyed but can only change form. Energy at the physical level makes waves, patterns, and fields that compose solid forms. There are energy fields at higher levels of vibration that make up consciousness. These fields can interpenetrate the physical forms, including human forms.

Our consciousness, not our physical form, is what has the potential of being eternal. What determines whether we live eternally as God does, and how wonderfully we live? As we have seen earlier, it is simply to include God in our lives.

 Christianity Affirms God is Eternal

For the invisible things of him from the creation of the world are clearly seen, being understood by the things that are made, even his eternal power and Godhead....
Romans 1:20

He that believeth on the Son of God hath the witness in himself: he
that believeth not God hath made him a liar; because he believeth
not the record that God gave of his Son.
And this is the record, that God hath given to us eternal life, and
this life is in his Son.
He that hath the Son hath life; and he that hath not the Son of God
hath not life.

 1 John 5:10-12

As we attune to the One Son, the Christ, which is the intermediary between God and man, we purify our consciousness. We
gradually rid ourselves of all that blocks our oneness with God.
We raise the level of our vibrations so that we can ultimately
flow into higher realms of the degrees of Heaven — for there are
many levels and worlds of vibration. We can do this while still in
embodiment, experiencing divine revelations especially at times
of peace, rest, and sleep.

Islam Affirms God is Eternal

Allah, (there is) no god but He, the Ever-living, the Self-subsisting,
by Whom all subsist.

 Qur'an 3:2

And there endures forever the person of thy Lord, the Lord of glory
and honour.

 Qur'an 55:27

Judaism Affirms God is Eternal

For thus said He who high aloft
Forever dwells, whose name is holy:
I dwell on high, in holiness;
Yet with the contrite and the lowly in spirit —
Reviving the spirits of the lowly,
Reviving the hearts of the contrite.
  (Tanakh) Isaiah 57:15

I say, "O my God, do not take me away
in the midst of my days,
You whose years go on for generations on end.
Of old You established the earth;
the heavens are the work of your hands.
They shall perish, but You shall endure;
they shall all wear out like a garment;
You change them like clothing and they pass away.
But You are the same, and Your years never end.
May the children of Your servants dwell securely
and their offspring endure in Your presence."
  (Tanakh) Psalms 102:25-29

 ## Hinduism Affirms God is Eternal

He is the one ruler of many who seem to act, but really do not act;
he makes the one seed manifold. The wise who perceive him within
their self, to them belongs eternal happiness, not to others. He is the
eternal among eternals, the thinker among thinkers, who, though
one, fulfils the desires of many.
  Svetasvatara Upanishad, VI

Of Time I am the Eternal Present....
I am the Beginning, the Middle and the End in creation....
I am Time inexhaustible; and I am the all-pervading Preserver.
    The Bhagavad Gita, chapter 10

 Buddhism Affirms God is Eternal

*Earnestness is the path of immortality (Nirvana), thoughtlessness
the path of death. Those who are in earnest do not die, those who
are thoughtless are as if dead already.*
    The Dhammapada, On Earnestness

*Who shall overcome this earth, and the world of Yama (the lord of the
departed), and the world of the gods? Who shall find out the plainly
shown path of virtue, as a clever man finds out the (right) flower?
The disciple will overcome the earth, and the world of Yama, and the
world of the gods. The disciple will find out the plainly shown path
of virtue, as a clever man finds out the (right) flower.*
*He who knows that this body is like froth, and has learnt that it is
as unsubstantial as a mirage, will break the flower-pointed arrow
of Mara, and never see the king of death.*
    The Dhammapada, Flowers

*Nothing can ever destroy the Buddha nature. The nature of self is
nothing but the undisclosed storehouse of the Tathagata. Such a
storehouse can never be broken, put to fire, or plundered. Though it
is not possible to destroy or see it, one can know it when one attains
the unsurpassed enlightenment.*
    The Mahaparinirvana, Sutra 220

Taoism Affirms God is Eternal

The Tao is like an empty bowl,
Which in being used can never be filled up....
It unites the world into one whole.
Hidden in the deeps,
Yet it seems to exist forever.
    Tao Teh Ching, chapter 4

...equipped with this timeless Tao,
You can harness present realities.
To know the origins is initiation into the Tao.
    Tao Teh Ching, chapter 14

 ## Confucianism Affirms God is Eternal

So large and substantial, the individual possessing it [sincerity] is
the co-equal of Earth. So high and brilliant, it makes him the co-
equal of Heaven. So far-reaching and long-continuing, it makes
him infinite.
    The Doctrine of the Mean

The ordinances of Heaven, how profound are they and unceasing!
    The Doctrine of the Mean

The sacred texts present us with a higher level of understanding life's purpose, as well as a greater appreciation of self and God. We learn that despite all the suffering we see in the world, life will be good, joyful, and filled with love, as we include a correct understanding of our intimate relationship with God in our life. We also learn that we do not have to feel or be separate from God by unnecessarily hanging on to self-condemnation.

As divine sons and daughters of God, we have unlimited potential to grow into an ever-greater union with Him while retaining our individuality. We learn that we are supposed to be loving co-creators with God in helping to build a wonderful life of peace and joy for all. As a result of learning the principles in part I, we see that life is well worth living. Knowing these divine truths establishes more fertile ground for divine love to establish itself in our life experience.

As your abilities and judgment develop, set your course with determination and include the goal of a closer relationship with God in your prayers and meditations. The entire process, although requiring willpower and effort, is a great joy.

Coming up next are our essential responsibilities for soul development as given to us by all the world religions. These essential responsibilities are in actuality a natural part of our divine nature.

PART II
Essential Responsibilities for Loving Living

FIRST, IT IS IMPORTANT TO UNDERSTAND, remember, and apply the first eleven principles of understanding. It is crucial to live life from the perspective of who you really are, a spirit, temporarily inhabiting a physical form, a son or daughter of God, unique, yet one with divine unlimited potential. It is helpful to regularly view life through the perspective of these principles.

It's a joyful experience to love the great God Self within others and within yourself. This is the best use of our divine energy. Every essential responsibility can be a joy to do, in loving service to God, others, or yourself. Ultimately, there is no difference, as we are one wonderful divine family.

The meaning and purpose of life is good, with love permeating through every particle of light/energy, as we are open to it. For this reason, we can enjoy the goodness of life while taking loving action to fulfill our responsibilities. Our responsibilities are part of our divine nature. A sense of our duty to perform them resides within our hearts, as they are a natural part of our Higher, Divine Selves.

Because we are continuously receiving the divine loving light of God through our being, and we have free will to qualify it as we choose, it is most natural to radiate that loving light:

1. *to God throughout the universe.*
     Section I: Love God (chapters 12-16)

2. *to God within ourselves.*
     Section II: Love Your Divine Self (chapters 17-21)

3. *to God within others.*
     Section III: Love Other's Divine Selves (chapters 22-29)

4. *to God within our projects in life.*
     Section IV: Love What You Do (chapters 30-33)

All of the universal principles presented have been grouped into these four categories to more readily organize and remember them. Each principle can also be applied to every other area of life. For example, although faith and hope are presented in section I, "Love God," it is also essential to have faith and hope in your Higher Self (God in you), the Higher Self of others, and in what you do. It is helpful to occasionally refer to an overview of the principles by looking at either the table of contents or "God's Code of Life and Love" in part III or Appendix A.

Section I

Love God

TO LOVE GOD IS TO SEARCH FOR GOD, to focus on God, and finally to rest and live in God. One of our primary responsibilities is to develop our spirituality, our true nature and self, and seek to satisfy what our souls truly yearn for. Jesus Christ encouraged us to do this:

And I say unto you, Ask, and it shall be given you; seek, and ye shall find; knock, and it shall be opened unto you.
For every one that asketh receiveth; and he that seeketh findeth; and to him that knocketh it shall be opened.
　　Luke 11:9-10

God can be seen and experienced in all aspects of life — if we look for Him. We may seek Him in every person, every flower, and even in every negative situation, though He may be more difficult to see. Even more powerful is the presence of God within our hearts and minds — if we look for Him. Only through this process of seeking and finding will we become more of God — for what we focus on we become.

143

We can learn to love more by reflecting upon those whom we love the most. First, remember that feeling of love, and then magnify that feeling toward those we love. Next, transfer that feeling — being totally loving and at one with that feeling, qualifying all of our light/energy with that feeling and radiate it out to everyone in our world, to God, ourselves, and our work. When we are radiating the feeling of love to all in our world we are in the flow of love, and it feels divine.

This section presents four divine qualities and actions that will magnify our love for God, Who contains all of life. Practice them and grow in the glorious flow of love.

Chapter 12

Faith and Hope

FAITH EMPOWERS US — it is our "extension cord" to God. It is essential to have faith in our ability to directly contact God. Faith can be gradually strengthened to a sure knowledge of all things divine. Your consciousness exists due to divine unlimited light/ energy. This energy can never be destroyed — it can only change. It's important to remember your divine identity as a son or daughter of God.

Examine your hopes and dreams and review them to affirm that they are only positive and good for all concerned. Then you will know that they are in alignment with God's will, and know that your Higher Self will manifest Itself in your life.

All of the twenty-two responsibilities contribute to your empowerment. Practicing every one will certainly cause your faith to grow. Incorporate them into your life and see the difference.

With your power of faith and belief, you will qualify God's energy every moment with right action, raising the positive experience of all in your world.

Let your faith keep you strong when you are enduring troubles in your life, including the loss of loved ones. Life's challenges are a refining fire. Gradually you will become the master over every situation.

It's important to not allow doubt into your life. Instead, open up to the power of God. This is an internal process in your mind and heart. Do not deny or doubt that power, or it will be blocked.

Consider meditating on the importance and power of faith.

Transcend all sense of guilt for past sins which would separate you from God and your true nature. If you truly regret your errors and do what can be done to repair any harm, the grace of God will always forgive you as you forgive others. Thus the slate is wiped clean, and you are sinless and whole again. This is empowerment.

We can do so much more when we grow in faith. Contemplate the mystical reality that God is indeed everywhere. It is God's Will that we strengthen and apply our faith. By so doing we can create life miracles.

When we expect good to come to us, when we love everyone else in our world (including those who have hurt us), the goodness and love that we have created will return to us.

 ## Christianity Affirms the Power of Faith and Hope

Now faith is the substance of things hoped for, the evidence of things not seen....
Through faith we understand that the worlds were framed by the word of God....
But without faith it is impossible to please him: for he that cometh to God must believe that He is, and that He is a rewarder of them that diligently seek Him.
   Hebrews 11:1, 3, 6

In the above quote, faith is referred to as a substance. As a substance, faith would be composed of spiritual energy of a very high vibration, and the raw material within all matter creation. Contemplate and practice the power of faith.

Jesus said unto him, If thou canst believe, all things are possible to him that believeth.
Mark 9:23

And in the fourth watch of the night Jesus went unto them, walking on the sea.
And when the disciples saw him walking on the sea, they were troubled, saying It is a spirit; and they cried out for fear.
But straightway Jesus spake unto them, saying, Be of good cheer; it is I; be not afraid.
And Peter answered him and said, Lord, if it be thou, bid me come unto thee on the water.
And he said, Come. And when Peter was come down out of the ship, he walked on the water, to go to Jesus.
But when he saw the wind boisterous, he was afraid; and beginning to sink, he cried, saying,
Lord, save me.
And immediately Jesus stretched forth his hand, and caught him, and said unto him, O thou of little faith, wherefore didst thou doubt?
Matthew 14:25-31

Islam Affirms the Power of Faith and Hope

There is no compulsion in religion — the right way is indeed clearly distinct from error. So whoever disbelieves in the devil and believes in Allah, he indeed lays hold on the firmest handle which shall never break. And Allah is Hearing, knowing.
Allah is the Friend of those who believe — He brings them out of darkness into light.
Qur'an 2:256-257

Those who believe and do good, their Lord guides them by their faith;
rivers will flow beneath them in Gardens of bliss.
Their cry therein will be, Glory to Thee, O Allah! and their greeting,
Peace! And the last of their cry will be: Praise be to Allah, the Lord
of the worlds!
　　Qur'an 10:9-10

Thou wilt not find a people who believe in Allah and the latter day
loving those who oppose Allah and His Messenger, even though they
be their fathers, or their sons, or their brothers, or their kinsfolk. These
are they into whose hearts He has impressed faith, and strengthened
them with a Spirit from Himself, and He will cause them to enter Gar-
dens wherein flow rivers, abiding therein. Allah is well-pleased with
them and they are well-pleased with Him. These are Allah's party.
Now surely it is Allah's party who are the successful!
　　Qur'an 58:22

Those who believe and do good deeds, for them the Beneficent will
surely bring about love.
　　Qur'an 19:96

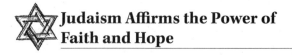 ## Judaism Affirms the Power of Faith and Hope

Those who trust in the Lord
are like Mount Zion
that cannot be moved,
enduring forever.
　　(Tanakh) Psalms 125:1

Blessed is the Lord,
for He has been wondrously faithful to me,

a veritable bastion.
Alarmed, I had thought,
"I am thrust out of Your sight;"
yet You listened to my plea for mercy
when I cried out to You.
So love the Lord, all you faithful;
the Lord guards the loyal,
and more than requites him who acts arrogantly.
Be strong and of good courage,
all you who wait for the Lord.
    (Tanakh) Psalms 31:22-25

Let us not forget two great stories in the Old Testament. The first is about Abraham, who was asked to sacrifice his son. At the last possible moment, an angel of the Lord stopped him, and told him how God would bless him for his willingness to obey. The second is the story of Job, who endured many trials but never lost his faith.

ॐ Hinduism Affirms the Power of Faith and Hope

The man who is full of faith obtaineth wisdom, and he also who hath mastery over his senses; and, having obtained wisdom, he goeth swiftly to the supreme peace. But the ignorant, faithless, doubting self goeth to destruction; nor this world, nor that beyond, nor happiness, is there for the doubting self.
    The Bhagavad Gita, chapter 4

They who have no faith in this teaching cannot find Me, but remain lost in the purlieus [outlying districts] of this perishable world.
    The Bhagavad Gita, chapter 9

Beyond the sense is the mind, beyond the mind is the highest created Being, higher than that Being is the Great Self, higher than the Great, the highest Undeveloped. Beyond the Undeveloped is the Person, the all-pervading and entirely imperceptible. Every creature that knows him is liberated, and obtains immortality. His form is not to be seen, no one beholds him with the eye. He is imagined by the heart, by wisdom, by the mind. Those who know this, are immortal.

He, the Self, cannot be reached by speech, by mind, or by the eye. How can it be apprehended except by him who says: "He is"? By the words "He is," is he to be apprehended, and by admitting the reality of both the invisible Brahman and the visible world, as coming from Brahman. When he has been apprehended by the words "He is," then his reality reveals itself.

Katha Upanishad, II, 6

 ## Buddhism Affirms the Power of Faith and Hope

South of Savatthi is a great river, on the banks of which lay a hamlet of five hundred houses. Thinking of the salvation of the people, the World-honored One resolved to go to the village and preach the doctrine. Having come to the riverside he sat down beneath a tree, and the villagers seeing the glory of his appearance approached him with reverence; but when he began to preach, they believed him not.

When the world-honored Buddha had left Savatthi Sariputta felt a desire to see the Lord and to hear him preach. Coming to the river where the water was deep and the current strong, he said to himself: "This stream shall not prevent me. I shall go and see the Blessed One, and he stepped upon the water which was as firm under his feet as a slab of granite. When he arrived at a place in the middle of the stream where the waves were high, Sariputta's heart gave way, and he began to sink. But rousing his faith and renewing his mental

effort, he proceeded as before and reached the other bank.
The people of the village were astonished to see Sariputta, and they
asked how he could cross the stream where there was neither a bridge
nor a ferry. Sariputta replied: "I lived in ignorance until I heard the
voice of the Buddha. As I was anxious to hear the doctrine of salva-
tion, I crossed the river and I walked over its troubled waters because
I had faith. Faith. nothing else, enabled me to do so, and now I am
here in the bliss of the Master's presence."
The World-honored One added: "Sariputta, thou hast spoken well.
Faith like thine alone can save the world from the yawning gulf of
migration and enable men to walk dryshod to the other shore." And
the Blessed One urged to the villagers the necessity of ever advanc-
ing in the conquest of sorrow and of casting off all shackles so as to
cross the river of worldliness and attain deliverance from death.

    Buddha, The Gospel: Walking on Water

By faith, you shall be free and go beyond the world of death.

    Sutta Nipata 1146

 ## Taoism Affirms the Power of Faith and Hope

If one lacks faith in himself, it is because he lacks faith in Tao.

    Laotzu's Tao and Wu-Wei, chapter 23

When you are lacking in faith,
Others will be unfaithful to you.

    Tao Teh Ching, chapter 17

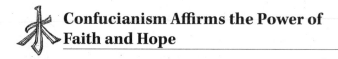 Confucianism Affirms the Power of Faith and Hope

Dze-kung asked Confucius, saying, "Allow me to ask the reason why the superior man sets a high value on jade, and but little on soapstone? Is it because jade is rare, and the soapstone plentiful?" Confucius replied, "It is not because soapstone is plentiful that he thinks but little of it, and because jade is rare that he sets a high value on it. Anciently superior men found the likeness of all excellent qualities in jade. Soft, smooth, and glossy, it appeared to them like benevolence; fine, compact, and strong — like intelligence; angular, but not sharp and cutting — like righteousness...its flaws not concealing its beauty, nor its beauty concealing its flaws — like loyalty; with an internal radiance issuing from it on every side — like good faith; bright as a brilliant rainbow — like heaven.

Li Ki (The Book of Rites), part II, book 45

It is only the able and virtuous man who can attain to this perfection; and can sacrifice when he has attained to it. Hence in the sacrifices of such a man he brings into exercise all sincerity and good faith, with all right-heartedness and reverence.

Li Ki (The Book of Rites), part II, book 22

Chapter 13

Praise and Gratitude

FEED YOUR INNER JOY by praise and gratitude to God for the many blessings of life. Doing so makes life an ongoing celebration, keeping you attuned with God.

Gratitude releases a feeling of love. As parents, we support our children who show their gratitude to us, and our Divine Father/ Mother God is much more powerful in Its ability to return the love that praise and gratitude generate. Both giving and receiving praise and gratitude creates a flow of energy within our consciousness that feels wonderful.

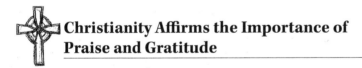 ## Christianity Affirms the Importance of Praise and Gratitude

And it came to pass, as he went to Jerusalem, that he passed through the midst of Samaria and Galilee.
And as he entered into a certain village, there met him ten men that were lepers, which stood afar off:
And they lifted up their voices, and said, Jesus, Master, have mercy on us.
And when he saw them, he said unto them, Go shew yourselves unto the priest. And it came to pass, that, as they went, they were cleansed.
And one of them, when he saw that he was healed, turned back, and

with a loud voice glorified God,
And fell down on his face at his feet, giving him thanks: and he was
a Samaritan.
And Jesus answering said, Were there not ten cleansed? but where
are the nine?
There are not found that returned to give glory to God, save this
stranger.
And he said unto him, Arise, go thy way: thy faith hath made thee
whole.
Luke 17:11-19

In every thing give thanks: for this is the will of God in Christ Jesus
concerning you.
1 Thessalonians 5:18

For every creature of God is good, and nothing to be refused, if it be
received with thanksgiving:
For it is sanctified by the word of God and prayer.
1 Timothy 4:4-5

And immediately I was in the spirit: and, behold, a throne was set
in heaven, and one sat on the throne.
And before the throne there was a sea of glass like unto crystal: and
in the midst of the throne, and round about the throne, were four
beasts full of eyes before and behind.
And the four beasts had each of them six wings about him; and they
were full of eyes within: and they rest not day and night, saying, Holy,
holy, holy, Lord God Almighty, which was, and is, and is to come.
And when those beasts give glory and honour and thanks to him
that sat on the throne, who liveth for ever and ever,
The four and twenty elders fall down before him that sat on the throne,
and worship him that liveth for ever and ever, and cast their crowns
before the throne, saying,

Thou art worthy, O Lord, to receive glory and honour and power: for thou hast created all things, and for thy pleasure they are and were created.
Revelation 4:2, 6, 8-11

 ## Islam Affirms the Importance of Praise and Gratitude

Praise be to Allah, the Lord of the worlds,
The Beneficent, the Merciful,
Master of the day of Requital.
Qur'an 1:1-3

If you are ungrateful, then surely Allah is above need of you. And He likes not ungratefulness in His servants. And if you are grateful, He likes it for you. And no bearer of a burden will bear another's burden. Then to your Lord is your return, then will He inform you of what you did. Surely He is Knower of what is in the breasts.
Qur'an 39:7

Allah is He Who made for you the night for resting in and the day for seeing. Surely Allah is Full of grace to men, but most men give not thanks.
Allah is He Who made the earth a resting-place for you and the heaven a structure, and He formed you, then made goodly your forms, and He provided you with goodly things. That is Allah, your Lord — so blessed is Allah, the Lord of the worlds.
Qur'an 40:61, 64

Judaism Affirms the Importance of Praise and Gratitude

Raise a shout for the Lord, all the earth; worship the Lord in gladness; come into His presence with shouts of joy.
Acknowledge that the Lord is God; He made us and we are His,
Enter His gates with praise, His courts with acclamation!
Praise Him! Bless His name!
For the Lord is good; His steadfast love is eternal;
His faithfulness is for all generations.
　　　(Tanakh) Psalms 100:1-5

Praise the Lord; call on His name; proclaim His deeds among the peoples.
Sing praises unto Him; speak of all His wondrous acts.
Exult in his holy name; let all who seek the Lord rejoice.
Turn to the Lord, to His might; seek His presence constantly.
Remember the wonders He has done; His portents and the judgments He has pronounced....
He is the Lord our God; His judgments are throughout the earth.
Be ever mindful of His covenant, the promise He gave for a thousand generations, that He made with Abraham, swore to Isaac, and confirmed in a decree for Jacob....
Sing to the Lord, all the earth. Proclaim His victory day after day.
Tell of His glory among the nations, His wondrous deeds among all peoples.
For the Lord is great and much acclaimed. He is held in awe by all divine beings.
All the gods of the peoples are mere idols, but the Lord made the heavens.
Glory and majesty are before Him; for He is coming to rule the earth.
Strength and joy are in His place.

Ascribe to the Lord, O families of the peoples, ascribe to the Lord glory and strength.

Ascribe to the Lord the glory of His name, bring tribute and enter before Him, bow down to the Lord majestic in holiness.

Tremble in His presence, all the earth! The world stands firm; it cannot be shaken.

Let the heavens rejoice and the earth exult; let them declare among the nations, "The Lord is King!"

Let the sea and all within it thunder, the fields and everything in them exult; then shall all the trees of the forest shout for joy at the presence of the Lord, for He is coming to rule the earth.

Praise the Lord for He is good; His steadfast love is eternal.

    (Tanakh) 1 Chronicles 16:8-34

Hinduism Affirms the Importance of Praise and Gratitude

I am the same to all beings. I favor none, and I hate none. But those who worship Me devotedly, they live in Me, and I in them.

Even the most sinful, if he worship Me with his whole heart, shall be considered righteous, for he is treading the right path.

He shall attain spirituality ere long, and Eternal Peace shall be his. O Arjuna! Believe me, My devotee is never lost.

    The Bhagavad Gita, chapter 9

But the Great Souls, O Arjuna! Filled with My Divine Spirit, they worship Me, they fix their minds on Me and on Me alone, for they know that I am the imperishable Source of being.

Always extolling Me, strenuous, firm in their vows, prostrating themselves before Me, they worship Me continually with concentrated devotion.

Others worship Me with full consciousness as the One, the Manifold, the Omnipresent, the Universal.

    The Bhagavad Gita, chapter 9

"Worship" is a form of praise and gratitude to God.

 Buddhism Affirms the Importance of Praise and Gratitude

Do not turn away what is given you,
Nor reach out for what is given to others,
Lest you disturb your quietness.
Give thanks
For what has been given you,
However little

The Dhammapada, chapter 25

The unworthy man is ungrateful, forgetful of benefits. This ingrati-
tude, this forgetfulness is congenial to mean people.... But the worthy
person is grateful and mindful of benefits done to him. This grati-
tude, this mindfulness, is congenial to the best people.

Anguttara Nikaya, i.61

 Taoism Affirms the Importance of Praise and Gratitude

Although different wording and concepts are used, it is not difficult to see praise and gratitude being acknowledged in Taoism
and Confucianism.

Tao gives them life,
Virtue nurses them,
Matter shapes them,
Environment perfects them.
Therefore all things without exception worship Tao and do homage
to Virtue.

Tao Teh Ching, chapter 51

Tao is always nameless.
Small as it is in its Primal Simplicity,
It is inferior to nothing in the world.
If only a ruler could cling to it,
Everything will render homage to him.
Heaven and earth will be harmonized
And send down sweet dew.
    Tao Teh Ching, chapter 32

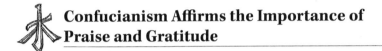

Confucianism Affirms the Importance of Praise and Gratitude

There are three things of which the superior man stands in awe. He stands in awe of the ordinances of Heaven. He stands in awe of great men. He stands in awe of the words of sages.
The mean man does not know the ordinances of Heaven, and consequently does not stand in awe of them.
    The Confucian Analects, book 16

By the ceremonies of the sacrifices to Heaven and Earth they served God, and by the ceremonies of the ancestral temple they sacrificed to their ancestors. He who understands the ceremonies of the sacrifices to Heaven and Earth, and the meaning of the several sacrifices to ancestors, would find the government of a kingdom as easy as to look into his palm!
    The Doctrine of the Mean

Chapter 14

Prayer and Meditation

PRAYER AND MEDITATION GO HAND IN HAND. When we pray, we usually ask, and when we meditate we usually receive. There are many ways that prayer can be answered, but if the answer involves receiving divine guidance, meditation is a wonderful way to encourage it. Other benefits of meditation and prayer are a lowering of stress and a balancing of our energies. In addition, the regular practice of meditation enables one to control and transcend the thought process.

Divine direction in answer to our prayers is receiving God's will. Doing God's will is not slavery as some would believe, but it is what will bring the greatest joy. It's tuning into the highest, purest, and most divine aspect of who we really are.

God, the angels, and masters are ready and willing to help us, but due to the law of free will many situations require us to ask for their assistance before they can help.

General Prayer Guidelines

Sincere prayer with good intention is always answered, sooner or later. It requires:
1. Requesting something aligned with God's will.
2. Faith in receiving an answer to your prayers.
3. Visualizing and feeling that you've already received an answer to your prayer.

Some important subjects for prayers might include:

1. Love — greater love to give to all.
2. Peace — both world peace and inner peace.
3. Thanks — acknowledgement of one's appreciation for life's blessings.
4. Divine wisdom — for making tough decisions.
5. Faith — can be increased significantly by praying for more.
6. Assistance and guidance in any area of one's life.

General Meditation Guidelines

1. Place yourself in a comfortable position (not lying down) where you will not be disturbed.
2. Close your eyes and relax every portion of your body. If necessary, relax each body area individually from the top down (eyes, mouth, throat, etc.).
3. Engage in a repetitious or singular activity to engage your mind (observing your breathing, watching a candle's flame, silently repeating a word or phrase).
4. Do this for 15-30 minutes one to three times a day. Work into this gradually.

Meditation will relax the mind with regular practice. The goal is to still your thoughts and quiet the mind, transcending the usual flow of mundane thoughts and clearing the way to receive divine energy, guidance, and grace.

Note how simple and logical the above guidelines are. No expensive courses are required. Communicating with God is a very natural thing to do.

The following meditation, if practiced consistently, will yield definite positive results:

The first step is the stilling of all OUTER ACTIVITY of both mind and body. Fifteen to thirty minutes at night before retiring and in the morning before beginning the day's work, using the following exercise, will do wonders for anyone who will make the necessary effort.

The second step: Make certain of being undisturbed, and after becoming very still, picture and FEEL your body enveloped in a Dazzling White Light. The first five minutes while holding this picture, recognize and FEEL INTENSELY the connection between the outer-self and Your Mighty God Within, focusing your attention upon the heart center and visualizing it as a Golden Sun.

The next step is the acknowledgement: "I now joyously accept the fullness of the Mighty God Presence — the Pure Christ." Feel the GREAT BRILLIANCY of the "Light" and INTENSIFY it in every cell of your body for at least ten minutes longer.

Then close the meditation by the command: "I Am a Child of the 'Light' — I Love the 'Light' — I serve the 'Light' — I live in the 'Light' — I am protected, illumined, supplied, sustained by the 'Light' — and I bless the 'Light.'"

Remember always: "One becomes THAT upon which he meditates." and since all things have come forth from the Light [Divine Energy, Frequency, Vibration], Light is the supreme perfection and control of all things.

CONTEMPLATION and ADORATION of the Light compels ILLUMINATION to take place in the mind — health, strength, and order to come into the body — and peace, harmony and success to manifest in the affairs of every individual who will really do it, and who seeks to maintain it.

Unveiled Mysteries, Godfre Ray King

Down through the centuries, under every condition, we are told by those who have expressed the greater accomplishments of life, that the Light is supreme — the Light is everywhere — and in the Light exist all things.

Consistent practice of meditation invites the divine "peace that passeth all understanding." Words cannot fully explain or describe it. Pray and meditate for a full and joyous life.

 ## Christianity Affirms the Power of Prayer and Meditation

And when thou prayest, thou shalt not be as the hypocrites are: for they love to pray standing in the synagogues and in the corners of the streets, that they may be seen of men. Verily I say unto you, They have their reward.

But thou, when thou prayest, enter into thy closet, and when thou hast shut thy door, pray to thy Father which is in secret; and thy Father which seeth in secret shall reward thee openly.

But when ye pray, use not vain repetitions, as the heathen do: for they think that they shall be heard for their much speaking.

Be not ye therefore like unto them: for your Father knoweth what things ye have need of, before ye ask him.

After this manner therefore pray ye: Our Father which art in heaven, Hallowed be thy name.

Thy Kingdom come. Thy will be done in earth, as it is in heaven.

Give us this day our daily bread.

And forgive us our debts, as we forgive our debtors.

And lead us not into tempation, but deliver us from evil: For thine is the Kingdom, and the power, and the glory, for ever. Amen.

Matthew 6:5-13

Ask, and it shall be given you; seek, and ye shall find; knock, and it shall be opened unto you:

For every one that asketh receiveth; and he that seeketh findeth; and to him that knocketh it shall be opened.

Or what man is there of you, whom if his son ask bread, will he give him a stone?

Or if he ask a fish, will he give him a serpent?

If ye then...know how to give good gifts unto your children, how much more shall your Father which is in heaven give good things to them that ask him?

Matthew 7:7-11

Meditate on these things; give thyself wholly to them; that thy profiting may appear to all.

1 Timothy 4:15

 ## Islam Affirms the Power of Prayer and Meditation

Recite that which has been revealed to thee of the Book [The Qur'an] and keep up prayer. Surely prayer keeps (one) away from indecency and evil; and certainly the remembrance of Allah is the greatest (force). And Allah knows what you do.

Qur'an 29:45

And when My servants ask thee concerning Me, surely I am nigh. I answer the prayer of the suppliant when he calls on Me, so they should hear My call and believe in Me that they may walk in the right way.

Qur'an 2:186

And your Lord says: Pray to Me, I will answer you. Those who disdain My service will surely enter hell, abased.
  Qur'an 40:60

Here, our Lord encourages us to pray to Him, and to include Him in our lives. If we do this, He promises to be of service to us.

 ## Judaism Affirms the Power of Prayer and Meditation

In those days Hezekiah fell dangerously ill. The prophet Isaiah son of Amoz came and said to him, "Thus said the Lord: Set your affairs in order, for you are going to die; you will not get well." Thereupon Hezekiah turned his face to the wall and prayed to the Lord. "Please, O lord," he said, "remember how I have walked before You sincerely and wholeheartedly, and have done what is pleasing to You." And Hezekiah wept profusely.
Then the word of the Lord came to Isaiah: "Go and tell Hezekiah: Thus said the Lord, the God of your father David: I have heard your prayer, I have seen your tears. I hereby add fifteen years to your life. I will also rescue you and this city from the hands of the king of Assyria. I will protect this city. And this is the sign for you from the Lord that the Lord will do the thing that He has promised: I am going to make the shadow on the steps, which has descended on the dial of Ahaz because of the sun, recede ten steps." And the sun['s shadow] receded ten steps, the same steps as it had descended.
  (Tanakh) Isaiah 38:1-8

In any plague and in any disease, any prayer or supplication offered by any person among all Your people Israel — each of whom knows his affliction and his pain — when he spreads forth his hands toward this House, may You hear in Your heavenly abode, and pardon.

Deal with each man according to his ways as You know his heart to be — for You alone know the hearts of all men — so that they may revere You all the days that they live on the land that You gave to our fathers.

Or if a foreigner who is not of Your people Israel comes from a distant land for the sake of Your great name, your mighty hand, and Your outstretched arm, if he comes to pray toward this House, may You hear in Your heavenly abode and grant whatever the foreigner appeals to You for. Thus all the peoples of the earth will know Your name and revere You, as does Your people Israel; and they will recognize that your name is attached to this House that I have built.

   (Tanakh) 2 Chronicles 6:29-33

May the words of my mouth
and the prayer ["meditation" in King James version] of my heart
be acceptable to You,
O Lord, my rock and my redeemer

   (Tanakh) Psalms 19:15

 ## Hinduism Affirms the Power of Prayer and Meditation

On whatever sphere of being the mind of a man may be intent at the time of death, thither will he go.
Therefore meditate always on Me, and fight; if thy mind and thy reason be fixed on Me, to Me shalt thou surely come.
He whose mind does not wander, and who is engaged in constant meditation, attains the Supreme Spirit.
Whoso meditates on the Omniscient, the Ancient, more Minute than the atom, yet the Ruler and Upholder of all, Unimaginable, Brilliant like the Sun, Beyond the reach of darkness;
He who leaves the body with mind unmoved and filled with devotion,

by the power of his meditation gathering between his eyebrows his
whole vital energy, attains the Supreme.
The Bhagavad Gita, chapter 8

But if a man will meditate on Me and Me alone, and will worship Me
always and everywhere, I will take upon Myself the fulfillment of his
aspiration, and I will safeguard whatsoever he shall attain.
The Bhagavad Gita, chapter 9

One should delight in prayer to God. If you make this your founda-
tion, the past will not tarnish you.
Svetasvatara Upanishad 2.3

 ## Buddhism Affirms the Power of Prayer and Meditation

Verily, from meditation arises wisdom. Without meditation wisdom
wanes.
Dhammapada 282

Sitting cross-legged, they should wish that all beings have firm and
strong roots of goodness and attain the state of immovability.
Cultivating concentration, they should wish that all beings conquer
their minds by concentration ultimately, with no remainder.
When practicing contemplation, they should wish that all beings see
truth as it is, and be forever free of opposition and contention.
Garland Sutra 11

 Taoism Affirms the Power of Prayer and Meditation

The following quotations reveal profound insight into the power of "non-ado" and silence, which strongly relate to the practice of meditation and prayer. Webster's dictionary defines "ado" as "fussy, bustling excitement: to-do."

The softest of all things
Overrides the hardest of all things.
Only Nothing can enter into no-space.
Hence I know the advantages of Non-Ado.
Few things under heaven are as instructive as the lessons of
Silence,
Or as beneficial as the fruits of Non-Ado.
　　Tao Teh Ching, chapter 43

Practice Non-Ado, and everything will be in order.
　　Tao Teh Ching, chapter 3

 Confucianism Affirms the Power of Prayer and Meditation

The Master being very sick, Tsze-lu asked leave to pray for him. He said, "May such a thing be done?" Tsze-lu replied, "It may. In the Eulogies it is said, 'Prayer has been made for thee to the spirits of the upper and lower worlds.'" The Master said, "My praying has been for a long time."
　· Confucian Analects, book 7

The Master said, "My children, why do you not study the Book of Poetry?

"The Odes serve to stimulate the mind.

"They may be used for purposes of self-contemplation."

Confucian Analects, book 17

Chapter 15

Humility

BEING HUMBLE IS ONE'S ACKNOWLEDGMENT that there is a Higher Power. It is knowing that there is a source of greater wisdom, love, and power than oneself. Although it's true that we can attune with that divinity, that we can ultimately be *at-one* with that divinity, the very nature of divinity is humble. Love is humbling. Not in a bow-and-scrape way, but in a way that always acknowledges the freedom and dignity of others.

Pride is the enemy of humility. Having a sense of dignity is appropriate for a spiritual seeker. Acknowledging the dignity of self and others promotes our Oneness. Pride, on the other hand, promotes separateness. Should we choose to honor the God Presence in a divinely attuned individual, that one will refer the glory back to God.

Pride goeth before destruction,
and an haughty spirit before a fall.
   Proverbs 16:18

Abide in me, and I in you. As the branch cannot bear fruit of itself,
except it abide in the vine; no more can ye, except ye abide in me.
I am the vine, ye are the branches: He that abideth in me, and I in
him, the same bringeth forth much fruit: for without me ye can do
nothing.
   John 15:4-5

We must humble ourselves by allowing our minds to be open to higher, divine wisdom that allows no more discord in our lives. Humility is an integral part of how we attune to spirit.

 ## Christianity Affirms the Importance of Humility

At the same time came the disciples unto Jesus, saying, Who is the greatest in the kingdom of heaven?
And Jesus called a little child unto him, and set him in the midst of them,
And said, Verily I say unto you, Except ye be converted, and become as little children, ye shall not enter into the kingdom of heaven.
Whosoever therefore shall humble himself as this little child, the same is greatest in the kingdom of heaven.
   Matthew 18:1-4

But he that is greatest among you shall be your servant.
And whosoever shall exalt himself shall be abased; and he that shall humble himself shall be exalted.
   Matthew 23:8-9

God resisteth the proud, but giveth grace unto the humble.
   James 4:6

Likewise, ye younger, submit yourselves unto the elder. Yea, all of you be subject one to another, and be clothed with humility: for God resisteth the proud, and giveth grace to the humble.
Humble yourselves therefore under the mighty hand of God, that he may exalt you in due time.
   1 Peter 5:5-6

Put on therefore, as the elect of God, holy and beloved, bowels of mercies, kindness, humbleness of mind, meekness, longsuffering; Forbearing one another, and forgiving one another, if any man have a quarrel against any: even as Christ forgave you, so also do ye.
Colossians 3:12-13

 ## Islam Affirms the Importance of Humility

And the servants of the Beneficent are they who walk on the earth in humility, and when the ignorant address them, they say, Peace!
Qur'an 25:63

And seek assistance through patience and prayer, and this is hard except for the humble ones,
Who know that they will meet their Lord and that to Him they will return.
Qur'an 2:45-46

Call on your Lord humbly and in secret. Surely He loves not the transgressors.
Qur'an 7:55

And remember thy Lord within thyself humbly and fearing, and in a voice not loud, in the morning and the evening, and be not of the heedless.
Surely those who are with thy Lord are not too proud to serve him, and they glorify Him and prostrate themselves before Him.
Qur'an 7:205-206

Judaism Affirms the Importance of Humility

The fear of the Lord is the discipline of wisdom;
Humility precedes honor.
    (Tanakh) Proverbs 15:33

He hath shewed thee, O man, what is good; and what doth the Lord
require of thee, but to do justly, and to love mercy, and to walk hum-
bly with thy God.
    (King James) Micah 6:8

When you seek the favor of Shaddai,
And lift up your face to God,
You will pray to Him, and He will listen to you,
And you will pay your vows.
You will decree and it will be fulfilled,
And light will shine upon your affairs.
When others sink low, you will say it is pride;
For He saves the humble.
    (Tanakh) Job 22:26-29

Pride goes before ruin,
Arrogance, before failure.
Better to be humble and among the lowly
Than to share spoils with the proud.
    (Tanakh) Proverbs 16:18-19

 Hinduism Affirms the Importance of Humility

Be humble, be harmless,
Have no pretension,

Be upright, forbearing;
Serve your teacher in true obedience,
Keeping the mind and body in cleanness,
Tranquil, steadfast, master of ego.
      The Bhagavad Gita, chapter 13

A brahmin should ever shrink from honor as from poison, and should
always be desirous of disrespect as if of ambrosia.
      The Laws of Manu 2.162

Shun all pride and jealousy. Give up all idea of "me" and "mine."
      Srimad Bhagavatam 11.4

 ## Buddhism Affirms the Importance of Humility

The body is impure, bad-smelling, and replete with various kinds of
stench which trickle here and there. If one, possessed of such a body,
thinks highly of himself and despises others — that is due to nothing
other than his lack of insight.
      Sutta Nipata 205-206

The fool who knows that he is a fool is for that very reason a wise
man; the fool who thinks he is wise is called a fool indeed.
      The Dhammapada, 63

Arrogance is haughtiness,
Non-conscientiousness is to neglect
Virtues, pride has seven forms
Each of which I will explain.
Boasting that one is lower than the lowly,
Or equal with the equal,
Or greater than or equal to the lowly

Is called the pride of selfhood.
Boasting that one is equal to those
Who by some good quality are better than oneself
Is the pride of being superior. Thinking
That one is higher than the extremely high,
Who fancy themselves to be superior,
Is pride greater than pride;
Like an abscess in a tumour
It is very vicious.
Conceiving an 'I' through ignorance
In the five empty [aggregates]
Which are called the appropriation
Is said to be the pride of thinking 'I'.
Thinking one has won fruits not yet
Attained is pride of conceit.
Praising oneself for faulty deeds
Is known by the wise as wrongful pride.
Deriding oneself, thinking
'I am senseless,' is called
The pride of lowliness.
Such briefly are the seven prides.
    The Precious Garland, 406-412

Taoism Affirms the Importance of Humility

After you have attained your purpose,
You must not parade your success,
You must not boast of your ability,
You must not feel proud.
   Tao Teh Ching, chapter 30

Truly, humility is the root from which greatness springs,
And the high must be built upon the foundation of the low.
That is why barons and princes style themselves
"The Helpless One," "The Little One," and "The Worthless one."
Perhaps they too realize their dependence upon the lowly.
Truly, too much honour means no honour.
It is not wise to shine like jade and resound like stone-chimes.
   Tao Teh Ching, chapter 39

How does the sea become the king of all streams?
Because it lies lower than they!
Hence it is the king of all streams.
Therefore, the Sage reigns over the people by humbling himself in
speech;
And leads the people by putting himself behind.
Thus it is that when a Sage stands above the people,
They do not feel the heaviness of his weight;
And when he stands in front of the people, they do not feel hurt.
Therefore all the world is glad to push him forward without getting
tired of him.
Just because he strives with nobody,
Nobody can ever strive with him.
   Tao Teh Ching, chapter 66

Confucianism Affirms the Importance of Humility

The Master said of Tsze-ch'an that he had four of the characteristics of a superior man — in the conduct of himself, he was humble; in serving his superior, he was respectful; in nourishing the people, he was kind; in ordering the people, he was just.

Confucian Analects, book 5

The Master said, "The superior man has a dignified ease without pride. The mean man has pride without a dignified ease."

Confucian Analects, book 13

Mesón de las Flores
Cotacachi - Ecuador

John & Kathleen!

Welcome to Ecuador!

Your room is ready &

We'll see you at

breakfast!

♡ Merri & Gary

Land of the Sun Foundation

García Moreno 13-67 y Sucre
Cotacachi-Ecuador
(593 6) 2916 009
Fax: (593 6) 2915 828
(336) 792 - 4767
mesondelasflores@gmail.com

Section II

Love Your Divine Self

ULTIMATELY, OUR SENSE of self may completely merge with the Godhead. As long as we have our unique perspective as a unit of awareness that is to some degree separate from the Divine One, it is important to love our Higher, Divine Self. People tend to easily acquire a sense of unworthiness, guilt, or shame resulting in an unnecessary sense of separateness from our one divine family.

It is not the Divine Self that needs forgiveness, but the acts we commit when operating from our lower, human self. In addition to making amends and asking for forgiveness, it is essential to forgive ourselves for past sins and errors. For how can we love ourselves, which is so essential, unless we let go of all guilt or shame that may accompany our non-forgiveness of ourselves? We need to do the very best that we can do, and then we need to call it good.

It is difficult to wisely love another if we don't love ourselves first. It is difficult to receive God's love or anyone else's love if we don't feel we deserve it. And it is difficult to radiate love to others when we've forgotten what it feels like to love. The following chapters represent responsibilities that will make it easy to stay in the divine flow of love.

Chapter 16

Loving the God in You

SINCE GOD IS EVERYWHERE, all-knowing and all-powerful, He is within us. God is within us as a loving father and loving mother. It is good and right to love the divinity within us — it is who we really are.

Loving the God in you does not mean to become self-centered. Nor does it mean that we are to love or reinforce our ego or any aspect of our lower, human self.

Our goal is the opposite of self-centeredness. It is to lose self-centeredness by constantly loving others in our world, God within and outside of us, and loving what we are doing. This is difficult to achieve if one has difficulty in practicing these twenty-two responsibilities.

The mysteries of the heart are fascinating to explore. God isn't just "out there" somewhere. God is within you, right now. When we love the God within ourselves, we focus the love and power of God back to God, our source. At those times, we are "recharging" ourselves and growing our attunement and ability to radiate out more divine love, wisdom, and power.

It is natural to love ourselves, if it is the good and divine aspect of our self.

This is such an important principle that it must be included with the other essential responsibilities, even though it is not precisely spelled out in all the religions. When reading the following quotations, if you can't find this essential teaching clearly expressed, look for it between the lines.

Christianity Affirms the Power of Loving the God in You

... I bow my knees unto the Father of our Lord Jesus Christ,
Of whom the whole family in heaven and earth is named,
That he would grant you, according to the riches of his glory, to be
strengthened with might by his Spirit in the inner man;
That Christ [the One Son of God] may dwell in your hearts by faith;
that ye, being rooted and grounded in love,
May be able to comprehend with all saints what is the breadth, and
length, and depth, and height;
And to know the love of Christ, which passeth knowledge, that ye
might be filled with all the fulness of God.
      Ephesians 3:14-19

No man hath seen God at any time. If we love one another, God dwell-
eth in us, and his love is perfected in us.
Hereby know we that we dwell in him, and he in us, because he hath
given us of his Spirit.
And we have known and believed the love that God hath to us. God
is love; and he that dwelleth in love dwelleth in God, and God in
him.
      1 John 4:12-13, 16

So ought men to love their wives as their own bodies. He that loveth
his wife loveth himself.
For no man ever yet hated his own flesh; but nourisheth and cher-
isheth it, even as the Lord the church:
For we are members of his body, of his flesh, and of his bones.
      Ephesians 5:28-30

Abide in me, and I in you. As the branch cannot bear fruit of itself, except it abide in the vine; no more can ye, except ye abide in me.

I am the vine, ye are the branches: He that abideth in me, and I in him, the same bringeth forth much fruit: for without me ye can do nothing.

If a man abide not in me, he is cast forth as a branch, and is withered; and men gather them, and cast them into the fire, and they are burned.

If ye abide in me, and my words abide in you, ye shall ask what ye will, and it shall be done unto you.

Herein is my Father glorified, that ye bear much fruit; so shall ye be my disciples.

As the Father hath loved me, so have I loved you: continue ye in my love.

If ye keep my commandments, ye shall abide in my love; even as I have kept my Father's commandments, and abide in his love.

These things have I spoken unto you, that my joy might remain in you, and that your joy might be full.

This is my commandment, That ye love one another, as I have loved you.

John 15:4-12

Jesus is speaking here as fully attuned with God and/or the one Son of God, the Christ. Either way, the power, wisdom, and love of God is speaking.

The kingdom of God is within you.

Luke 17:21

Islam Affirms the Power of Loving the God in You

And those who disbelieve say: Why is not a sign sent down to him by his Lord? Say: Allah leaves in error whom He pleases, and guides to Himself those who turn (to Him) —
Those who believe and whose hearts find rest in the remembrance of Allah. Now surely in Allah's remembrance do hearts find rest.
    Qur'an 13:27-28

When I love him, I am his hearing by which he hears; and his sight by which he sees; his hand by which he strikes; and his foot by which he walks.
    Forty Hadith of An-Nawawi 38

Heaven and earth contain me not, but the heart of my faithful servant contains me.
    Hadith of Suhrawardi

Islam tells us how close God is to us. Because God is omnipresent, omniscient, and omnipotent, He could not be closer to us. God is infused within our being.

Islam also tells us to love God. From this can be seen how we are prompted to love the God within us.

And certainly We created man, and We know what his mind suggests to him — and We are nearer to him than his life-vein.
    Qur'an 50:16

He is so near to us that nothing can be nearer.
    Nahjul Balagha, sermon 54

Judaism Affirms the Power of Loving the God in You

You shall not hate your kinsfolk in your heart. Reprove your kinsman but incur no guilt because of him. You shall not take vengeance or bear a grudge against your countrymen. Love your fellow as yourself: I am the Lord.
   (Tanakh) Leviticus 19:17-18

The above quotation affirms the naturalness of loving your self. What follows are affirmations to love God with all of our heart or inner Spirit.

You shall love the Lord your God with all your heart and with all your soul and with all your might.
   (Tanakh) Deuteronomy 6:5

For Your just ways, O Lord, we look to You;
We long for the name by which You are called.
At night I yearn for You with all my being,
I seek you with all the spirit within me.
   (Tanakh) Isaiah 26:8-9

For thus said He who high aloft
Forever dwells, whose name is holy:
I dwell on high, in holiness;
Yet (also) with the contrite and the lowly in spirit —
Reviving the spirits of the lowly,
Reviving the hearts of the contrite.
   (Tanakh) Isaiah 57:15

*And Moses said unto God, Behold, when I come unto the children
of Israel, and shall say unto them, The God of your fathers hath sent
me unto you; and they shall say to me, What is his name? What shall
I say unto them?*
*And God said unto Moses, I AM THAT I AM: and he said, Thus shalt
thou say unto the children of Israel, I AM hath sent me unto you.*
    (King James) Exodus 3:13-14

It is an excellent example of God's divine wisdom that he chose
the one name for Himself that, when spoken by others, "I AM THAT
I AM," includes them in the divine one. Thus, when we call to God
by using the name that He chose for Himself, we are attuning to
our own Higher/Divine Self.

ॐ Hinduism Affirms the Power of Loving the God in You

*The supreme Lord who pervades all existence, the true Self of all
creatures, may be realized through undivided love.*
    The Bhagavad Gita, chapter 8

With this teaching we are directed to totally love God, our
True Self.

Bright but hidden the Self dwells in the heart.
Everything that moves, breathes, opens and closes
Lives in the Self. He is the source of love
And may be known through love but not through thought.
He is the goal of life. Attain this goal!
The shining Self dwells hidden in the heart.
Everything in the cosmos, great and small,
Lives in the Self. He is the source of life,

Truth beyond the transience of this world.
He is the goal of life. Attain this goal!
    Mundaka Upanishad 2.2:1-2

The door of the Truth is covered by a golden disc. Open it, O
Nourisher!
Remove it so that I who have been worshipping the Truth may
behold It.
O Nourisher, lone Traveller of the sky! Controller! O Sun…Gather
your rays; withdraw your light. I would see, through your grace, that
form of yours which is the fairest.
He that Person who dwells there — is I myself!
    Isha Upanishad 15-16

Supreme Bliss is the lot of the sage, whose mind attains Peace, whose
passions subside, who is without sin, and who becomes one with the
Absolute.
Thus, free from sin, abiding always in the Eternal, the saint enjoys
without effort the Bliss which flows from realization of the Infinite.
He who experiences the unity of life sees his own Self in all beings,
and all beings in his own Self, and looks on everything with an
impartial eye;
He who sees Me in everything and everything in Me, him shall I never
forsake, nor shall he lose Me.
The sage who realizes the unity of life and who worships Me in all
beings, lives in Me, whatever may be his lot.
O Arjuna! He is the perfect saint who, taught by the likeness within
himself, sees the same Self everywhere, whether the outer form be
pleasurable or painful.
    The Bhagavad Gita, chapter 6

What follows are two different translations of the same sacred
text. Both are presented to illustrate how different these translations

can be. Though different, they lead to the same conclusion: to focus on God within.

Meditate upon Him and transcend physical consciousness. Thus will you reach union with the Lord of the universe. Thus will you become identified with Him who is One without a second. In Him all your desires will find fulfillment.
The truth is that you are always united with the Lord. But you must know *this.*

    Svetasvatara Upanishad 1:11-12,

    from "The Spiritual Heritage of India"

From meditating on him there arises, on the dissolution of the body, the third state, that of universal lordship; but he only who is alone, is satisfied.
This, which rests eternally within the self, should be known; and beyond this not anything has to be known.

    Svetasvatara Upanishad 1:11-12

    from "The Upanishads, Part II"

 ## Buddhism Affirms the Power of Loving the God in You

Love yourself and watch — today, tomorrow, always.

    Dhammapada, chapter 12

For the sake of others' welfare, however great, let not one neglect one's own welfare. Clearly perceiving one's own welfare, let one be intent on one's own goal.

    Dhammapada, 166

The Dwelling of the Tathagata is the great compassionate heart within all the living. The Robe of the Tathagata is the gentle and forbearing heart. The Seat of the Tathagata is the "spirituality of all existence."
　　Lotus Sutra 10

O good man! One who acts good is the "true thinking."
The true thinking is compassion.
Compassion is the Tathagata....
O good man! Compassion acts as parent to all beings.
The parent is compassion.
Know that compassion is the Tathagata.
O good man! Compassion is the Buddha nature of all beings.
　　Mahaparinirvana Sutra 259

Oneself, indeed, is one's savior, for what other savior could there be? With oneself well controlled one obtains a savior difficult to find.
　　Dhammapada, 160

Taoism Affirms the Power of Loving the God in You

The Sage knows himself,
But makes no show of himself;
Loves himself,
But does not exalt himself.
He prefers what is within to what is without.
　　Tao Teh Ching, chapter 72

Tao is really nothing but that which you Westerns call 'God.' Tao is the One; the beginning and the end. It embraces all things, and to it all things return....

Think not that I would teach you to banish love from your heart;
for that would be to go against Tao. Love what you love, and be
not misled by the thought that love is a hindrance which holds you
in bondage. To banish love from your heart would be a mad and
earthly action, and would put you further away from Tao than you
have ever been.

Wu Wei, chapter 1

 ## Confucianism Affirms the Power of Loving the God in You

If a man does not understand what is good, he will not attain sin-
cerity in himself.
Sincerity is the way of Heaven. The attainment of sincerity is the way
of men. He who possesses sincerity is he who, without an effort, hits
what is right, and apprehends, without the exercise of thought — he
is the sage who naturally and easily embodies the right way.

The Doctrine of the Mean

Without recognizing the ordinances of Heaven, it is impossible to
be a superior man.

Confucian Analects, book 20

The "ordinances of Heaven" are well known within the heart of
the superior man, who loves and applies them to the very best
of his ability.

It is said in the Book of Poetry,
"Heaven in producing mankind,
Gave them their various faculties and relations with their specific
laws.
These are the invariable rules of nature for all to hold,

And all love this admirable virtue."
Confucius said, "The maker of this ode knew indeed the principle
of our nature!"
We may thus see that every faculty and relation must have its law,
and since there are invariable rules for all to hold, they consequently
love this admirable virtue.

Mencius, chapter 21

Chapter 17

Inner Peace

INNER PEACE IS THE DOORWAY to spiritual attunement and an integral part of our divine nature. Lack of peace is a resistance to the divine flow of life.

Be still and know that I am God.
   Psalms 46:10

Be still and sense the peaceful presence within you. It is always there, available as an important part of your conscious life, waiting for your recognition.

Order in your world is conducive to maintaining inner peace. Order is essential for good mental health. Being organized and tidy makes every task more efficient. Loving one's personal environment and maintaining order in it makes life significantly easier, for greater clarity is facilitated when everything is in its place.

It is important to control your thoughts and include God in them. It is also important, with the help of regular meditation, to periodically transcend your thoughts. You can control your destiny and master life with regular practice of these twenty-two essential responsibilities. If you can maintain a positive outlook on life regardless of circumstances, your feelings and your life experience will be more positive.

Christianity Affirms the Importance of Inner Peace

Jesus, upon return to his disciples after his crucifixion, said several times *Peace be unto you.* (John 20:19, 21, 26).

And the peace of God, which passeth all understanding, shall keep your hearts and minds through Christ Jesus.
    Philippians 4:7

And suddenly there was with the angel a multitude of the heavenly host praising God, and saying,
Glory to God in the highest, and on earth peace, good will toward men.
    Luke 2:13-14

For the kingdom of God is not meat and drink; but righteousness, and peace, and joy in the Holy Ghost.
For he that in these things serveth Christ is acceptable to God, and approved of men.
Let us therefore follow after the things which make for peace, and things wherewith one may edify another.
    Romans 14:17-19

Blessed are the peacemakers; for they shall be called the children of God.
    Matthew 5:9

But the wisdom that is from above is first pure, then peaceable, gentle, and easy to be intreated, full of mercy and good fruits, without partiality, and without hypocrisy.
And the fruit of righteousness is sown in peace of them that make peace.
    James 3:17-18

*For he that will love life, and see good days, let him refrain his tongue
from evil, and his lips that they speak no guile:
Let him eschew evil, and do good; let him seek peace, and ensue it.*
　　1 Peter 3:10-11

 ## Islam Affirms the Importance of Inner Peace

The standard greeting between Muslims is *Peace be upon you.*

*And this is the path of thy Lord, (a) straight (path). Indeed We have
made the messages clear for a people who mind.
Theirs is the abode of peace with their Lord, and He is their Friend
because of what they do.*
　　Qur'an 6:126-127

*Those who believe and do good, their Lord guides them by their faith;
rivers will flow beneath them in Gardens of bliss.
Their cry therein will be, Glory to Thee, O Allah! and their greeting,
Peace!*
　　Qur'an 10:9-10

*The believers are brethren so make peace between your brethren,
and keep your duty to Allah that mercy may be had on you.*
　　Qur'an 49:10

*And Allah invites to the abode of peace, and guides whom he pleases
to the right path.*
　　Qur'an 10:25

*And their prophet said to them: Surely the sign of his kingdom is
that there shall come to you the heart in which there is tranquility
from your Lord and the best of what the followers of Moses and the
followers of Aaron have left, the angels bearing it.*
　　Qur'an 2:248

He it is Who sent down tranquility into the hearts of the believers
that they might add faith to their faith. And Allah's are the hosts of
the heavens and the earth, and Allah is ever Knowing, Wise —
    Qur'an 48:4

 ## Judaism Affirms the Importance of Inner Peace

For the work of righteousness shall be peace,
And the effect of righteousness, calm and confidence forever.
Then my people shall dwell in peaceful homes,
In secure dwellings,
In untroubled places of rest.
    (Tanakh) Isaiah 32:17-18

Happy is the man who finds wisdom,
The man who attains understanding.
Her value in trade is better than silver,
Her yield, greater than gold.
She is more precious than rubies;
All of your goods cannot equal her.
In her right hand is length of days,
In her left, riches and honor.
Her ways are pleasant ways,
And all her paths, peaceful.
    (Tanakh) Proverbs 3:13-17

Great peace have they which love thy law: and nothing shall offend
them.
    (King James) Psalms 119:165

The righteous man perishes,
And no one considers;

Pious men are taken away,
And no one gives thought
That because of evil
The righteous was taken away.
Yet he shall come to peace,
He shall have rest on his couch
Who walked straightforward.
(Tanakh) Isaiah 57:1-2

ॐ Hinduism Affirms the Importance of Inner Peace

As rivers flow into the ocean but cannot make the vast ocean over-
flow, so flow the streams of the sense-world into the sea of peace
that is the sage.
The Bhagavad Gita, chapter 2

By His grace you will find supreme peace, and the state which is
beyond all change.
The Bhagavad Gita, chapter 18

Peace be to earth and to airy spaces!
Peace be to heaven, peace to the waters, peace to the plants and
peace to the trees!
May all the gods grant me peace!
By this invocation of peace may peace be diffused!
By this invocation of peace may peace bring peace!
With this peace the dreadful I appease, with this peace the cruel I
appease, with this peace all evil I appease, so that peace may pre-
vail, happiness prevail!
May everything for us be peaceful!
Atharva Veda 19.9.14

Buddhism Affirms the Importance of Inner Peace

Just as a deep lake is clear and still, even so, on hearing the teachings and realizing them, the wise become exceedingly peaceful.
The Dhammapada, 82

Victory breeds hatred, for the defeated live in pain. Happily live the peaceful, giving up victory and defeat.
The Dhammapada, 201

The monk looks for peace within himself, and not in any other place. For when a person is inwardly quiet, there is nowhere a self can be found; where, then, could a not-self be found?
There are no waves in the depths of the sea; it is still, unbroken. It is the same with the monk. He is still, without any quiver of desire, without a remnant on which to build pride and desire.
Sutta Nipata, 919-920

 Taoism Affirms the Importance of Inner Peace

Attain to utmost Emptiness.
Cling single-heartedly to interior peace.
While all things are stirring together,
I only contemplate the Return.
For flourishing as they do,
Each of them will return to its root.
To return to the root is to find peace.
To find peace is to fulfill one's destiny.
Tao Teh Ching, chapter 16

Fine weapons of war augur evil.
Even things seem to hate them.
Therefore, a man of Tao does not set his heart upon them.
...peace and quiet are dearest to his heart.
     Tao Teh Ching, chapter 31

The peaceful and serene
Is the Norm of the World.
     Tao Teh Ching, chapter 45

 ## Confucianism Affirms the Importance of Inner Peace

The Master said, "The superior man is satisfied and composed; the mean man is always full of distress."
     Confucian Analects, book 7

The Master said, "The wise are free from perplexities; the virtuous from anxiety; and the bold from fear."
     Confucian Analects, book 9

Chapter 18

Perfection and Purity

PERFECTION AND PURITY ARE CONCEPTS used to describe a soul's ideal attainment. This includes a cleansing from past sins. Achieving perfection and purity, one can be fully attuned to God. One is no longer held back or subject to illusions caused by baggage from past errors. One is free from negative karma. The individual's desires are one with the will of God, and no more sense of separation exists.

It's important to strive for perfection, and also to avoid self-condemnation when we're not successful. God looks at our intent as well as our results. We are entitled to make mistakes, as that is how we learn. It's helpful to not identify with our mistakes, to affirm that we are *not* our mistakes. If we follow our inner guide, our conscience (an aspect of our Higher/Divine Self), we'll always do what is right. It's important to feel worthy, and to not feel isolated from God.

According to the sacred teachings, serious mistakes — when someone is harmed — can be forgiven if forgiveness is asked for with true sincerity, along with making amends to the fullest extent possible. Doing this will transmute all or part of the karma (misqualified energy). The karma also may be partially or fully lifted by God's grace. The measure of grace received may be influenced by what the individual has learned since the act — empathizing with the person one has injured and truly regretting the act is necessary for this to occur. We are forgiven as we forgive.

Some believe they will be saved by God's grace without any effort on their part. God's grace will save those who make the necessary efforts and strive for perfection. Our goal is to be able to live in perfect harmony with all of life.

Gautama Buddha said sex is the greatest temptation. During sex there is an exchange of energies that creates karmic ties. For this reason sex is a serious activity. Ideally it is an expression of love within marriage. It is best to not use sex merely for momentary thrills. It's helpful to ask for divine assistance when dealing with this energy.

Marriage is a dedication of the couple's energies in the service of God and thus includes God intimately in the relationship.

God never gives us a test too difficult to pass.

 ## Christianity Affirms the Power of Perfection and Purity

Be ye therefore perfect, even as your Father which is in heaven is perfect.
Matthew 5:44

That they all may be one; as thou, Father art in me, and I in thee, that they also may be one in us: that the world may believe that thou hast sent me.
And the glory which thou gavest me I have given them; that they may be one, even as we are one:
I in them, and thou in me, that they may be made perfect in one; and that the world may know that thou hast sent me, and hast loved them, as thou hast loved me.
John 17:21-23

The disciple is not above his master: but every one that is perfect shall be as his master.
    Luke 6:40

And he gave some, apostles; and some, prophets; and some, evangelists; and some, pastors and teachers;
For the perfecting of the saints, for the work of the ministry, for the edifying of the body of Christ:
Till we all come in the unity of the faith, and of the knowledge of the Son of God unto a perfect man, unto the measure of the stature of the fullness of Christ.
    Ephesians 4:11-13

 ## Islam Affirms the Power of Perfection and Purity

He indeed is successful who purifies himself,
And remembers the name of his Lord, then prays.
    Qur'an 87:14-15

In the name of Allah, the Beneficent, the Merciful.
By the sun and his brightness!
And the moon when she borrows light from him!
And the day when it exposes it to view!
And the night when it draws a veil over it!
And the heaven and its make!
And the earth and its extension!
And the soul and its perfection! —
So He reveals to it its way of evil and its way of good;
He is indeed successful who causes it to grow.
    Qur'an 91:1-9

The author of this excellent translation of the Koran, Maulana Muhammad Ali, included the following helpful commentary regarding the above passage:

The mention of the perfection of the soul of man in this verse is a sequel to what is stated in the first six verses. Man is here spoken of as possessing the highest of qualities which are met with in nature. The sun is a source of light, even so is the perfect man a source of spiritual light. The moon borrows the light of the sun, even so is the perfect man, whose light is really borrowed from the Divine source, which is the real source of all light. The day makes things manifest and thus enables man to carry on his struggle, while the night casts a veil over light and brings rest; the perfect man possesses both these qualities, as he carries on a very hard struggle for the attainment of great ends, and at the same time his mind is at rest and he possesses the quality of contentment. The heaven is raised high, and the earth is spread out for men to walk over, being thus a manifestation of humility; the perfect man possesses both these qualities, having the highest of aspirations and being at the same time humble and lowly. The perfect man thus possesses the opposite qualities of giving light and receiving light, severe exertion and complete rest, greatness and humility. These qualities were possessed by the Prophet, who invited others to make the same the goal of their lives.
Maulana Muhammad Ali

Judaism Affirms the Power of Perfection and Purity

Who may ascend the mountain of the Lord?
Who may stand in His holy place? —
He who has clean hands and a pure heart, who has not taken a false oath by My life or sworn deceitfully.

He shall carry away a blessing from the Lord, a just reward from God, his deliverer.
(Tanakh) Psalms 24:3-5

The Tanakh uses the word "wholehearted" instead of being "perfect" in this next Old Testament quotation, so the King James version is given.

Thou shalt be perfect with the Lord thy God.
(King James) Deuteronomy 18:13

Here are a few more quotes from the Old Testament's King James version, which use the term "perfect."

And when Abram was ninety years old and nine, the Lord appeared to Abram, and said unto him, I am the Almighty God; walk before me, and be thou perfect.
(King James) Genesis 17:1

Let your heart therefore be perfect with the Lord our God, to walk in his statutes, and to keep his commandments.
(King James) 1 Kings 8:61

For the eyes of the Lord run to and fro throughout the whole earth, to shew himself strong in the behalf of them whose heart is perfect toward him.
(King James) 2 Chronicles 16:9

Mark the perfect man, and behold the upright: for the end of that man is peace.
(King James) Psalms 37:37

Hinduism Affirms the Power of Perfection and Purity

He, indeed, is the great Purusha, the Lord, who inspires the mind to attain the state of stainlessness. He is the Ruler and the imperishable Light.

    Svetasvatara Upanishad 3:12

When the light of knowledge gleams forth from all the gates of the body, then be sure that Purity prevails....
When Purity prevails, the soul on quitting the body passes on to the pure regions where live those who know the Highest.

    The Bhagavad Gita, chapter 14

To him who thinks constantly of me, and of nothing else, to such an ever-faithful devotee, O Arjuna, am I ever accessible.
Coming thus unto Me, these great souls go no more to the misery and death of earthly life, for they have gained perfection.

    The Bhagavad Gita, chapter 8

Smaller than the smallest, greater than the greatest, this Self forever dwells within the hearts of all. When a man is free from desire, his mind and senses purified, he beholds the glory of the Self and is without sorrow.
Though seated, he travels far; though at rest, he moves all things. Who but the purest of the pure can realize this Effulgent Being, who is joy and who is beyond joy.

    Katha Upanishad 1.2:20-21

The Atman, resplendent and pure, whom the sinless disciples behold residing within the body, is attained by unceasing practice of truthfulness, austerity, right knowledge and continence.

    Mundaka Upanishad 3.1.5

Buddhism Affirms the Power of Perfection and Purity

Whosoever in this world has overcome good and evil, both ties, who is free from grief and defilement, and is pure, him I call a Bramana.
The Sutta-Nipata, Part III

All that we are is the result of what we have thought: it is founded on our thoughts, it is made up of our thoughts. If a man speaks or acts with a pure thought, happiness follows him, like a shadow that never leaves him.
The Dhammapada, chapter 1

Not to do any evil, to cultivate good, to purify one's mind — this is the teaching of the Buddhas.
The Dhammapada, 183

Make thyself an island, work hard, be wise! When thy impurities are blown away, and thou art free from guilt, thou wilt enter into the heavenly world of the elect....
Let a wise man blow off the impurities of his self, as a smith blows off the impurities of silver one by one, little by little, and from time to time....
The fault of others is easily perceived, but that of oneself is difficult to perceive; a man winnows his neighbour's faults like chaff, but his own fault he hides, as a cheat hides the bad die from the gambler.
The Dhammapada, chapter 18

Taoism Affirms the Power of Perfection and Purity

In keeping the spirit and the vital soul together,
Are you able to maintain their perfect harmony?
In gathering your vital energy to attain suppleness,
Have you reached the state of a new-born babe?
In washing and clearing your inner vision,
Have you purified it of all dross?
Tao Teh Ching, chapter 10

Know the white,
Keep to the black,
And be the Pattern of the World.
To be the Pattern of the World is
To move constantly in the path of Virtue
Without erring a single step
And to return again to the Infinite
Tao Teh Ching, chapter 28

 ## Confucianism Affirms the Power of Perfection and Purity

Perfection is (seen in) the beginning and end of (all) creatures and
things. Without this perfection there would be no creature or thing.
Therefore the superior man considers perfection as the noblest of
all attainments.
He who is perfect does not only complete himself; his perfection
enables him to complete all other beings also. The completion of
himself shows the complete virtue of his nature; the completion of
other beings shows his Wisdom.
Li Ki (The Book of Rites), part II, book 28

Let every attainment in what is good be firmly grasped.
Let perfect virtue be accorded with.
    Confucian Analects, book 7.

The Master said, "By extensively studying all learning, and keeping himself under the restraint of the rules of propriety, one may thus likewise not err from what is right."
The Master said, "The superior man seeks to perfect the admirable qualities of men, and does not seek to perfect their bad qualities. The mean man does the opposite of this."
    Confucian Analects, book 12

Chapter 19

Moderation and Balance

MODERATION APPLIES TO OUR DIET, how much we work, and all extremes of behavior, thought, and feeling. It is tied closely with the other chapters in this section and with discipline and effort. The middle way is usually the best way. It is best to avoid extremes, unless the extreme is the correct goal for a situation.

Recommendations for moderation and balance in life can be found in every world religion.

 Christianity Affirms the Importance of Moderation and Balance

Let your moderation be known unto all men.
Philippians 4:5

And every man that striveth for the mastery is temperate in all things.
1 Corinthians 9:25

Add to your faith virtue; and to virtue knowledge;
And to knowledge temperance; and to temperance patience; and to patience godliness;
And to godliness brotherly kindness; and to brotherly kindness charity.
2 Peter 1:5-7

For a bishop must be blameless, as the steward of God; not self-willed, not soon angry, not given to wine, no striker, not given to filthy lucre;
But a lover of hospitality, a lover of good men, sober, just, holy, temperate.

Titus 1:7-8

 ## Islam Affirms the Importance of Moderation and Balance

O children of Adam, attend to your adornment at every time of prayer, and eat and drink and be not prodigal [recklessly extravagant]; surely He loves not the prodigals.

Qur'an 7:31

Observe moderation in all you do, and if that is not possible, try to be near moderation.

Hadith

 ## Judaism Affirms the Importance of Moderation and Balance

The wicked crows about his unbridled lusts;
The grasping man reviles and scorns the Lord.

(Tanakh) Psalms 10:3

Listen, my son, and get wisdom;
Lead your mind in a [proper] path.
Do not be of those who guzzle wine,
Or glut themselves on meat;
For guzzlers and gluttons will be impoverished,

And drowsing will clothe you in tatters.
   (Tanakh) Proverbs 23:19-21

Two things I ask of you; do not deny them to me before I die:
Keep lies and false words far from me;
Give me neither poverty nor riches,
But provide me with my daily bread,
Lest, being sated, I renounce, saying, "Who is the Lord?"
Or, being impoverished, I take to theft
And profane the name of my God.
   (Tanakh) Proverbs 30:7-9

ॐ Hinduism Affirms the Importance of Moderation and Balance

Meditation is not for him who eats too much, nor for him who eats not at all; nor for him who is overmuch addicted to sleep, nor for him who is always awake.
But for him who regulates his food and recreation, who is balanced in action, in sleep and in waking, it shall dispel all unhappiness.
   The Bhagavad Gita, chapter 6

Under the sway of strong impulse, the man who is devoid of self-control willfully commits deeds that he knows to be fraught with future misery. But the man of discrimination, even though moved by desires, at once becomes conscious of the evil that is in them, and does not yield to their influence but remains unattached.
   Srimad Bhagavatam 11:7

These eight qualities glorify a man: wisdom, high birth, self-restraint, learning, prowess, moderation in speech, gift according to one's power, and gratitude.
   The Mahabharata, book 5, section 33

Buddhism Affirms the Importance of Moderation and Balance

The Tathagata, the Buddha continued, does not seek salvation in austerities, but neither does he for that reason indulge in worldly pleasure, nor live in abundance. The Tathagata has found the middle path.

There are two extremes, O bhikkhus, which the man who has given up the world ought not to follow — the habitual practice, on the one hand, of self-indulgence which is unworthy, vain and fit only for the world-minded and the habitual practice, on the other hand, of self-mortification, which is painful, useless and unprofitable.

Neither abstinence from fish and flesh, nor going naked, nor shaving the head, nor wearing matted hair, nor dressing in a rough garment, nor covering oneself with dirt, nor sacrificing to Agni, will cleanse a man who is not free from delusions....

A middle path, O bhikkhus avoiding the two extremes, has been discovered by the Tathagata — a path which opens the eyes, and bestows understanding, which leads to peace of mind, to the higher wisdom, to full enlightenment, to Nirvana! ...By suffering, the emaciated devotee produces confusion and sickly thoughts in his mind. Mortification is not conducive even to worldly knowledge; how much less to a triumph over the senses!

...And how can any one be free from self by leading a wretched life, if he does not succeed in quenching the fires of lust, if he still hankers after either worldly or heavenly pleasures? But he in whom self has become extinct is free from lust; he will desire neither worldly nor heavenly pleasures, and the satisfaction of his natural wants will not defile him. However, let him be moderate, let him eat and drink according to the need of the body.

Buddha, The Gospel: The Sermon at Benares

In the body restraint is good, good is restraint in speech, in thought
restraint is good, good is restraint in all things. A Bhikshu, restrained
in all things, is freed from all pain.
The Dhammapada, chapter 25

He in whom there is truth, virtue, love, restraint, moderation, he who
is free from impurity and is wise, he is called an elder.
The Dhammapada, chapter 19

 ## Taoism Affirms the Importance of Moderation and Balance

The Yellow Emperor sighed heavily and said, "My fault is want of
moderation. The misery I suffer comes from over-attention to my
own self, and the troubles of the Empire from over-regulation in
everything."
The Book of Lieh-Tzu, book II

For all things there is a time for going ahead, and a time for follow-
ing behind;
A time for slow-breathing and a time for fast-breathing;
A time to grow in strength and a time to decay;
A time to be up and a time to be down.
Therefore, the Sage avoids all extremes, excesses and
extravagances.
Tao Teh Ching, chapter 29

An excessive love for anything will cost you dear in the end.
The storing up of too much goods will entail a heavy loss.
To know when you have enough is to be immune from disgrace.
To know when to stop is to be preserved from perils.
Only thus can you endure long.
Tao Teh Ching, chapter 44

Confucianism Affirms the Importance of Moderation and Balance

Tsze-kung asked which of the two, Shih or Shang, was the superior. The Master said, "Shih goes beyond the due mean, and Shang does not come up to it."
"Then," said Tsze-kung, "the superiority is with Shih, I suppose."
The Master said, "To go beyond is as wrong as to fall short."
    Confucian Analects, book 11

Mencius said, "When it appears proper to take a thing, and afterwards not proper, to take it is contrary to moderation."
    Mencius, chapter 16

Chapter 20

Vigilance

BECAUSE WE NEED TO BELIEVE in our potential for perfection and strive for it, we need to be constantly vigilant. Our vigilance needs to include all of our thoughts, feelings, words, and actions. We need to stand at the doorway of our consciousness and sound the alarm whenever any negative or impure thinking comes in. We need to immediately deny its truth, not giving it any power by accepting it. Instead, substitute a positive truth that will counteract any impure or negative thoughts. This is the necessary way, the vigilant way.

We need to be aware whenever we violate the spiritual teachings we want to adhere to. Be aware of those first thoughts or feelings that would oppose our plan of spiritual liberation. Without vigilance, it is easy to simply revert back to our old habits.

 Christianity Affirms the Importance of Vigilance

Be sober, be vigilant; because your adversary the devil, as a roaring lion, walketh about, seeking whom he may devour:
Whom resist stedfast in the faith, knowing that the same afflictions are accomplished in your brethren that are in the world.
But the God of all grace, who hath called us unto his eternal glory by Christ Jesus, after that ye have suffered a while, make you perfect, stablish, strengthen, settle you.
1 Peter 5:8-10

*Ye are all the children of light, and the children of the day: we are
not of the night, nor of darkness.*
*Therefore let us not sleep, as do others; but let us watch and be
sober.*
    1 Thessalonians 5:5-6

*Now I Paul myself beseech you by the meekness and gentleness of
Christ, who in presence am base among you, but being absent am
bold toward you:*
*But I beseech you, that I may not be bold when I am present with
that confidence, wherewith I think to be bold against some, which
think of us as if we walked according to the flesh.*
For though we walk in the flesh, we do not war after the flesh:
*(For the weapons of our warfare are not carnal, but mighty through
God to the pulling down of strong holds);*
*Casting down imaginations, and every high thing that exalteth itself
against the knowledge of God, and bringing into captivity every
thought to the obedience of Christ;*
    2 Corinthians 10:1-5

Here, Paul is stating that our struggle is not with battling physical beings, but "every thought" that is not in accord with the
teachings of the Christ.

 ## Islam Affirms the Importance of Vigilance

The Muslim practice of praying several times every day provides
Islam's followers a significant degree of vigilance and protection.
Also, the Qur'an contains numerous instructions to remember
God.

And watch, surely I too am watching with you.
Qur'an 11:93

When anything pricketh your conscience, foresake it.
Hadith

*And certainly We have repeated (warnings) in this Koran that they
[men] may be mindful.*
Qur'an 17:41

The most excellent jihad [holy war] is that for the conquest of self.
Hadith

 ## Judaism Affirms the Importance of Vigilance

Evil thoughts are an abomination to the Lord,
But pleasant words are pure....
The heart of the righteous man rehearses his answer,
But the mouth of the wicked blurts out evil things.
(Tanakh) Proverbs 15:26, 28

More than all that you guard, guard your mind,
For it is the source of life.
Put crooked speech away from you;
Keep devious talk far from you.
Let your eyes look forward,
Your gaze be straight ahead.
Survey the course you take,
And all your ways will prosper.
Do not swerve to the right or the left;
Keep your feet from evil.
(Tanakh) Proverbs 4:23-27

I look to the Lord;
I look to Him;
I await His word.
I am more eager for the Lord than watchmen for the morning
    (Tanakh) Psalms 130:5-6

All the ways of a man seem right to him,
But the Lord probes the mind.
To do what is right and just
Is more desired by the Lord than sacrifice.
    (Tanakh) Proverbs 21:2-3

Hinduism Affirms the Importance of Vigilance

That intellect which understands the creation and dissolution of life, what actions should be done and what not, which discriminates between fear and fearlessness, bondage and deliverance, that is Pure....
And that which, shrouded in Ignorance, thinks wrong right, and sees everything perversely, O Arjuna, that intellect is ruled by Darkness.
The conviction and steady concentration by which the mind, the vitality and the senses are controlled — O Arjuna! They are the product of Purity.
    The Bhagavad Gita, chapter 18

Let him seek liberation by the help of his highest Self, and let him never disgrace his own Self. For that Self is his only friend; yet it may also be his enemy.
To him who has conquered his lower nature by Its help, the Self is a friend, but to him who has not done so, It is an enemy.
    The Bhagavad Gita, chapter 6

The firm control of the senses is what is called yoga. One must then be vigilant; for yoga can be both beneficial and injurious.
Katha Upanishad 2.3.11

 ## Buddhism Affirms the Importance of Vigilance

Let the wise man guard his thoughts, for they are difficult to perceive, very subtle, and they rush wherever they list; thoughts well-guarded bring happiness.

Those who bridle their mind, which travels far, moves about alone, is incorporeal, and hides in the chamber of the heart, will be free from the bonds of Mara, the tempter.

If a man's faith is unsteady, if he does not know the true law, if his peace of mind is troubled, his knowledge will never be perfect.

If a man's thoughts are not scattered, if his mind is not perplexed, if he has ceased to think of good or evil, then there is no fear in him while he is watchful.

Knowing that his body is fragile like a jar, and making his thought firm like a fortress, one should attack Mara, the tempter, with the weapon of knowledge; one should watch him when conquered, and should never rest.

Whatever a hater may do to a hater, or an enemy to an enemy, a wrongly-directed mind will do us greater mischief.
The Dhammapada , chapter 3

Vigilance is the road to immortality. Negligence is the road to death. Those who are vigilant do not die. Those who are negligent are as if dead.

To those who are inconstant in thought, ignorant of the true law, or wavering confidence, wisdom comes not to fullness.
The Dhammapada

An evil deed is better left undone, for a man repents of it afterwards; a good deed is better done, for having done it, one does not repent. Like a well-guarded frontier fort, with defences within and without, so let a man guard himself. Not a moment should escape, for they who allow the right moment to pass, suffer pain when they are in hell.

They who are ashamed of what they ought not to be ashamed of, and are not ashamed of what they ought to be ashamed of, such men, embracing false doctrines enter the evil path.

They who fear when they ought not to fear, and fear not when they ought to fear, such men, embracing false doctrines, enter the evil path.

They who forbid when there is nothing to be forbidden, and forbid not when there is something to be forbidden, such men, embracing false doctrines, enter the evil path.

They who know what is forbidden as forbidden, and what is not forbidden as not forbidden, such men, embracing the true doctrine, enter the good path.

The Dhammapada, chapter 22

 ## Taoism Affirms the Importance of Vigilance

To keep the rule and measure constantly in your mind is what we call Mystical Virtue. Deep and far-reaching is Mystical Virtue! It leads all things to return, till they come back to Great harmony!

Tao Teh Ching, chapter 65

He who adheres assiduously to the path of Tao is a man of steady purpose.

Tao Teh Ching, chapter 33

Confucianism Affirms the Importance of Vigilance

Tsze-lu asked what constituted the superior man. The Master said, "The cultivation of himself in reverential carefulness."
Confucian Analects, book 14

Tsze-chang asked how a man should conduct himself, so as to be everywhere appreciated.
The Master said, "Let his words be sincere and truthful and his actions honorable and careful."
Confucian Analects, book 15

The superior man honors his virtuous nature, and maintains constant inquiry and study, seeking to carry it out to its breadth and greatness, so as to omit none of the more exquisite and minute points which it embraces, and to raise it to its greatest height and brilliancy.
The Doctrine of the Mean

Chapter 21

Health Maintenance

WE DON'T NEED ANY SACRED TEXTS to know how essential it is to take good care of our bodies. When we make healthy choices we can lead happy, productive lives.

It is difficult to find within the sacred texts excerpts that simply state the importance of maintaining one's health. Many of the following quotations refer to health maintenance indirectly.

In today's world of junk food, fast food, additives, soil depletion, and environmental health factors, it is more and more challenging to maintain ideal health. At the time the sacred texts were written, health issues were more basic. In times past, the health care plan for most was simply having enough food, avoiding disease, and avoiding violent death!

Today, we need to be vigilant about the quality and quantity of our food. We need to exercise regularly. We need to keep our stress levels to a minimum by including stress reduction techniques. We need to minimize our use of drugs to treat our ailments, as they usually have negative side effects and often don't treat the source of health problems. We need to avoid the use of drugs for "recreational" purposes and realize that there is an abundance of ways to get "high" naturally, with God.

Our bodies are temples for our souls to temporarily inhabit. They are on loan from God, and we need to treat them with the utmost respect. Glorify God in your body by taking good care of it.

Christianity Affirms the Importance of Maintaining Good Health

What doth it profit, my brethren, though a man say he hath faith, and have not works? Can faith save him?
If a brother or sister be naked, and destitute of daily food,
And one of you say unto them, Depart in peace, by ye warmed and filled; notwithstanding ye give them not those things which are needful to the body; what doth it profit?
    James 2:14-16

So ought men to love their wives as their own bodies. He that loveth his wife loveth himself.
For no man ever yet hated his own flesh; but nourisheth and cherisheth it, even as the Lord the church:
For we are members of his body, of his flesh, and of his bones.
    Ephesians 5:28-30

I beseech you therefore, brethren, by the mercies of God, that ye present your bodies a living sacrifice, holy, acceptable unto God, which is your reasonable service.
    Romans 12:1

According to my earnest expectation and my hope, that in nothing I shall be ashamed, but that with all boldness, as always, so now also Christ shall be magnified in my body, whether it be by life, or by death.
    Philippians 1:20

What? Know ye not that your body is the temple of the Holy Ghost which is in you, which ye have of God, and ye are not your own?
For ye are bought with a price: therefore glorify God in your body, and in your spirit, which are God's.
    1 Corinthians 6:19-20

Know ye not that ye are the temple of God, and that the Spirit of God dwelleth in you?

If any man defile the temple of God, him shall God destroy; for the temple of God is holy, which temple ye are.

1 Corinthians 3:16-17

The light of the body is the eye: if therefore thine eye be single, thy whole body shall be full of light.

But it thine eye be evil, thy whole body shall be full of darkness. If therefore the light that is in thee be darkness, how great is that darkness!

Matthew 6:22-23

 ## Islam Affirms the Importance of Maintaining Good Health

Whoever among you is sick or has an ailment of the head, he (may effect) a compensation by fasting or alms or sacrificing.

Qur'an 2:196

While man is in this world, two things are necessary for him: first, the protection and nurture of his soul; secondly, the care and nurture of his body. The proper nourishment of the soul...is the knowledge and love of God, and to be absorbed in the love of anything but God is the ruin of the soul. The body, so to speak, is simply the riding-animal of the soul, and perishes while the soul endures. The soul should take care of the body, just as a pilgrim on his way to Mecca takes care of his camel; but if the pilgrim spends his whole time in feeding and adorning his camel, the caravan will leave him behind, and he will perish in the desert.

The Alchemy of Happiness, Chapter 3

O you who believe, when you rise up for prayer, wash your faces, and your hands up to the elbows, and wipe your heads, and (wash) your feet up to the ankles. And if you are under an obligation, then wash (yourselves).

And if your are sick or on a journey, or one of you comes from the privy, or you have had contact with women and you cannot find water, betake yourselves to pure earth and wipe your faces and your hands therewith. Allah desires not to place a burden on you but He wishes to purify you, and that He may complete His favour on you, so that you may give thanks.

    Qur'an 5:6

 ## Judaism Affirms the Importance of Maintaining Good Health

For I the Lord am he who brought you up from the land of Egypt to be your God: you shall be holy, for I am holy.

These are the instructions concerning animals, birds, all living creatures that move in water, and all creatures that swarm on earth, for distinguishing between the unclean and the clean, between the living things that may be eaten and the living things that may not be eaten.

    (Tanakh) Leviticus 11:45-47

Is it such a fast that I have chosen? A day for a man to afflict his soul? Is it to bow down his head as a bulrush, and to spread sackcloth and ashes under him? Wilt thou call this a fast, and an acceptable day to the Lord?

Is not this the fast that I have chosen? To loose the bands of wickedness, to undo the heavy burdens, and to let the oppressed go free, and that ye break every yoke?

Is it not to deal thy bread to the hungry, and that thou bring the poor

that are cast out to thy house? When thou seest the naked, that thou cover him; and that thou hide not thyself from thine own flesh?
Then shall thy light break forth as the morning, and thine health shall spring forth speedily: and thy righteousness shall go before thee; the glory of the Lord shall be thy reward.
Then shalt thou call, and the Lord shall answer; thou shalt cry, and he shall say, Here I am. If thou take away from the midst of thee the yoke, the putting forth of the finger, and speaking vanity;
And if thou draw out thy soul to the hungry, and satisfy the afflicted soul; then shall thy light rise in obscurity and thy darkness be as the noon day.

(King James) Isaiah 58:5-10

My son, attend to my words; incline thine ear unto my sayings.
Let them not depart from thine eyes; keep them in the midst of thine heart.
For they are life unto those that find them, and health to all their flesh.
Keep thy heart with all diligence; for out of it are the issues of life.
Put away from thee a froward mouth, and perverse lips put far from thee.
Let thine eyes look right on, and let thine eyelids look straight before thee.
Ponder the path of thy feet, and let all thy ways be established.
Turn not to the right hand nor to the left: remove thy foot from evil.

(King James) Proverbs 4:20-27

Let a man always consider himself as if the Holy One dwells within him.

The Babylonian Talmud, Taanit, 11b

ॐ Hinduism Affirms the Importance of Maintaining Good Health

Those who practise austerities not commanded by scripture, who are slaves to hypocrisy and egotism, who are carried away by the fury of desire and passion,
They are ignorant. They torment the organs of the body; and they harass Me also, Who lives within. Know that they are devoted to evil.
The food which men enjoy is also threefold, like the ways of sacrifice, austerity and almsgiving. Listen to the distinction.
The foods that prolong life and increase purity, vigour, health, cheerfulness and happiness are those that are delicious, soothing, substantial and agreeable. These are loved by the Pure.
Those in whom Passion is dominant like foods that are bitter, sour, salt, over-hot, pungent, dry and burning. These produce unhappiness, repentance and disease.
The ignorant love food which is stale, not nourishing, putrid and corrupt, the leavings of others and unclean.
     The Bhagavad Gita, chapter 17

...in the Waters there is healing balm
Be swift, ye Gods, to give them praise.
Within the Waters — Soma thus hath told me — dwell all balms that heal,
And Agni, he who blesseth all. The Waters hold all medicines.
O Waters, teem with medicine to keep my body safe from harm,
So that I long may see the Sun.
     The Rig Veda, book 1: hymn XXIII

Ayurveda is part of the sacred texts of Hinduism known as the Vedas. As a preventive science and a medical system, it is contained within the Rig Veda, which was written 5,000 years ago.

Ayurveda is considered by many to be the oldest form of health care in the world, and has had a significant influence upon other health care systems.

Buddhism Affirms the Importance of Maintaining Good Health

But to satisfy the necessities of life is not evil. To keep the body in good health is a duty, for otherwise we shall not be able to trim the lamp of wisdom, and keep our minds strong and clear.
      Buddha, The Gospel: The Sermon at Benares

The Blessed One said, "Truly, the body is full of impurity and its end is the charnel house, for it is impermanent and destined to be dissolved into its elements. But being the receptacle of karma, it lies in our power to make it a vessel of truth and not of evil. It is not good to indulge in the pleasure of the body, but neither is it good to neglect our bodily needs and to heap filth upon impurities. The lamp that is not cleansed and not filled with oil will be extinguished, and a body that is unkempt, unwashed, and weakened by penance will not be a fit receptacle for the light of truth. Attend to your body and its needs as you would treat a wound which you care for without loving it. Severe rules will not lead the disciple on the middle path which I have taught.
      Buddha, The Gospel: The Jealousy of Devadatta

Said the king, "Bhante Nagasena, are they who have retired from the world fond of their bodies?"
"No, your majesty, they who have retired from the world are not fond of their bodies."
"Then why, bhante, do you indulge your body, and lavish attention on it?"

"Pray, your majesty, have you ever at any time been hit in battle by an arrow?"

"Yes, bhante; I have."

"And was the wound, your majesty, anointed with ointment, smeared with oil, and bandaged with a strip of fine cloth?"

"Yes, bhante. It was anointed with ointment, smeared with oil, and bandaged with a strip of fine cloth."

"In exactly the same way, your majesty, they who have retired from the world are not fond of their bodies; but, without being attached to them, they take care of their bodies in order to advance in the religious life. The body, your majesty, has been likened to a wound by The Blessed One; and therefore, they who have retired from the world take care of their bodies as though they were wounds, without thereby becoming attached to them.

The Millindapanha

 ## Taoism Affirms the Importance of Maintaining Good Health

To realize that our knowledge is ignorance,
This is a noble insight.
To regard our ignorance as knowledge,
This is mental sickness.
Only when we are sick of our sickness
Shall we cease to be sick.
The Sage is not sick, being sick of sickness;
This is the secret of health.

Tao Teh Ching, chapter 71

The five colours blind the eye.
The five tones deafen the ear.
The five flavours cloy the palate.

Racing and hunting madden the mind.
Rare goods tempt men to do wrong.
Therefore, the Sage takes care of the belly, not the eye.
He prefers what is within to what is without.
     Tao Teh Ching, chapter 12

Confucianism Affirms the Importance of Maintaining Good Health

When fasting, he thought it necessary to change his food, and also to change the place where he commonly sat in the apartment.
He did not dislike to have his rice finely cleaned, or to have his mince meat cut quite small.
He did not eat rice which had been injured by heat or damp and turned sour, nor fish or flesh which was gone. He did not eat what was discolored, or what was of a bad flavor, nor anything which was ill-cooked, or was not in season.
He did not eat meat which was not cut properly, nor what was served without its proper sauce.
Though there might be a large quantity of meat, he would not allow what he took to exceed the due proportion for the rice....
He did not partake of wine and dried meat bought in the market.
He was never without ginger when he ate. He did not each much.
     Confucian Analects, book 10

Suppose me in a year of great drought — I will use you as a copious rain. Open your mind, and enrich my mind. (Be you) like medicine, which must distress the patient, in order to cure his sickness. (Think of we) as walking barefoot, whose feet are sure to be wounded, if he does not see the ground.
     Shu King, part IV, book 8

Section III
Love Other's Divine Selves

IT IS FAR EASIER TO LOVE GOD within others and within our-selves when we know our true divine identity, and remember that love is the ultimate purpose of life. It is easier to love some-one when we look for and see the God and good in them. When we remember our true identity, it is easy to apply the essential responsibilities in the following chapters.

Chapter 2, "Love Creates Joyous Living," already established the importance of love as integral to the meaning and purpose of life. Every religion has abundant teachings on the importance of lov-ing others. The chapters included in this section contain impor-tant ways we can love others. There is much overlap between the following eight responsibilities for loving other's Divine Selves. With some practice, their application can become automatic, as we reprogram our subconscious mind to automatically respond in a divine way.

We are, ultimately, one huge universal family. We are unique viewpoints of consciousness as part of the One Consciousness. We are units of awareness, all equal in rights, all beautiful and divine. We all started equally, yet uniquely. Unfortunately, many have lost their way, and consequently made poor choices causing negative experiences and a sense of separation.

We need to honor everyone in our world, except those who clearly oppose goodness, love, and peace. It is far easier to love the good people in our world than our enemies. Yet we need to love our enemies, even if we have to stand up to them.

May the Light constantly flow through each of us as we focus on loving every other person, animal, place, object, and situation that comes into our lives. Let us accept each challenge to grow and refine our mastery in all situations.

Chapter 22

The Golden Rule

THE GOLDEN RULE IS BEAUTIFUL, concise, and captures the spirit of loving others. This principle contains so much of what we need to know and apply. Its beauty, power, and simplicity are found within all religions.

The Golden Rule contains simple guidance that, if followed, would make earth a paradise. It is clearly evident within every other principle of this section. It makes destructive qualities such as dishonesty, envy, hatred, bigotry, and greed impossible. When purely practiced, justice is achieved for all, and good is returned for evil. Is that not how we would like to be treated?

It is easier to apply the Golden Rule when we look for and see the God/good in others. The love and practice of the Golden Rule creates a bond of fellowship with all.

 Christianity Affirms the Importance of The Golden Rule

Therefore all things whatsoever ye would that men should do to you, do ye even so to them: for this is the law and the prophets.
Matthew 7:12

And as ye would that men should do to you, do ye also to them likewise.
Luke 6:31

Master, which is the great commandment in the law? Jesus said unto him, Thou shalt love the Lord thy God with all thy heart, and with all thy soul, and with all thy mind.

This is the first and great commandment.

And the second is like unto it, Thou shalt love thy neighbour as thyself.

On these two commandments hang all the law and the prophets.

Matthew 7:36-40

 ## Islam Affirms the Importance of The Golden Rule

Not one of you is a believer until he loves for his brother what he loves for himself.

Forty Hadith of An-Nawawi, 13

Whoever submits himself entirely to Allah and he is the doer of good (to others), he has his reward from his Lord, and there is no fear for such nor shall they grieve.

Qur'an 2:112

On the day of judgment God Most High will say, "Son of Adam, I was sick and you did not visit Me." He will reply, "My Lord, how could I visit Thee when Thou art the Lord of the Universe?" He will say, "Did you not know that My servant so-and-so was ill and yet you did not visit him? Did you not know that if you had visited him you soon would have found Me with him?"

Hadith of Muslim

Be good to the parents and to the near of kin and the orphans and the needy and the neighbour of (your) kin and the alien neighbour, and the companion in a journey and the wayfarer.

Qur'an 4:36

Judaism Affirms the Importance of The Golden Rule

You shall not take vengeance or bear a grudge against your countrymen. Love your fellow as yourself: I am the Lord.
(Tanakh) Leviticus 19:18

What is hateful to you, do not do to your neighbor: that is the whole Torah; all the rest of it is commentary; go and learn.
Talmud, Shabbat 31a

Hinduism Affirms the Importance of The Golden Rule

One should not behave towards others in a way which is disagreeable to oneself. This is the essence of morality. All other activities are due to selfish desire.
Mahabharata, Anusasana Parva 113.8

"Is this one of our tribe or a stranger?" is the calculation of the narrow-minded; but to those of a noble disposition the world itself is but one family.
The Hitopadesa

From the Upanishads we have a quotation urging us to love the Self/God in all persons (meaning the Higher/Christ Self) and things. This is guidance to hold the "immaculate concept" of perfection for all. Doing so makes continuous application of the Golden Rule possible, in the knowledge of our Oneness.

Verily, a husband is not dear, that you may love the husband, but that you may love the Self through the husband, therefore a husband is dear.

Verily, a wife is not dear, that you may love the wife; but that you may love the Self through the wife, therefore a wife is dear.

Verily, sons are not dear, that you may love the sons; but that you may love the Self through the sons, therefore sons are dear.

Verily, wealth is not dear, that you may love wealth; but that you may love the Self through the wealth, therefore wealth is dear....

Verily, the worlds are not dear, that you may love the worlds; but that you may love the Self through the worlds, therefore the worlds are dear....

Verily, everything is not dear, that you may love everything; but that you may love the Self through everything, therefore everything is dear.

Verily, the Self is to be seen, to be heard, to be perceived, to be marked, O Maitreyi! When we see, hear, perceive, and know the Self, then all this is known.

As all waters find their center in the sea, all touches in the skin, all tastes in the tongue, all smells in the nose, all colors in the eye, all sounds in the ear, all precepts in the mind, all knowledge in the heart, all actions in the hands, all movements in the feet, and all the Vedas in speech;

As a lump of salt, when thrown into water, becomes dissolved into water, and could not be taken out again, but wherever we taste (the water) it is salt — thus verily, O Maitreyi, does this great Being, endless, unlimited, consisting of nothing but knowledge, rise from out these elements, and vanish again in them. This is enough, O beloved, for wisdom.

For when there is duality, then one sees the other, one smells the others, one hears the others, one salutes the others, one perceives the other, one knows the other; but when the Self only is all this, how should he smell another, how should he see another, how should he hear another, how should he salute another, how should he perceive another, how should he know another? How should he know him by whom he knows all this? How, O beloved, should he know himself, the knower?

Brihadaranyaka Upanishad, IV, 5

 ## Buddhism Affirms the Importance of The Golden Rule

As a man traversing the whole earth,
Finds not anywhere an object more loveable than himself;
Therefore, since the self is so universally loved by all,
The man who loves himself so much,
Should do no injury to others.

The Udana, chapter 5

Comparing oneself to others in such terms as "Just as I am so are they, just as they are so am I," he should neither kill nor cause others to kill.

The Sutta Nipata, 705

 ## Taoism Affirms the Importance of The Golden Rule

By doing to others as you would wish to be done by, and being sincere and honest in all your dealings, you may attract all men to become your friends.

The Su Shu, Part III

The Sage does not take to hoarding.
The more he lives for others, the fuller is his life.

The more he gives, the more he abounds.
The Way of Heaven is to benefit, not to harm.
   Tao Teh Ching, chapter 81

 ## Confucianism Affirms the Importance of The Golden Rule

Tsze-kung asked, saying, "Is there one word which may serve as
a rule of practice for all one's life?" The Master said, "Is not RECI-
PROCITY such a word? What you do not want done to yourself, do
not do to others."
   Confucian Analects, book 15

Chung-kung asked about perfect virtue. The Master said, "It is, when
you go abroad, to behave to every one as if you were receiving a great
guest; to employ the people as if you were assisting at a great sacri-
fice; not to do to others as you would not wish done to yourself."
   Confucian Analects, book 12

When one cultivates to the utmost the principles of his nature, and
exercises them on the principle of reciprocity, he is not far from
the path. What you do not like when done to yourself, do not do to
others.
   The Doctrine of the Mean

Chapter 23

Patience

WEBSTER'S DICTIONARY DEFINES "PATIENT" AS: "1. bearing pains or trials calmly or without complaint. 2. manifesting forbearance under provocation or strain. 3. not hasty or impetuous. 4. steadfast despite opposition, difficulty, or adversity." Patience is needed for all of life's difficulties. And, its quality of constancy is needed regarding any situation that appears to take too long. The more patience we have, the more peaceful we are.

One way the divine quality of patience translates into ideal behavior is it helps us to be slow to anger. Ideally, anger is never allowed to take over our behavior. We need to be the masters of our anger, and remain in control at a higher level of awareness than any anger we may feel.

When we allow ourselves to become angry, we descend to a lower level of vibration. Once in that energy state, it can be difficult to rise above it. When we are angry, it is easy to misqualify our energy, which will eventually return to us. Angry people can create karmic conditions that may continue even after the anger is gone. As long as we are angry, we are not free.

Patience also means not giving up before we have finished our work. Patience is the staying power that we all need to successfully complete our projects.

Our patience is tested every day. The more we can master ourselves and be patient, the stronger we will be.

Christianity Affirms the Importance of Patience

My brethren, count it all joy when ye fall into divers temptations; Knowing this, that the trying of your faith worketh patience. But let patience have her perfect work, that ye may be perfect and entire [whole], wanting nothing.
James 1:2-4

In your patience possess ye your souls.
Luke 21:19

Here is the patience of the saints: here are they that keep the commandments of God, and the faith of Jesus.
Revelation 14:12

Be patient therefore, brethren, unto the coming of the Lord. Behold, the husbandman waiteth for the precious fruit of the earth, and hath long patience for it, until he receive the early and latter rain.
Be ye also patient; stablish your hearts: for the coming of the Lord draweth nigh.
Grudge not one against another, brethren, lest ye be condemned: behold, the judge standeth before the door.
Take, my brethren, the prophets, who have spoken in the name of the Lord, for an example of suffering affliction, and of patience.
Behold, we count them happy which endure. Ye have heard of the patience of Job, and have seen the end of the Lord; that the Lord is very pitiful, and of tender mercy.
James 5:7-11

Patience requires inner strength and endurance.

Islam Affirms the Importance of Patience

So be patient; surely the promise of Allah is true; and ask protection for thy sin and celebrate the praise of thy Lord in the evening and the morning.
Qur'an 40:55

O you who believe, seek assistance through patience and prayer; surely Allah is with the patient.
Qur'an 2:153

Surely man is in loss,
Except those who believe and do good, and exhort one another to Truth, and exhort one another to patience.
Qur'an 103:2-3

But if you show patience, it is certainly best for the patient.
And be patient and thy patience is not but by (the help of) Allah.
Qur'an 16:126-127

The conscious intent and effort to be patient is strengthened by God.

 ## Judaism Affirms the Importance of Patience

The Lord is good to those who trust in Him,
To the one who seeks Him;
It is good to wait patiently
Till rescue comes from the Lord.
It is good for a man, when young,
To bear a yoke;

Let him sit alone and be patient,
When He has laid it upon him.
(Tanakh) Lamentations 3:25-28

Do not be vexed by evil men; do not be incensed by wrongdoers; for
they soon wither like grass, like verdure fade away.
Trust in the Lord and do good, abide in the land and remain loyal.
Seek the favor of the Lord, and He will grant you the desires of your
heart.
Leave all to the Lord; trust in Him; He will do it.
He will cause your vindication to shine forth like the light, the justice
of your case, like the noonday sun.
Be patient and wait for the Lord, do not be vexed by the prospering
man who carries out his schemes.
(Tanakh) Psalms 37:1-7

The end of a matter is better than the beginning of it.
Better a patient spirit than a haughty spirit.
Don't let your spirit be quickly vexed, for vexation abides in the
breasts of fools.
(Tanakh) Ecclesiastes 7:8-9

Hinduism Affirms the Importance of Patience

Be peaceful; have patience; when a difficulty comes, one should not,
all of a sudden, lose one's patience.... Victory or defeat is completely
under the control of destiny: therefore intelligent ones should always
be patient.
The Srimad Devi Bhagavatam, book 5

Self-control consists in never wishing for another man's possessions,
in gravity and patience and capacity to allay the fears of others in
respect to one's own self, and immunity from disease....

That virtue which forgives for the sake of virtue and profit is called endurance. It is a form of forgiveness. It is acquired through patience.
The Mahabharata, book 12

 ## Buddhism Affirms the Importance of Patience

One should cherish ideals of charity, good behavior, patience, zeal, thoughtfulness and wisdom.
Lankavatara Sutra, chapter 9

Patience and pleasant speech...religious conversation at due seasons, this is the highest blessing.
The Sutta Nipata, Part II

The Awakened call patience the highest penance, long-suffering the highest Nirvana.
The Dhammapada, chapter 14

 ## Taoism Affirms the Importance of Patience

In handling affairs, people often spoil them just at the point of success.
With heedfulness in the beginning and patience at the end, nothing will be spoiled.
Tao Teh Ching, chapter 64

Your first duty is patience without limit, your second, tireless perseverance.
T'ai-Shang Kan-Ying P'ien, The Spirit of the Hearth

Confucianism Affirms the Importance of Patience

Want of forbearance in small matters confounds great plans.
Confucian Analects, book 15

The Master said, "Never flagging when I set forth anything to him — ah! that is Hui." The Master said of Ken Yuan... "I saw his constant advance. I never saw him stop in his progress."
Confucian Analects, book 9

The Master said, "The people of the south have a saying — 'A man without constancy cannot be either a wizard or a doctor.' Good! Inconstant in his virtue, he will be visited with disgrace."
Confucian Analects, book 13

Chapter 24

Harmlessness

WHEN WE RADIATE LOVE TO OTHERS it prevents us from intentionally causing harm. When our love is accompanied by adequate wisdom, we have the absolute ability to act without hurting others.

Because it's natural that we want no harm to come to ourselves, and because the Golden Rule states that we should treat others as we'd like to be treated, it follows that we should not want to cause harm to others. It is important to remember that almost everyone's feelings are similar in similar situations. Let us embrace each other with higher levels of love for our one divine family. In doing so, we can empathize with others and be guided to do no harm.

 ## Christianity Affirms the Importance of Harmlessness

Behold, I send you forth as sheep in the midst of wolves: be ye therefore wise as serpents, and harmless as doves.
Matthew 10:16

For it is God which worketh in you both to will and to do of his good pleasure.
Do all things without murmurings and disputings:

That ye may be blameless and harmless, the sons of God, without rebuke, in the midst of a crooked and perverse nation, among whom ye shine as lights in the world.
    Philippians 2:13-15

For the eyes of the Lord are over the righteous, and his ears are open unto their prayers: but the face of the Lord is against them that do evil.
And who is he that will harm you, if ye be followers of that which is good?
But and if ye suffer for righteousness' sake, happy are ye: and be not afraid of their terror, neither be troubled.
    1 Peter 3:12-14

And, behold, one of them which were with Jesus stretched out his hand, and drew his sword, and struck a servant of the high priest's and smote off his ear.
Then said Jesus unto him, Put up again thy sword into his place: for all they that take the sword shall perish with the sword.
    Matthew 26:51-52

Islam Affirms the Importance of Harmlessness

There should be neither harm nor reciprocating of harm.
    Hadith

And whoever kills a believer intentionally, his punishment is hell, abiding therein; and Allah is wroth with him and He has cursed him and prepared for him a grievous chastisement.
    Qur'an 4:93

...whoever kills a person, unless it be for manslaughter or for mischief in the land, it is as though he had killed all men. And whoever saves a life, it is as though he had saved the lives of all men.
        Qur'an 5:32

And keep your duty to Allah, and know that you will be gathered together to Him.
And of men is he whose speech about the life of this world pleases thee, and he calls Allah to witness as to that which is in his heart, yet he is the most violent of adversaries.
And when he holds authority, he makes effort in the land to cause mischief in it and destroy tilth and offspring; and Allah loves not mischief.
And when it is said to him, Be careful of thy duty to Allah, pride carries him off to sin — so hell is sufficient for him. And certainly evil is the resting-place.
        Qur'an 2:203-206

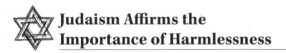 Judaism Affirms the Importance of Harmlessness

Do not devise harm against your fellow
Who lives trustfully with you.
Do not quarrel with a man for no cause,
When he has done you no harm.
        (Tanakh) Proverbs 3:29-30

If anyone kills any human being, he shall be put to death. One who kills a beast shall make restitution for it: life for life. If anyone maims his fellow, as he has done so shall it be done to him: fracture for fracture, eye for eye, tooth for tooth. The injury he inflicted on another shall be inflicted on him. One who kills a beast shall make restitution

for it; but one who kills a human being shall be put to death. You shall have one standard for stranger and citizen alike: for I the Lord am your God.
    (Tanakh) Leviticus 24:17-22

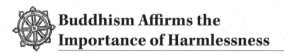 Hinduism Affirms the Importance of Harmlessness

The mode of living which is founded upon a total harmlessness toward all creatures or (in case of necessity) upon a minimum of such harm, is the highest morality.
    Mahabharata, Shanti Parva 262.5-6

Let him not, even though in pain, (speak words) cutting (others) to the quick; let him not injure others in thought or deed; let him not utter speeches which make (others) afraid of him, since that will prevent him from gaining heaven.
    The Laws of Manu 2:161

He who does not harm the world, and whom the world cannot harm, who is not carried away by any impulse of joy, anger or fear, such a one is My beloved.
    The Bhagavad Gita, chapter 12

Buddhism Affirms the Importance of Harmlessness

Hurt·none by word or deed, be consistent in well-doing.
    The Dhammapada

All men tremble at punishment, all men fear death; remember that
you are like unto them, and do not kill, nor cause slaughter.
All men tremble at punishment, all men love life; remember that thou
art like unto them, and do not kill, nor cause slaughter.
He who seeking his own happiness punishes or kills beings who also
long for happiness, will not find happiness after death.

The Dhammapada, chapter 10

Comparing oneself to others in such terms as "Just as I am so are
they, just as they are so am I," he should neither kill nor cause oth-
ers to kill.

The Sutta Nipata 705

 Taoism Affirms the Importance of Harmlessness

Fine weapons of war augur evil.
Even things seem to hate them.
Therefore, a man of Tao does not set his heart upon them....
As weapons are instruments of evil,
They are not properly a gentleman's instruments;
Only on necessity will he resort to them.
For peace and quiet are dearest to his heart,
And to him even a victory is no cause for rejoicing.
To rejoice over a victory is to rejoice over the slaughter of men!
Hence a man who rejoices over the slaughter of men cannot expect
to thrive in the world of men.

Tao Teh Ching, chapter 31

What another has taught let me repeat:
"A Man of violence will come to a violent end."
Whoever said this can be my teacher and my father.

Tao Teh Ching, chapter 42

Confucianism Affirms the Importance of Harmlessness

Chi K'ang asked Confucius about government, saying, "What do you say to killing the unprincipled for the good of the principled?" Confucius replied, "Sir, in carrying on your government, why should you use killing at all? Let your evinced desires be for what is good, and the people will be good. The relation between superiors and inferiors is like that between the wind and the grass. The grass must bend, when the wind blows across it."

Confucianism Analects, book 12

This great mutual consideration and harmony would ensure the constant nourishment of the living.... However greatly things might accumulate, there would be no entanglement among them. They would move on together without error, and the smallest matters would proceed without failure. However deep some might be, they would be comprehended. However thick and close their array, there would be spaces between them. They would follow one another without coming into contact. They would move about without doing any hurt to one another. This would be the perfection of such a state of mutual harmony.

Li Ki (The Book of Rites), part I, book 7

Chapter 25

Charity and Helping Others

WE HAVE ALL HAD TIMES IN OUR LIVES when we needed help of one kind or another. Sometimes it was given and other times it was not. We felt grateful and close to those who offered us assistance.

Our help and charity are needed by all who don't have adequate food, clean water, a roof over their heads, and other life essentials. God does not want His children to suffer from lack and be forced to struggle just to survive.

Those who have more than enough can do more. Our conscience or Higher Self tells us it is right to help those in need. It is part of our true nature to be giving. There is much more that can be done for those who are less fortunate.

It is not wrong to be wealthy, if we use that wealth to help others. There is more than enough for everyone, if we are willing to share. Every religion asks us to do what we can for those in need.

 Christianity Affirms the Importance of Charity and Helping Others

And above all things have fervent charity among yourselves: for charity shall cover the multitude of sins.
Use hospitality one to another without grudging.
As every man hath received the gift, even so minister the same one to another, as good stewards of the manifold grace of God.
1 Peter 4:8-10

Brethren, if a man be overtaken in a fault, ye which are spiritual, restore such an one in the spirit of meekness; considering thyself, lest thou also be tempted.
Bear ye one another's burdens, and so fulfill the law of Christ.
    Galatians 6:1-2

Look not every man on his own things but every man also on the things of others.
    Philippians 2:4

But Jesus called them unto him, and said, Ye know that the princes of the Gentiles exercise dominion over them, and they that are great exercise authority upon them.
But it shall not be so among you: but whosoever will be great among you, let him be your minister;
And whosoever will be chief among you, let him be your servant....
    Matthew 20:25-27

Give to him that asketh thee, and from him that would borrow of thee turn not thou away.
Ye have heard that it hath been said, Thou shalt love thy neighbour, and hate thine enemy.
But I say unto you, Love your enemies, bless them that curse you, do good to them that hate you, and pray for them which despitefully use you, and persecute you.
    Matthew 5:42-44

Give, and it shall be given unto you; good measure, pressed down, and shaken together, and running over, shall men give into your bosom. For with the same measure that ye mete withal it shall be measured to you again.
    Luke 6:38

Islam Affirms the Importance of Charity and Helping Others

It is not righteousness that you turn your faces toward the East and the West, but righteous is the one who believes in Allah, and the Last Day, and the angels and the Book and the prophets, and gives away wealth out of love for Him to the near of kin and the orphans and the needy and the wayfarer and to those who ask and to set slaves free and keeps up prayer and pays the poor-rate.

Qur'an 2:177

So give to the near of kin his due, and to the needy and the wayfarer. This is best for those who desire Allah's pleasure, and these it is who are successful.

And whatever you lay out at usury, so that it may increase in the property of men, it increases not with Allah; and whatever you give in charity, desiring Allah's pleasure — these will get manifold.

Qur'an 30:38-39

Surely man is created impatient —
Fretful when evil afflicts him,
And niggardly when good befalls him —
Except those who pray,
Who are constant at their prayer,
And in whose wealth there is a known right
For the beggar and the destitute.

Qur'an 70:19-25

The men who give in charity and the women who give in charity and set apart for Allah a goodly portion, it will be doubled for them, and theirs is a generous reward.

Qur'an 57:18

The best of men are those who are useful to others.
    Hadith of Bukhari

The Prophet said: "Give in charity and do not withhold it otherwise Allah will withhold it back from you."
    Hadith of Bukhari 3.763

 ## Judaism Affirms the Importance of Charity and Helping Others

A light shines for the upright in the darkness; he is gracious, compassionate, and beneficent.
All goes well with the man who lends generously, who conducts his affairs with equity.
He shall never be shaken; the beneficent man will be remembered forever.
He is not afraid of evil tidings; his heart is firm, he trusts in the Lord.
His heart is resolute, he is unafraid; in the end he will see the fall of his foes.
He gives freely to the poor; his beneficence lasts forever; his horn is exalted in honor.
    (Tanakh) Psalms 112:4-9

He who is generous to the poor makes a loan to the Lord;
He will repay him his due.
    (Tanakh) Proverbs 19:17

Hinduism Affirms the Importance of Charity and Helping Others

Bounteous is he who gives unto the beggar who comes to him in want of food and feeble.
Rig Veda Book 10, hymn CXVII

In the beginning, when God created all beings by the sacrifice of Himself, He said unto them: 'Through sacrifice you can procreate, and it shall satisfy all your desires.
Worship the Powers of Nature thereby, and let them nourish you in return; thus supporting each other, you shall attain your highest welfare.
For, fed on sacrifice, nature will give you all the enjoyment you can desire. But he who enjoys what she gives without returning is, indeed, a robber.'
The sages who enjoy the food that remains after the sacrifice is made are freed from all sin; but the selfish who spread their feast only for themselves feed on sin only.
The Bhagavad Gita, chapter 3

Lord Shri Krishna continued: Fearlessness, clean living, unceasing concentration on wisdom, readiness to give, self-control, a spirit of sacrifice, regular study of the scriptures, austerities, candour,
Harmlessness, truth absence of wrath, renunciation, contentment, straightforwardness, compassion towards all, uncovetousness, courtesy, modesty, constancy,
Valour, forgiveness, fortitude, purity, freedom from hate and vanity; these are his who possesses the Godly Qualities, O Arjuna!
The Bhagavad Gita, chapter 16

He who gives liberally goes straight to the gods; on the high ridge of heaven he stands exalted.
   Rig Veda 1.125.5

 ## Buddhism Affirms the Importance of Charity and Helping Others

Verily, misers go not to the celestial realms. Fools do not indeed praise liberality. The wise man rejoices in giving and thereby becomes happy thereafter.
   The Dhammapada, 177

The Buddha said, "When you see someone practicing the Way of giving, aid him joyously, and you will obtain vast and great blessings." A shramana asked, "Is there an end to those blessings?" The Buddha said, "Consider the flame of a single lamp. Though a hundred thousand people come and light their own lamps from it so that they can cook their food and ward off the darkness, the first lamp remains the same as before. Blessings are like this, too."
   Sutra of Forty-Two Sections, 10

As a full jar overflowing pours out the liquid and keeps back nothing, even so shall your charity be without reserve — as a jar overturned.
   Sutta-Pitaka

 ## Taoism Affirms the Importance of Charity and Helping Others

The Way of Heaven diminishes the more-than-enough to supply the less-than-enough. The way of man is different: it takes from the less-

than-enough to swell the more-than-enough. Who except a man of the Tao can put his superabundant riches to the service of the world?
Tao Teh Ching, chapter 77

The Sage does not take to hoarding.
The more he lives for others, the fuller is his life.
The more he gives, the more he abounds.
Tao Teh Ching, chapter 81

Confucianism Affirms the Importance of Charity and Helping Others

The Master said, "Though a man have abilities as admirable as those of the Duke of Chau, yet if he be proud and niggardly, those other things are really not worth being looked at."
Confucian Analects, book 7

I have heard that a superior man helps the distressed, but does not add to the wealth of the rich.
Confucian Analects, book 6

Tsze-chang asked Confucius about perfect virtue. Confucius said, "To be able to practice five things everywhere under heaven constitutes perfect virtue." He begged to ask what they were, and was told, "Gravity, generosity of soul, sincerity, earnestness, and kindness. If you are grave, you will not be treated with disrespect. If you are generous, you will win all. If you are sincere, people will repose trust in you. If you are earnest, you will accomplish much. If you are kind, this will enable you to employ the services of others."
Confucian Analects, book 17

Chapter 26

Loving Speech and Kindness

SINCE LOVE IS A SIGNIFICANT ASPECT of the meaning and purpose of life, and the highest and best use of our energy, what we say to others is very important. Speech is one of the primary vehicles we have to convey the flow of love to others.

Kindness and loving speech truly come from within. It is difficult to fake. Practice kindness daily with everyone in your life. This will elevate your life experience to new heights of joy as you increase your radiance of the divine flow of love. Being in love's flow feels fantastic — it is living life to the fullest. All doubts and fears will vanish.

All religions encourage us to love more — kindness and speaking lovingly are an integral part of our divine evolution.

 Christianity Affirms the Importance of Loving Speech and Kindness

Finally, be ye all of one mind, having compassion one of another, love as brethren, be pitiful, be courteous:
Not rendering evil for evil, or railing for railing: but contrariwise blessing; knowing that ye are thereunto called, that ye should inherit a blessing.
For he that will love life, and see good days, let him refrain his tongue from evil, and his lips that they speak no guile:
Let him eschew evil, and do good; let him seek peace, and ensue it.

For the eyes of the Lord are over the righteous, and his ears are open unto their prayers; but the face of the Lord is against them that do evil.

1 Peter 3:8-12

Let all bitterness, and wrath, and anger, and clamour, and evil speaking, be put away from you, with all malice:
And be ye kind one to another, tenderhearted, forgiving one another, even as God for Christ's sake hath forgiven you.

Ephesians 4:31-32

Rebuke not an elder, but intreat him as a father; and the younger men as brethren;
The elder women as mothers; the younger as sisters, with all purity.

1 Timothy 5:1-2

Let your speech be always with grace, seasoned with salt, that ye may know how ye ought to answer every man.

Colossians 4:6

 ## Islam Affirms the Importance of Loving Speech and Kindness

Those who spend their wealth in the way of Allah, then follow not up what they have spent with reproach or injury, their reward is with their Lord, and they shall have no fear nor shall they grieve.
A kind word with forgiveness is better than charity followed by injury. And Allah is Self-sufficient, forbearing.
O you who believe, make not your charity worthless by reproach and injury, like him who spends his wealth to be seen of men and believes not in Allah and the Last Day.

Qur'an 2:262-264

And when you are greeted with a greeting, greet with one better than it, or return it. Surely Allah ever takes account of all things.
Qur'an 4:86

You shall serve none but Allah. And do good to (your) parents, and to the near of kin and to orphans and the needy, and speak good (words) to (all) men.
Qur'an 2:83

In the name of Allah, the Beneficent, the Merciful
Hast thou seen him who belies religion?
That is the one who is rough to the orphan,
And urges not the feeding of the needy.
So woe to the praying ones,
Who are unmindful of their prayer!
Who do [good] to be seen,
And refrain from acts of kindness!
Qur'an 107:1-7

Allah loves not the public utterance of hurtful speech, except by one who has been wronged. And Allah is ever Hearing, Knowing.
If you do good openly or keep it secret or pardon an evil, Allah surely is ever Pardoning, Powerful.
Qur'an 4:148-149

Like golden apples in silver showpieces
Is a phrase well turned.
Like a ring of gold, a golden ornament,
Is a wise man's reproof in a receptive ear....
Like clouds, wind — but no rain —
Is one who boasts of gifts not given.
Through forbearance a ruler may be won over;
A gentle tongue can break bones.
Qur'an 25:11-12, 14-15

Anas and Abdullah reported God's Messenger as saying, "All [human] creatures are God's children, and those dearest to God are those who treat His children kindly."

Hadith of Baihaqi

A man once asked the Prophet what was the best thing in Islam, and the latter replied, "It is to feed the hungry and to give the greeting of peace both to those one knows and to those one does not know."

Hadith of Bukhari

 ## Judaism Affirms the Importance of Loving Speech and Kindness

She openeth her mouth with wisdom; and in her tongue is the law of kindness.
Her children arise up, and call her blessed; her husband also, and he praiseth her.

(King James) Proverbs 31:26, 28

A brother offended is more formidable than a stronghold;
Such strife is like the bars of a fortress.
A man's belly is filled by the fruit of his mouth;
He will be filled by the produce of his lips.
Death and life are in the power of the tongue;
Those who love it will eat its fruit.

(Tanakh) Proverbs 18:19-21

On three things the world is stayed; on the Thorah [Torah], and on the Worship, and on the bestowal of Kindnesses.

Sayings of the Jewish Fathers, 1.2

Hinduism Affirms the Importance of Loving Speech and Kindness

Words that cause no woe, words always true, gentle and pleasing words — these mark the true religious speech.
The Bhagavad Gita, chapter 7

He who is incapable of hatred towards any being, who is kind and compassionate, free from selfishness, without pride, equable in pleasure and in pain, and forgiving,
Always contented, self-centered, self-controlled, resolute, with mind and reason dedicated to Me, such a devotee of Mine is My beloved.
The Bhagavad Gita, chapter 12

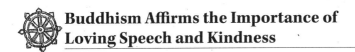 Buddhism Affirms the Importance of Loving Speech and Kindness

The bhikkhu who abides in loving-kindness, who is pleased with the Buddha's teachings, attains to that state of peace and happiness, the stilling of conditioned things, Nibbana.
Let him be cordial in all his ways and refined in conduct; filled thereby with joy, he will make an end of ill.
The Dhammapada, 368, 376

Do not speak harshly to anybody; those who are spoken to will answer thee in the same way. Angry speech is painful, blows for blows will touch thee.
If, like a shattered metal plate (gong), thou utter not, then thou hast reached Nirvana; contention is not known to thee.
The Dhammapada, 133-134

Taoism Affirms the Importance of Loving Speech and Kindness

In dealing with others, know how to be gentle and kind.
In speaking, know how to keep your words.
　　Tao Teh Ching, chapter 8

The Sage has no interests of his own,
But takes the interests of the people as his own.
He is kind to the kind;
He is also kind to the unkind:
For Virtue is kind.
　　　Tao Teh Ching, chapter 49

 ## Confucianism Affirms the Importance of Loving Speech and Kindness

The Master said, "The superior man is affable, but not adulatory;
the mean man is adulatory, but not affable."
　　Confucian Analects, book 13

The Master said, "Superior men, and yet not always virtuous, there
have been, alas! But there never has been a mean man, and, at the
same time, virtuous."
　　Confucian Analects, book 14

Tsze-lu said, "I should like, sir, to hear your wishes." The Master
said, "They are, in regard to the aged, to give them rest; in regard
to friends, to show them sincerity; in regard to the young, to treat
them tenderly."
　　Confucian Analects, book 5

Chapter 27

Forgiveness and Mercy

WE ARE FORGIVEN AS WE FORGIVE. Our goal must be to forgive everyone, so that we can be totally forgiven in turn. Any lack of forgiveness will hold us back from our divine destiny of peace, joy, and love.

Errors in life are inevitable. Those that hurt us are not perfect. It is easier to forgive another if we first understand why they have hurt us, and then peacefully accept the fact that they have caused insult or injury. This makes it far easier to practice forgiveness.

Although we may have to pay a price in the future for hurting another, that doesn't mean that we are not already forgiven through God's grace, if we have sincere regret. Repentance for our sins is essential, as well as making amends whenever possible.

Remember that self-forgiveness is just as important as forgiving others. Some people who have forgiven others have not forgiven themselves for their own past actions. These people do not realize how much they hold themselves back.

 ## Christianity Affirms the Power of Forgiveness and Mercy

Jesus demonstrated divinity through forgiveness and love for others. Now that two thousand years have gone by, mankind has evolved to a place of greater opportunity to more fully comprehend

and manifest the pure attunement that Jesus introduced. We can
merge with our Higher/Christ Self through forgiveness and love.

And forgive us our debts, as we forgive our debtors.
And lead us not into temptation, but deliver us from evil: For thine
is the kingdom, and the power, and the glory, for ever. Amen
For if ye forgive men their trespasses, your heavenly Father will also
forgive you:
But if ye forgive not men their trespasses, neither will your Father
forgive your trespasses.
    Matthew 6:12-15

But love ye your enemies, and do good, and lend, hoping for nothing
again; and your reward shall be great, and ye shall be the children
of the Highest: for he is kind unto the unthankful and to the evil.
Be ye therefore merciful, as your Father also is merciful.
    Luke 6:35-36

Ye have heard that it hath been said, Thou shalt love thy neighbour,
and hate thine enemy.
But I say unto you, Love your enemies, bless them that curse you, do
good to them that hate you, and pray for them which despitefully
use you, and persecute you;
That ye may be the children of your Father which is in heaven: for
he maketh his sun to rise on the evil and on the good, and sendeth
rain on the just and on the unjust.
For if ye love them which love you, what reward have ye? Do not even
the publicans [tax collectors] the same?
And if ye salute your brethren only, what do ye more than others?
Do not even the publicans so?
Be ye therefore perfect, even as your Father which is in heaven is
perfect.
    Matthew 5:43-48

Jesus is saying that it's easy to love those that love you, but it is essential that we love our enemies as well.

And when ye stand praying, forgive, if ye have ought against any: that your Father also which is in heaven may forgive you your trespasses.
But if ye do not forgive, neither will your Father which is in heaven forgive your trespasses.
    Mark 11:25-26

Therefore is the kingdom of heaven likened unto a certain king, which would take account of his servants.
And when he had begun to reckon, one was brought unto him, which owed him ten thousand talents.
But forasmuch as he had not to pay, his lord commanded him to be sold, and his wife, and children, and all that he had, and payment to be made.
The servant therefore fell down, and worshipped him, saying, Lord, have patience with me, and I will pay thee all.
Then the lord of that servant was moved with compassion, and loosed him, and forgave him the debt.
But the same servant went out, and found one of his fellowservants, which owed him an hundred pence: and he laid hands on him, and took him by the throat, saying, Pay me that thou owest.
And his fellowservant fell down at his feet, and besought him, saying, Have patience with me, and I will pay thee all.
And he would not: but went and cast him into prison, till he should pay the debt.
So when his fellowservants saw what was done, they were very sorry, and came and told unto their lord all that was done.
Then his lord, after that he had called him, said unto him, O thou wicked servant, I forgave thee all that debt, because thou desiredst me:

Shouldest not thou also have had compassion on thy fellowservant,
even as I had pity on thee?
And his lord was wroth, and delivered him to the tormentors, till he
should pay all that was due unto him.
So likewise shall my heavenly Father do also unto you, if ye from your
hearts forgive not every one his brother their trespasses.
     Matthew 18:23-35

 ## Islam Affirms the Power of Forgiveness and Mercy

Take to forgiveness and enjoin good and turn away from the
ignorant.
     Qur'an 7:199

So whatever you are given is but a provision of this world's life, and
that which Allah has is better and more lasting for those who believe
and rely on their Lord;
And those who shun the great sins and indecencies, and whenever
they are angry they forgive;
And those who respond to their Lord and keep up prayer, and whose
affairs are (decided) by counsel among themselves, and who spend
out of what We have given them;
And those who, when great wrong afflicts them, defend
themselves.
And the recompense of evil is punishment like it; but whoever for-
gives and amends, his reward is with Allah. Surely He loves not the
wrongdoers....
And whoever is patient and forgives — that surely is an affair of
great resolution.
     Qur'an 42:36-40, 43

If you pardon and forbear and forgive, surely Allah is Forgiving, Merciful.
Qur'an 64:14

Moses son of Imran said, "My Lord, who is the greatest of Thy servants in Thy estimation?" and received the reply, "The one who forgives when he is in a position of power."
Hadith of Baihaqi

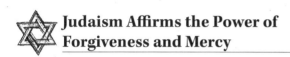 ## Judaism Affirms the Power of Forgiveness and Mercy

No longer will they need to teach one another and say to one another, "Heed the Lord;" for all of them, from the least of them to the greatest, shall heed Me — declares the Lord.
For I will forgive their iniquities,
And remember their sins no more.
(Tanakh) Jeremiah 31:34

"Come, let us reach an understanding," — says the Lord.
"Be your sins like crimson,
They can turn snow-white;
Be they red as dyed wool,
They can become like fleece."
If, then, you agree and give heed,
You will eat the good things of the earth;
But if you refuse and disobey,
You will be devoured (by) the sword.
For it was the Lord who spoke.
(Tanakh) Isaiah 1:18-20

Seek the Lord while He can be found,
Call to Him while He is near.
Let the wicked give up his ways,
The sinful man his plans;
Let him turn back to the Lord,
And He will pardon him;
To our God,
For he freely forgives.

(Tanakh) Isaiah 55:6-7

Who is a God like unto thee, that pardoneth iniquity, and passeth
by the transgression of the remnant of his heritage? He retaineth not
his anger for ever, because He delighteth in mercy.
He will turn again, He will have compassion upon us; he will sub-
due our iniquities; and thou wilt cast all their sins into the depths
of the sea.

(King James) Micah 7:18-19

Hinduism Affirms the Power of Forgiveness and Mercy

...Anger is the root of all prosperity and all adversity. O thou beau-
tiful one, he that suppresseth his anger earneth prosperity. That
man, again, who always giveth way to anger, reapeth adversity
from his fierce anger. It is seen in this world that anger is the cause
of destruction of every creature. How then can one like me indulge
his anger which is so destructive of the world? The angry man com-
miteth sin. The angry man killeth even his preceptors. The angry
man insulteth even his superiors in harsh words. The man that is
angry faileth to distinguish between what should be said and what
should not. There is no act that an angry man may not do, no word
that an angry man may not utter. From anger a man may slay one

that deserveth not to be slain, and may worship one that deserveth to be slain.

...the virtuous applaud them that have conquered their wrath. Indeed, it is the opinion of the virtuous that the honest and forgiving man is ever victorious....

If amongst men there were not persons equal unto the earth in forgiveness, there would be no peace among men but continued strife caused by wrath. If the injured return their injuries, if one chastised by his superior were to chastise his superior in return, the consequence would be the destruction of every creature, and sin also would prevail in the world....

Forgiveness is virtue; forgiveness is sacrifice, forgiveness is the Vedas.... He that knoweth this is capable of forgiving everything. Forgiveness is Brahma; forgiveness is truth; forgiveness is stored ascetic merit; forgiveness protecteth the ascetic merit of the future; forgiveness is asceticism; forgiveness is holiness; and by forgiveness is it that the universe is held together....

Forgiveness is the might of the mighty; forgiveness is sacrifice; forgiveness is quiet of mind. How, O Krishna, can one like us abandon forgiveness, which is such, and in which are established Brahma, and truth, and wisdom and the worlds? The man of wisdom should ever forgive, for when he is capable of forgiving everything, he attaineth to Brahma. The world belongeth to those that are forgiving: the other world is also theirs. The forgiving acquire honours here, and a state of blessedness hereafter. Those men that ever conquer their wrath by forgiveness, obtain the higher regions. Therefore hath it been said that forgiveness is the highest virtue.

The Mahabharata, book 3, section XXIX

Even the most sinful, if he worship Me with his whole heart, shall be considered righteous, for he is treading the right path.
He shall attain sprituality ere long, and Eternal Peace shall be his.
O Arjuna! Believe me, My devotee is never lost.

The Bhagavad Gita, chapter 9

Buddhism Affirms the Power of Forgiveness and Mercy

Be not far-sighted, be not near-sighted, for not by hatred is hatred appeased; hatred is appeased by not-hatred only!
People will forgive great wrongs which they have suffered, but they will never be at ease about the wrong which they themselves have done....
And if I should deprive thee of thy life, then thy partisans in turn would take away my life; my partisans again would deprive thine of their lives. Thus by hatred, hatred would not be appeased. But now, O king, thou has granted me my life, and I have granted thee thine; thus by not-hatred hatred has been appeased.

Buddha, The Gospel: The Re-establishment of Concord

...you shall not do evil for evil nor return hate for hate. Neither think that you can destroy wrong by retaliating evil for evil and thus increasing wrong. Leave the wicked to their fate and their evil deeds will sooner or later in one way or another bring on their own punishment....
Who harms the man who does no harm,
Or strikes at him who strikes him not,
Shall soon some punishment incur
Which his own wickedness begot,
One of the gravest ills in life,
Either a loathsome dread disease,
Or sad old age, or loss of mind,
Or wretched pain without surcease,
Or conflagration, loss of wealth;
Or of his nearest kin he shall
See some one die that's dear to him,
And then he'll be reborn in hell.

Buddha, The Gospel: The Patient Elephant

Taoism Affirms the Power of Forgiveness and Mercy

Do the Non-Ado.
Strive for the effortless.
Savour the savourless.
Exalt the low.
Multiply the few.
Requite injury with kindness.
  Tao Teh Ching, chapter 63

I have Three Treasures, which I hold fast and watch over closely. The first is Mercy. The second is Frugality. The third is Not Daring to Be First in the World. Because I am merciful, therefore I can be brave. Because I am frugal, therefore I can be generous. Because I dare not be first, therefore I can be the chief of all vessels....
*Mercy alone can help you to win a war. Mercy alone can help you to defend your state. For Heaven will come to the rescue of the merciful, and protect him with **its** Mercy.*
  Tao Teh Ching, chapter 67

Confucianism Affirms the Power of Forgiveness and Mercy

To show forbearance and gentleness in teaching others; and not to revenge unreasonable conduct — this is the energy of southern regions, and the good man makes it his study.
  The Doctrine of the Mean

To assail one's own wickedness and not assail that of others; is not this the way to correct cherished evil?
  Confucian Analects, book 12

A public and common spirit ruled all under the sky; they chose men of talents, virtue, and ability; their words were sincere, and what they cultivated was harmony.... They showed kindness and compassion to widows, orphans, childless men, and those who were disabled by disease, so that they were all sufficiently maintained.

Li Ki (The Book of Rites), part I, book 7

Chapter 28

Honesty and Truthfulness

THE WORLD CANNOT FUNCTION at a higher level without honesty and truthfulness. How can we work with others if we cannot trust what they say? How can peace, joy, and love reign supreme when those operating from their lower self practice deception for selfish purposes? The truth of life and our destiny is so wonderful. It would be foolish to deny it.

Occasionally, what are known as "white lies" may be appropriate, when they truly cause no harm but rather avoid causing another unnecessary pain. Great care, however, must be taken in practicing any white lie. This must only be considered when absolutely necessary to avoid causing pain, and then only for the right reason. The intent must be pure and the result always for the good.

Here are some examples of how the religions affirm the importance of honesty and truthfulness.

 Christianity Affirms the Importance of Honesty and Truthfulness

Then said Jesus to those Jews which believed on him, If ye continue in my word, then are ye my disciples indeed;
And ye shall know the truth, and the truth shall make you free.
  John 8:31-32

Now I pray to God that ye do no evil; not that we should appear approved, but that ye should do that which is honest....
For we can do nothing against the truth, but for the truth.
     2 Corinthians 13:7-8

Finally, brethren, whatsoever things are true, whatsoever things are honest, whatsoever things are just, whatsoever things are pure, whatsoever things are lovely, whatsoever things are of good report; if there be any virtue, and if there be any praise, think on these things.
     Philippians 4:8

Pray for us: for we trust we have a good conscience, in all things willing to live honestly.
     Hebrews 13:18

I exhort therefore, that, first of all, supplications, prayers, intercessions, and giving of thanks, be made for all men;
For kings, and for all that are in authority; that we may lead a quiet and peaceable life all godliness and honesty.
     1 Timothy 2:1-2

If we say that we have no sin, we deceive ourselves, and the truth is not in us.
If we confess our sins, he is faithful and just to forgive us our sins, and to cleanse us from all unrighteousness.
If we say that we have not sinned, we make him a liar, and his word is not in us.
     1 John 1:8-10

Islam Affirms the Importance of Honesty and Truthfulness

And give full measure when you measure out, and weigh with a true balance. This is fair and better in the end.
Qur'an 17:35

Woe on that day to the rejectors!
Who give the lie to the day of Judgement.
And none gives the lie to it but every exceeder of limits, every sinful one;
When Our messages are recited to him, he says, Stories of those of yore!
Nay, rather, what they earned is rust upon their hearts.
Nay, surely they are that day debarred from their Lord.
Qur'an 83:10-15

Surely Allah guides not him who is a liar, ungrateful.
Qur'an 39:3

Who is then more unjust than he who utters a lie against Allah and denies the truth, when it comes to him? Is there not in hell an abode for the disbelievers?
And he who brings the truth and accepts the truth — such are the dutiful.
They shall have with their Lord what they please. Such is the reward of the doers of good —
Qur'an 39:32-34

Surely those who forge a lie against Allah will not prosper.
Qur'an 16:116

*Seest thou not how Allah sets forth a parable of a good word as a
good tree, whose root is firm and whose branches are high,
Yielding its fruit in every season by the permission of its Lord? And
Allah sets forth parables for men that they may be mindful.
And the parable of an evil word is as an evil tree pulled up from the
earth's surface; it has no stability.
Allah confirms those who believe with the sure word in this world's
life and in the Hereafter; and Allah leaves the wrongdoers in error;
and Allah does what He pleases.*
        Qur'an 14:24-27

*O you who believe, why say you that which you do not?
It is most hateful in the sight of Allah that you say that which you
do not.*
        Qur'an 61:2-3

*There are three characteristics of a hypocrite: when he speaks, he
lies; when he makes a promise, he acts treacherously; and when he
is trusted, he betrays.*
        Hadith of Muslim

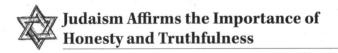 **Judaism Affirms the Importance of
Honesty and Truthfulness**

*You shall not steal.
You shall not bear false witness against your neighbor.*
        (Tanakh) Exodus 20:13

*These are the things you are to do: Speak the truth to one another,
render true and perfect justice in your gates. And do not contrive
evil against one another, and do not love perjury, because all those
are things that I hate — declares the Lord.*
        (Tanakh) Zechariah 8:16-17

Let not mercy and truth forsake thee: bind them about thy neck;
write them upon the table of thine heart:
So shalt thou find favour and good understanding in the sight of
God and man.
  (King James) Proverbs 3:3-4

There is blunt talk like sword-thrusts,
But the speech of the wise is healing.
Truthful speech abides forever,
A lying tongue for but a moment.
Deceit is in the minds of those who plot evil;
For those who plan good there is joy.
No harm befalls the righteous,
But the wicked have their fill of misfortune.
Lying speech is an abomination to the Lord,
But those who act faithfully please Him.
  (Tanakh) Proverbs 12:18-22

ॐ Hinduism Affirms the Importance of Honesty and Truthfulness

Truth is said to be the one unequalled means of purification of the
soul. Truth is the ladder by which man ascends to heaven, as a ferry
plies from one bank of a river to another.
  Narada Dharma Sutra 1.210

For he is the Breath shining forth in all beings, and he who under-
stands this becomes truly wise, not a talker only. He revels in the Self,
he delights in the Self, and having performed his works (truthfulness,
penance, meditation, etc.) he rests, firmly established in Brahman,
the best of those who know Brahman.
By truthfulness, indeed, by penance, right knowledge, and abstinence

must that Self be gained...
The true prevails, not the untrue; by the true the path is laid out, the
way of the gods, on which the old sages, satisfied in their desires,
proceed to where there is that highest place of the True One.
   Mundaka Upanishad 3.1.4-6

Say what is true! Do thy duty! Do not neglect the study of the Veda!...
Do not swerve from the truth! Do not swerve from duty!
   Taittiriyaka Upanishad I, 11

 **Buddhism Affirms the Importance of
Honesty and Truthfulness**

*He in whom there is truth, virtue, love, restraint, moderation, he who
is free from impurity and is wise, he is called an elder.*
*An envious, greedy, dishonest man does not become respectable by
means of much talking only, or by the beauty of his complexion.*
   The Dhammapada, chapter 19

*He who says what is not goes to hell; he also who, having done a
thing, says I have not done it. After death, both are equal, they are
men with evil deeds in the next world*
   The Dhammapada, chapter 22

*If a man has transgressed one law, and speaks lies, and scoffs at
another world, there is no evil he will not do.*
   The Dhammapada, chapter 13

Taoism Affirms the Importance of Honesty and Truthfulness

But if any person acts in opposition to what is right and turns his back upon the truth...deceives the simple, slanders his fellow students, bring false accusations against others...calling good evil and evil good...if a man is guilty of any of these crimes, the God who rules over human destinies will, according as the sin is trivial or serious, abbreviate his span of life.

The Book of Recompenses

Yet there are some people whose behavior is unrighteous.
Their deportment is irrational.
In evil they delight.
With brutality they do harm and damage.
Insidiously they injure the good and the law-abiding.
Stealthily they despise their superiors and parents.
They disregard their seniors and rebel against those whom they serve.
They deceive the uninformed.
They slander their fellow-students.
Liars they are, bearing false witness, deceivers, and hypocrites; malevolent exposers of kith and kin; mischievous and malignant; not humane, cruel and irrational; self-willed.
Right and wrong they confound. Their avowals and disavowals are not as they ought to be.

T'ai-Shang Kan-Ying P'ien, A Description of Evil-Doers

Confucianism Affirms the Importance of Honesty and Truthfulness

The Master said, "I do not know how a man without truthfulness is to get on. How can a large carriage be made to go without the cross-bar for yoking the oxen to, or a small carriage without the arrangement for yoking the horses?"
Confucian Analects, book 2

Tsze-chang asked how a man should conduct himself, so as to be everywhere appreciated.
The Master said, "Let his words be sincere and truthful and his actions honorable and careful."
Confucian Analects, book 15

Chapter 29

Respect for Others and Non-Judgment

WE NEED OUR COURT SYSTEMS of justice to protect the innocent. Let us, however, refrain from judging another unless we are presented with clear evidence of wrong-doing. Let wisdom, compassion, and mercy be foundations for helping us to protect what is good and correct what is not good.

The terms "judge" and "judgment" used in the sacred texts, when not referring to God's judgment, are often referring to people establishing a negative or condemnatory opinion of others. God's teaching within the sacred texts guides us to not get caught up in negative feelings that can imprison us and lead us to a sense of separation, even from misguided souls.

One of the basic freedoms of life is freedom of religion, the right to worship God as one wants. It is essential that we give due respect to the spiritual beliefs of others. It is easy to offend someone by judging or not respecting their beliefs. Let us respect others as we want to be respected.

Every religion shares the same core principles we can all embrace. Let us respect the truth in every religion.

Christianity Affirms the Importance of Respect for Others and Non-Judgment

But why dost thou judge thy brother? Or why dost thou set at nought thy brother? For we shall all stand before the judgment seat of Christ.

For it is written, As I live, saith the Lord, every knee shall bow to me, and every tongue shall confess to God.

So then every one of us shall give account of himself to God.

Let us not therefore judge one another any more: but judge this rather, that no man put a stumbling block or an occasion to fall in his brother's way.

    Romans 14:10-13

Speak not evil one of another, brethren. He that speaketh evil of his brother, and judgeth his brother, speaketh evil of the law, and judgeth the law: but if thou judge the law, thou art not a doer of the law, but a judge.

There is one lawgiver, who is able to save and to destroy: who art thou that judgest another?

    James 4:11-12

Judge not, that ye be not judged.

For with what judgment ye judge, ye shall be judged: and with what measure ye mete, it shall be measured to you again.

And why beholdest thou the mote that is in thy brother's eye, but considerest not the beam that is in thine own eye?

Or how wilt thou say to thy brother, Let me pull out the mote out of thine eye; and, behold, a beam is in thine own eye?

Thou hypocrite, first cast out the beam out of thine own eye; and then shalt thou see clearly to cast out the mote out of thy brother's eye.

    Matthew 7:1-5

Therefore thou art inexcusable, O man, whosoever thou art that judgest: for wherein thou judgest another, thou condemnest thyself; for thou that judgest does the same things.
But we are sure that the judgment of God is according to truth against them which commit such things.
And thinkest thou this, O man, that judgest them which do such things, and doest the same, that thou shalt escape the judgment of God?

Romans 2:1-3

Judge not, and ye shall not be judged: condemn not, and ye shall not be condemned: forgive, and ye shall be forgiven.

Luke 6:37

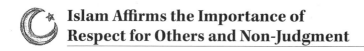 ## Islam Affirms the Importance of Respect for Others and Non-Judgment

We believe in Allah and that which is revealed to us, and that which was revealed to Abraham and Ishmael and Isaac and Jacob and the tribes, and that which was given to Moses and Jesus and to the prophets from their Lord; we make no distinction between any of them, and to Him we submit.

Qur'an 3:84

Islam acknowledges that Jesus Christ, along with other prophets, received divine teachings from God to share with those who would listen. What Jesus received and taught is closely aligned with the principles presented here that are common among the world religions.

And follow what is revealed to thee and be patient till Allah give judgment, and he is the Best of the judges.
    Qur'an 10:109

Surely Allah commands...that when you judge between people, you judge with justice. Surely Allah admonishes you with what is excellent. Surely Allah is ever Hearing, Seeing.
    Qur'an 4:58

Surely Allah enjoins justice and the doing of good (to others) and the giving to the kindred, and he forbids indecency and evil and rebellion. He admonishes you that you may be mindful.
    Qur'an 16:90

Happy is the person who finds fault with himself instead of finding fault with others.
    Hadith

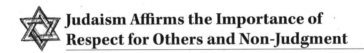 ## Judaism Affirms the Importance of Respect for Others and Non-Judgment

Do not judge thy comrade until thou hast stood in his place.
    Mishnah, Abot 2.5

Thus said the Lord: Do what is just and right; rescue from the defrauder him who is robbed; do not wrong the stranger, the fatherless, and the widow; commit no lawless act, and do not shed the blood of the innocent....
    (Tanakh) Jeremiah 22:3

Moses spoke to his people, saying:

"I cannot bear the burden of you by myself. The Lord your God has multiplied you until you are today as numerous as the stars in the sky. —

May the Lord, the God of your fathers, increase your numbers a thousandfold, and bless you as He promised you. —

How can I bear unaided the trouble of you, and the burden, and the bickering!

Pick from each of your tribes men who are wise, discerning, and experienced, and I will appoint them as your heads."

You answered me and said, "What you propose to do is good."

So I took your tribal leaders, wise and experienced men, and appointed them heads over you: chiefs of thousands, chiefs of hundreds, chiefs of fifties, and chiefs of tens, and officials for your tribes.

I charged your magistrates at that time as follows, "Hear out your fellow men, and decide justly between any man and a fellow Israelite or a stranger.

You shall not be partial in judgment: hear out low and high alike. Fear no man, for judgment is God's. And any matter that is too difficult for you, you shall bring to me and I will hear it."

(Tanakh) Deuteronomy 1:9-17

You shall not render an unfair decision: do not favor the poor or show deference to the rich; judge your kinsman fairly. Do not deal basely with your countrymen. Do not profit by the blood of your fellow: I am the Lord.

You shall not hate your kinsfolk in your heart. Reprove your kinsman but incur no guilt because of him. You shall not take vengeance or bear a grudge against your countrymen. Love your fellow as yourself: I am the Lord.

(Tanakh) Leviticus 19:15-17

ॐ Hinduism Affirms the Importance of Respect for Others and Non-Judgment

Howsoever men try to worship Me, so do I welcome them.
By whatever path they travel, it leads to Me at last.
    The Bhagavad Gita, chapter 4

In varying ways the sages have described
The same unvarying and essential truths;
There is no real conflict between them all.
    Shrimad Bhagavatam 4.4.19

The vile are ever prone to detect the faults of others, though they be
as small as mustard seeds, and persistently shut their eyes against
their own, though they be as large as Vilva fruit.
    Garuda Purana 112

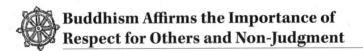

☸ Buddhism Affirms the Importance of Respect for Others and Non-Judgment

...you shall not do evil for evil nor return hate for hate. Neither
think that you can destroy wrong by retaliating evil for evil and
thus increasing wrong. Leave the wicked to their fate and their evil
deeds will sooner or later in one way or another bring on their own
punishment....
Who harms the man who does no harm,
Or strikes at him who strikes him not,
Shall soon some punishment incur
Which his own wickedness begot.
    Buddha, The Gospel: The Patient Elephant

He who sees others' faults is ever irritable — his corruptions grow.
He is far from the destruction of the corruptions.
The Dhammapada, 252-253

He who treads the Path in earnest
Sees not the mistakes of the world;
If we find fault with others
We ourselves are also in the wrong.
When other people are in the wrong, we should ignore it,
For it is wrong for us to find fault.
By getting rid of this habit of fault-finding
We cut off a source of defilement.
Sutra of Hui Neng 2

 ## Taoism Affirms the Importance of Respect for Others and Non-Judgment

All deeds originate in the heart.
All...good acts...begin in the heart and are completed, too, in the heart. The heart's inmost recess is the very spot where there is Heaven and where there is Hell.
The difference between sages such as Yao and Shun and wretches such as Chieh or Chou, simply pivots here around this puny little thing. Unexpected blessings grow, as it were, in a very actual field, which can be ploughed and harvested. The heart, though spiritual and mysterious, yet possesses a solid, tangible soil, which can be watered and tilled.
The soul of a true, earnest gentleman has its root in this obscure recess, which he examines and purifies in solemn silence and privacy. Merely this, a heart to save the world; not one mote of a heart for worldliness. Merely this, a heart to love mankind; not a mote of a heart for hatred of people. Merely this, a heart to have respect for

others; not a mote of a heart for making light of the world....
This is the way of self-purification and the sure foundation of bliss.
     Yin Chih Wen

Accumulate virtue, and store up merit; treat all with gentleness and
love; be loyal, be dutiful; be respectful to your elder brothers and
kind to your juniors.
     The Book of Recompenses

We can achieve the correct interpretation or judgment of something through our own internal attunement with our Higher/
Divine Self.

Without going out of your door,
You can know the ways of the world.
Without peeping through your window,
You can see the Way of Heaven.
The farther you go,
The less you know.
Thus the Sage knows without travelling,
Sees without looking,
And achieves without Ado.
     Tao Teh Ching, chapter 47

 ## Confucianism Affirms the Importance of Respect for Others and Non-Judgment

Let the superior man never fail reverentially to order his own con-
duct, and let him be respectful to others and observant of propri-
ety — then all within the four seas will be his brothers.
     Confucian Analects, book 12

The Master was mild, and yet dignified; majestic, and yet not fierce; respectful, and yet easy.

Confucian Analects, book 7

Section IV

Love What You Do

FOR LOVE TO FLOW FREELY, it's important to love what you do. Whatever you do for a living should help others in some way. By serving your fellow man you will experience greater levels of inner peace and fulfillment.

The previous section demonstrated the abundance of sacred scripture on the subject of loving the Divine Self of others and doing good works for others. It is important that doing so carries on in whatever work we do.

A man asked the Prophet what was the mark whereby a man might know the reality of his faith. He said, "If thou derive pleasure from the good which thou hast done, and be grieved for the evil which thou hast committed, thou art a true believer."
Hadith

Earning a living is not presented as a separate responsibility. It is a foregone conclusion, just like the importance of breathing, that the world does not owe us a living. Ideally, we love our work.

If, however, you're stuck in a job you don't like, then work on what you love in your spare time, keeping in mind that your regular job makes this possible. Look harder for things to appreciate in your job, including finding new ways that your industry helps others.

Certain aspects of any job can be boring or stressful. The practice of non-attachment, discussed in "Divine Passion, Zeal, and Enthusiasm," can be a big help in getting through difficult times. Excessive focusing on the negative aspects of any job will certainly amplify their unpleasantness.

If necessary, make plans to move on from your current employment into an area that you will enjoy more. This could require years of spare-time education and other preparation. It might require relocation. If retired, consider "un-retiring" yourself to do more of something you love. If handicapped, do whatever you can that you truly love. There are many excellent books available on changing jobs and experiencing greater fulfillment at work.

Just as loving God, loving God in ourselves, and loving God in others is essential, it is vital to find divine joy in your work, so that it can be a further offering of love for God. Of course, the highest work we can do is to find God and be attuned with Him.

Chapter 30

Your Perfect Vision

YOUR PERFECT VISION IS YOUR PURPOSE IN LIFE. In Part I, the general meaning and purpose of life was addressed. Here, your individual divine plan or mission is addressed.

Each one of us has a unique purpose in life. It's important to create and maintain the perfect vision for one's divine plan. Faith plays a strong role in holding this vision steady — which will help negative images, thoughts, and feelings to fade away. It is far easier to receive what can be seen, and often impossible to receive what cannot be seen.

Let "Thy will be done" by attuning to your Higher/Divine Self, using the prayer and meditation techniques given. It is better to allow the Higher Self to guide our reception of divine images than to force a mental picture. Allowing divine guidance assures working with and maintaining only plans that are for good. Applying the principles within this book will allow greater clarity of attunement with your Higher Self to realize its divine plan for you.

It is helpful to include any insights about your concept of duty in your divine plan. Establish noble goals and pursue them. Minimize and eliminate habits that can lower and contaminate your energy, such as excessive television watching or overeating.

Excellent results have been reported by a number of people who have created a personal treasure map. This is accomplished by starting with a piece of poster board and using colored pens to draw your various future accomplishments, or by cutting out and pasting on pictures from magazines. Include all those projects that are dear to your heart, that help others, and harm no one. Visualizing these projects as achieved results in a sense of fulfillment. Many have placed their finished treasure maps upon their personal altar in their home. A significant number of people I know who have practiced working daily with their treasure maps have expressed to me their joy due to receiving within a short period of time what they had regularly visualized using their treasure map. This is a successful form of using correct prayer technique — praying with a feeling of having already accomplished the object of your prayer. It is difficult to accomplish a goal that is not consistently envisioned.

Inner vision, as an extension of faith, is a great key to divine power.

Christianity Affirms the Power of Your Perfect Vision

I therefore, the prisoner of the Lord, beseech you that ye walk worthy of the vocation wherewith ye are called....
Endeavouring to keep the unity of the Spirit in the bond of peace.
There is one body, and one Spirit, even as ye are called in one hope of your calling;
One Lord, one faith, one baptism,
One God and Father of all, who is above all, and through all, and in you all.
But unto every one of us is given grace according to the measure of the gift of Christ.
Wherefore he saith, When he ascended up on high, he led captivity captive, and gave gifts unto men....
And he gave some, apostles; and some, prophets; and some, evangelists; and some, pastors and teachers;

For the perfecting of the saints, for the work of the ministry, for the edifying of the body of Christ:
Till we all come in the unity of the faith, and of the knowledge of the Son of God, unto a perfect man, unto the measure of the stature of the fulness of Christ:
That we henceforth be no more children, tossed to and fro, and carried about with every wind of doctrine, by the sleight of men, and cunning craftiness, whereby they lie in wait to deceive…
Wherefore be ye not unwise, but understanding what the will of the Lord is.
    Ephesians 4:1, 3-8, 11-14; 5:17

For God hath not given us the spirit of fear; but of power, and of love, and of a sound mind.
Be not thou therefore ashamed of the testimony of our Lord, nor of me [St. Paul] his prisoner: but be thou partaker of the afflictions of the gospel according to the power of God;
Who hath saved us, called us with an holy calling, not according to our works, but according to his own purpose and grace, which was given us in Christ Jesus before the world began.
    2 Timothy 1:7-9

God has a holy calling, a perfect vision, and divine plan for every one of His children. According to St. Paul, this was given to us through the One Son, the Christ "before the world began." This would be at the time of creation of each unique spiritual being from the Godhead.

Islam Affirms the Power of Your Perfect Vision

And everyone has a goal to which he turns (himself), so vie with one another in good works. Wherever you are, Allah will bring you all together. Surely Allah is Possessor of power over all things.
    Qur'an 2:148

Indeed, there has come to you from Allah, a Light and a clear Book,
Whereby Allah guides such as follow His pleasure into the ways of peace, and brings them out of darkness into light by His will, and guides them to the right path.
    Qur'an 5:15-16

Judaism Affirms the Power of Your Perfect Vision

Where there is no vision, the people perish.
    (King James) Proverbs 29:18

I will pour out My spirit on all flesh;
Your sons and daughters shall prophesy;
Your old men shall dream dreams,
And your young men shall see visions.
    (Tanakh) Joel 3:1

ॐ Hinduism Affirms the Power of Your Perfect Vision

As the ignorant act, because of their fondness for action, so should the wise act without such attachment, fixing their eyes, O Arjuna, only on the welfare of the world.

But a wise man should not perturb the minds of the ignorant, who are attached to action; let him perform his own actions in the right spirit, with concentration on Me, thus inspiring all to do the same.

Action is the product of the Qualities inherent in nature. It is only the ignorant man who, misled by personal egotism, says: 'I am the doer.'

But he, O Mighty One, who understands correctly the relation of the Qualities to action, is not attached to the act, for he perceives that it is merely the action and reaction of the Qualities among themselves.
    The Bhagavad Gita, chapter 3

In soul-vision the wise man perceives in his heart the reality free from growth and change, whose being is beyond perception, the essence of equalness, unequalled, immeasurable, perfectly taught by the words of inspiration, eternal, praised by us.

In soul-vision the wise man perceives in his heart the unfading, undying reality, which by its own being can know no setting, like the shimmering water of the ocean, bearing no name, where quality and change have sunk to rest, eternal, peaceful, one.

Through intending the inner mind to it, gain vision of the Self, in its own form, the partless sovereignty. Sever thy bonds that are stained with the stain of life, and effortfully make thy manhood fruitful.
    The Crest-Jewel of Wisdom, Free Even in Life

The human heart is my favorite dwelling place.
    Srimad Bhagavatam 11.2

Buddhism Affirms the Power of Your Perfect Vision

Never neglect your work
For another's,
However great his need.
Your work is to discover your work
And then with all your heart
To give yourself to it.
>   The Dhammapada, chapter 12

If your purpose wavers,
You will not find light.
>   The Dhammapada, chapter 22

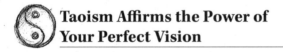

Taoism Affirms the Power of Your Perfect Vision

Except those people who have a vision of the higher life, others do
not realize that existence isn't worth lusting for: except those who
have heard the great (divine) words, others do not understand that
empire is not worth hankering after.
>   Huai Nan Tzu, Life and Soul

"When the mind is convinced of the unreality of visible things and
holds steadfastly to the undisturbed state, though the whole creation
is spread out before the eyes, I look to the mind."
...All these loyal men had a vision of something beyond the present.
Their spirits were indifferent to life and death, and so they were not
to be beguiled by any material conditions or worldly goods.
>   Huai Nan Tzu, Response of Matter to the Cosmic Spirit

In ancient times, Emperor Kun of Hsia built a tower wall; but the Lords rebelled and the distant people became suspicious and wily. And so Yu, seeing the opposition of the kingdoms, razed this wall to the ground and filled in the moats, scattered the wealth accumulated, burnt the implements of war and administered the empire on the principle of virtue, not of force. As a result, the distant people brought their tributes and the barbarian tribes their offerings. The concord sealed at the conclave of the Lords, at T'u Shan, resulted in valuable tributes from myriad kingdoms. From this we see that when a scheming mind is cherished, the sincerity of purpose is not perfect nor the spiritual energies complete; (singleness of mind is lacking.) The ruler whose vision is narrow fails to appreciate how to command the services of those who are far away.

Huai Nan Tzu, The Cosmic Spirit

Thus the Sages yearned over the people.... Such was their clear-sighted vision.

Huai Nan Tzu, Endeavour and Duty

Confucianism Affirms the Power of Your Perfect Vision

Tsze-hsia said, "Even in inferior studies and employments there is something worth being looked at; but if it be attempted to carry them out to what is remote, there is a danger of their proving inapplicable. Therefore, the superior man does not practice them."

Tsze-hsia said, "He, who from day to day recognizes what he has not yet, and from month to month does not forget what he has attained to, may be said indeed to love to learn."

Tsze-hsia said, "There are learning extensively, and having a firm and sincere aim; inquiring with earnestness, and reflecting with self-application — virtue is in such a course."

Confucian Analects, book 19

Tsze-chang asked what constituted intelligence. The Master said, "He with whom neither slander that gradually soaks into the mind, nor statements that startle like a wound in the flesh, are successful may be called intelligent indeed. Yea, he with whom neither soaking slander, nor startling statements are successful may be called farseeing."

Confucian Analects, book 12

Chapter 31

Divine Passion, Zeal, and Enthusiasm

CREATING AND MAINTAINING your perfect vision provides the stimulating force and connection to divine energy and zeal. Faith in God and your perfect vision are prime factors for divine passion. Know that the same divine power that points you to your dreams will help you make your dreams come true. This knowledge provides an abundance of enthusiasm and energy to do your work.

Divine passion also contains divine peace and non-attachment. Non-attachment is a prime aspect of our internal peace. The Eastern religions, in particular, contain teachings that advocate non-attachment and desirelessness. Yet they also contain teachings endorsing zeal and holding your perfect vision. This apparent dichotomy can be explained by the distinction between human passion and divine passion. Divine passion lies in the mind and a knowingness of the heart and radiates a vibration of peace along with its power. It is a byproduct of holding noble, altruistic goals that energize our divine nature of selfless giving and service. Divine passion is love. Human passion is much more emotional, physical, and less peaceful. It often refers to sexual passion.

Much time is spent on achieving various goals. It is important to be enthused about the achievement of those goals, yet we have a tendency to allow a greater degree of stress or discord when goals aren't met as we desire. At those times, remember divine peace and non-attachment by reaffirming important goals and setting a new timetable for their completion.

Having divine passion guides and energizes us to focus on our goals. At the same time, divine passion transcends the level of experiencing stress regarding the results, for faith and patience go hand in hand with it. Faith in our perfect vision and patient persistence lead to a successful outcome.

After a life of achievement it is possible to reach a point of no desire for achievement or having specific goals. Simply being and flowing with life is total fulfillment. Yet even that is a goal of divine passion.

Meditation on the balance between divine passion and divine peace in life can add insight and guidance to this important subject.

 ## Christianity Affirms the Power of Divine Passion, Zeal, and Enthusiasm

And whatsoever ye do, do it heartily, as to the Lord, and not unto men:
Colossians 3:23

For the grace of God that bringeth salvation hath appeared to all men,
Teaching us that, denying ungodliness and worldly lusts, we should live soberly, righteously, and godly, in this present world;
Looking for that blessed hope, and the glorious appearing of the great God and our Saviour Jesus Christ;
Who gave himself for us, that he might redeem us from all iniquity, and purify unto himself a peculiar people, zealous of good works.
Titus 2:11-14

But it is good to be zealously affected always in a good thing and not only when I am present with you.

Galatians 4:18

I know thy works, that thou art neither cold nor hot: I would thou wert cold or hot.

So then because thou art lukewarm, and neither cold nor hot, I will spue thee out of my mouth.

Because thou sayest, I am rich, and increased with good, and have need of nothing; and knowest not that thou art wretched, and miserable, and poor, and blind, and naked:

I counsel thee to buy of me gold tried in the fire, that thou mayest be rich; and white raiment, that thou mayest be clothed, and that the shame of thy nakedness do not appear; and anoint thine eyes with eyesalve, that thou mayest see.

As many as I love, I rebuke and chasten: be zealous therefore, and repent.

Revelation 3:15-19

Seeing ye have purified your souls in obeying the truth through the Spirit unto unfeigned love of the brethren, see that ye love one another with a pure heart fervently.

1 Peter 1:22

For if the trumpet give an uncertain sound, who shall prepare himself to the battle?

1 Corinthians 14:8

Islam Affirms the Power of Divine Passion, Zeal, and Enthusiasm

Of the People of the Book there is an upright party who recite Allah's messages in the night-time and they adore (Him).
They believe in Allah and the Last Day, and they enjoin good and forbid evil and vie one with another in good deeds. And those are among the righteous.
    Qur'an 3:113-114

So vie one with another in virtuous deeds.
    Qur'an 5:48

In the following two quotations, a definite love and divine passion for pleasing Allah is described.

So I warn you of the Fire that flames.
None will enter it but the most unfortunate,
Who rejects (the truth) and turns (his) back.
And away from it shall be kept the most faithful to duty,
Who gives his wealth, purifying himself,
And none has with him any boon for a reward,
Except the seeking of the pleasure of his Lord, the Most High.
And he will soon be well-pleased.
    Qur'an 92:14-21

There is no good except (in) him who enjoins charity or goodness or reconciliation between people. And whoever does this, seeking Allah's pleasure, We shall give him a mighty reward.
    Qur'an 4:114

Judaism Affirms the Power of Divine Passion, Zeal, and Enthusiasm

Whatever it is in your power to do, do with all your might.
(Tanakh) Ecclesiastes 9:10

He donned victory like a coat of mail,
With a helmet of triumph on His head;...
Wrapped himself in zeal as in a robe.
(Tanakh) Isaiah 59:17

Hinduism Affirms the Power of Divine Passion, Zeal, and Enthusiasm

Thy heart with strength and courage stay,
And cast this weakling mood away.
Our fainting hopes in vain revive
Unless with firm resolve we strive.
The zeal that fires the toiler's breast
Mid earthly powers is first and best.
Zeal every check and bar defies,
And wins at length the loftiest prize,
In woe and danger, toil and care,
Zeal never yields to weak despair.
With zealous heart thy task begin,
And thou once more thy spouse shalt win.
The Ramayana, book IV, canto I

When one obtains happiness then one proceeds to act.
No one acts without first obtaining happiness.
Only by obtaining happiness does one act.
Chandogya Upanishad 7.22

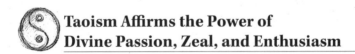

Buddhism Affirms the Power of Divine Passion, Zeal, and Enthusiasm

If anything is to be done, let a man do it, let him attack it vigorously!
The Dhammapada, 313

Through zeal knowledge is gotten, through lack of zeal knowledge is lost; let a man who knows this double path of gain and loss thus place himself that knowledge may grow.
The Dhammapada, 282

Just, O king, as the pilot, day and night, with continuous and unceasing zeal and effort, navigates his ship; just so, O king, does the strenuous Bhikshu, earnest in effort, when regulating his mind continue night and day unceasingly zealous and earnest in regulating his mind by careful thought.
The Questions of King Milinda

Taoism Affirms the Power of Divine Passion, Zeal, and Enthusiasm

When you hear a noble word, you are for the moment carried away with zeal and emulation, while if you witness a good action, your heart leaps for very joy. But as soon as these things are out of your sight and hearing, you forget them at once. Faith has not planted her roots deeply in your heart, and therefore your good principles have no solid foundation. Then, too, the good words and actions of your whole life have never been anything but empty show. Have you ever done a single thing that betrayed a noble motive?

...From this time forward, arm yourself with courage, and banish all impure and unworthy thoughts that may present themselves to your mind. You must first bring forth a crop of pure and noble thoughts, and after that you may direct your efforts to the accomplishment of good. If an opportunity comes to do a good action which is within the limits of your strength, hasten to do it with a firm and resolute heart, without calculating whether is it large or small, difficult or easy, or whether it will bring you any advantage. If this good act is above your strength, use the same zeal and effort in order to show your sincere intention.

T'ai-Shang Kan-Ying P'ien, The Spirit of the Hearth

Let us consider those sages who were the people of the cotton clothes (started life as common people), and the foot travellers. There was Yi-yun who had his first acquaintance with T'ang, the emperor, when he was a cook and carried the saucepan; there was Yu-wang who made the acquaintance of the future emperor of Chou when he was a butcher; Peh-li-hsi, a man of Yu, who sold himself for five pieces of hide to the Duke Mu of Ts'in and became Prime Minister; there was Kuan Chung who became a captive and later rose to great power; there was Confucius whose cooking stove was never warm for he was always out travelling; and there was Mei Tzu but who seldom warmed his domestic bed in his zeal for the public good.
These sages thought no mountain too high, no river too broad to traverse in the pursuit of their work: they bore every buffeting, by waiting on kings. It wasn't because they lusted after emoluments or sought positions of power that they did so; but they desired rather to advance the good of the empire and to expel everything hurtful to the people.

Huai Nan Tzu, Endeavour and Duty

Confucianism Affirms the Power of Divine Passion, Zeal, and Enthusiasm

The Master said, "To be fond of learning is to be near to knowledge. To practice with vigor is to be near to magnanimity."
    The Doctrine of the Mean

The superior man honors his virtuous nature, and maintains constant inquiry and study, seeking to carry it out to its breath and greatness, so as to omit none of the more exquisite and minute points which it embraces, and to raise it to its greatest height and brilliancy, so as to pursue the course of the Mean. He cherishes his old knowledge, and is continually acquiring new. He exerts an honest, generous earnestness, in the esteem and practice of all propriety.
    The Doctrine of the Mean

I will follow after that which I love.
    Confucian Analects, book 7

Chapter 32

Knowledge and Wisdom

THE WORD "WISDOM" PERTAINS TO "wise dominion." By God's grace, we are destined to have dominion in our world to the degree that we can attune to divine wisdom and apply it.

Knowledge is the knowing of facts. The highest knowledge is how to reach God. Wisdom requires knowledge, experience, and attunement with God. Knowledge and wisdom together are what enable us to accomplish what we desire.

We need to develop our knowledge and attunement before we can fully succeed in manifesting our natural desire and perfect vision for the creation of goodness. Therefore we need to study to acquire knowledge. In addition, it is important that we meditate and pray so that we can reach our necessary divine attunement. We gather wisdom as we contemplate and apply these principles that God has given us.

Some may want to consider learning from a spiritual teacher in embodiment, or invoke the guidance and assistance of God, an angel, or a master for spiritual growth or to help with specific life circumstances. Once you have reached the level of direct and pure attunement with your Divine Self, divine assistance is always available from within.

Christianity Affirms the Power of Acquiring Knowledge and Wisdom

If any of you lack wisdom, let him ask of God, that giveth to all men liberally, and upbraideth not; and it shall be given him.

But let him ask in faith, nothing wavering. For he that wavereth is like a wave of the sea driven with the wind and tossed.

For let not that man think that he shall receive any thing of the Lord.

    James 1:5-7

Simon Peter, a servant and an apostle of Jesus Christ, to them that have obtained like precious faith with us through the righteousness of God and our Saviour Jesus Christ:

Grace and peace be multiplied unto you through the knowledge of God, and of Jesus our Lord,

According as his divine power hath given unto us all things that pertain unto life and godliness, through the knowledge of him that hath called us to glory and virtue:

Whereby are given unto us exceeding great and precious promises: that be these ye might be partakers of the divine nature, having escaped the corruption that is in the world through lust.

And beside this, giving all diligence, add to your faith virtue; and to virtue knowledge;

And to knowledge temperance; and to temperance patience; and to patience godliness;

And to godliness brotherly kindness; and to brotherly kindness charity.

For if these things be in you, and abound, they make you that ye shall neither be barren nor unfruitful in the knowledge of our Lord Jesus Christ.

    2 Peter 1:1-8

Woe unto you, lawyers! For ye have taken away the key of knowledge: ye entered not in yourselves, and them that were entering in ye hindered.

Luke 11:52

And this I pray, that your love may abound yet more and more in knowledge and in all judgment;
That ye may approve things that are excellent; that ye may be sincere and without offence till the day of Christ;
Being filled with the fruits of righteousness, which are by Jesus Christ, unto the glory and praise of God.

Philippians 1:9-11

But as touching brotherly love ye need not that I write unto you: for ye yourselves are taught of God to love one another.
And indeed ye do it toward all the brethren which are in all Macedonia: but we beseech you, brethren, that ye increase more and more;
And that ye study to be quiet, and to do your own business, and to work with your own hands, as we commanded you;
That ye may walk honestly toward them that are without, and that ye may have lack of nothing.

1 Thessalonians 4:9-12

 ## Islam Affirms the Power of Acquiring Knowledge and Wisdom

He grants wisdom to whom He pleases. And whoever is granted wisdom, he indeed is given a great good.

Qur'an 2:269

With knowledge man rises to the heights of goodness and a noble position, associates with the sovereigns of this world, and attains the perfection of happiness in the next world.
   Hadith

Allah will exalt those of you who believe, and those who are given knowledge, to high ranks. And Allah is aware of what you do.
   Qur'an 58:11

And when they hear that which has been revealed to the Messenger thou seest their eyes overflow with tears because of the truth they recognize. They say: Our Lord, we believe, so write us down with the witnesses.
   Qur'an 5:83

The search for knowledge is an obligation laid on every Muslim.
   Hadith of Baihaqi

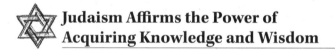 ## Judaism Affirms the Power of Acquiring Knowledge and Wisdom

The Lord God took the man and placed him in the garden of Eden, to till it and tend it.
And the Lord God commanded the man, saying, "Of every tree of the garden you are free to eat;
But as for the tree of knowledge of good and bad, you must not eat of it; for as soon as you eat of it, you shall die."
And the serpent said to the woman, "You are not going to die, but God knows that as soon as you eat of it your eyes will be opened and you will be live divine beings who know good and bad."
And the Lord God said, "...the man has become like one of us, knowing good and bad...."
   (Tanakh) Genesis 2:15-17; 3:4-5, 22

A house is built by wisdom,
And is established by understanding;
By knowledge are its rooms filled
With all precious and beautiful things.
A wise man is strength;
A knowledgeable man exerts power.
　　(Tanakh) Proverbs 24:3-5

Wisdom is more of a stronghold to a wise man than ten magnates
that a city may contain.
For there is not one good man on earth who does what is best and
doesn't err.
　　(Tanakh) Ecclesiastes 7:19-20

The wicked flee though no one gives chase,
But the righteous are as confident as a lion.
When there is rebellion in the land, many are its rulers;
But with a man who has understanding and knowledge, stability
will last.
　　(Tanakh) Proverbs 28:1-2

Acquire wisdom, acquire discernment;
Do not forget and do not swerve from my words.
Do not forsake her and she will guard you;
Love her and she will protect you.
The beginning of wisdom is — acquire wisdom;
With all your acquisition, acquire discernment.
Hug her to you and she will exalt you;
She will bring you honor if you embrace her.
　　(Tanakh) Proverbs 4:5-8

How much better to acquire wisdom than gold;
To acquire understanding is preferable to silver.
　　(Tanakh) Proverbs 16:16

ॐ Hinduism Affirms the Power of Acquiring Knowledge and Wisdom

I am the source of all; from me everything flows. Therefore the wise worship Me with unchanging devotion.

With minds concentrated on Me, with lives absorbed in Me, and enlightening each other, they ever feel content and happy.

To those who are always devout and who worship Me with love, I give the power of discrimination, which leads them to Me.

By My grace, I live in their hearts; and I dispel the darkness of ignorance by the shining light of wisdom.

The Bhagavad Gita, chapter 10

O Arjuna! The righteous who worship Me are grouped by stages: first they who suffer, next they who desire knowledge, then they who thirst after truth, and lastly they who attain wisdom.

Of all these, he who has gained wisdom, who meditates on Me without ceasing, devoting himself only to Me, he is the best; for by the wise man I am exceedingly beloved and the wise man, too, is beloved by Me.

Noble-minded are they all, but the wise man I hold as my own Self; for he, remaining always at peace with Me, makes Me his final goal.

The Bhagavad Gita, chapter 7

The sacrifice of wisdom is superior to any material sacrifice, for, O Arjuna, the climax of action is always Realisation.

This shalt thou learn by prostrating thyself at the Master's feet, by questioning Him and by serving Him. The wise who have realized the Truth will teach thee wisdom.

Having known That, thou shalt never again be confounded; and, O Arjuna, by the power of that wisdom, thou shalt see all these people as if they were thine own Self, and therefore as Me.

Be thou the greatest of all sinners, yet thou shalt cross over all sin by the ferryboat of wisdom.

As the kindled fire consumes the fuel, so, O Arjuna, in the flame of wisdom the embers of action are burnt to ashes.

There is nothing in the world so purifying as wisdom; and he who is a perfect saint finds that at last in his own Self.

He who is full of faith attains wisdom, and he too who can control his senses. Having attained that wisdom, he shall ere long attain the Supreme Peace.

But the ignorant man, and he who has no faith, and the sceptic are lost. Neither in this world nor elsewhere is there any happiness in store for him who always doubts.

But the man who has renounced his action for meditation, who has cleft his doubt in twain by the sword of wisdom, who remains always enthroned in his Self, is not bound by his acts.

Therefore, cleaving asunder with the sword of wisdom the doubts of thy heart, which thine own ignorance has engendered, follow the Path of Wisdom and arise!"

The Bhagavad Gita, chapter 4

 ## Buddhism Affirms the Power of Acquiring Knowledge and Wisdom

A good, all-around education, appreciation of the arts, a highly trained discipline and pleasant speech; this is the highest blessing.

Sutta Nipata 261

Without knowledge there is no meditation, without meditation there is no knowledge: he who has knowledge and meditation is near unto Nirvana.

The Dhammapada, chapter 25

There is a taint worse than all taints — ignorance is the greatest taint. O mendicants! Throw off that taint, and become taintless!

The Dhammapada, chapter 18

As a fletcher makes straight his arrow, a wise man makes straight his trembling and unsteady thought, which is difficult to guard, difficult to hold back.

As a fish taken from his watery home and thrown on the dry ground, our thought trembles all over in order to escape the dominion of Mara, the tempter.

It is good to tame the mind, which is difficult to hold in and flighty, rushing wherever it lists; a tamed mind brings happiness.

Let the wise man guard his thoughts, for they are difficult to perceive, very subtle, and they rush wherever they list; thoughts well-guarded bring happiness.

Those who bridle their mind, which travels far, moves about alone, is incorporeal, and hides in the chamber of the heart, will be free from the bonds of Mara, the tempter.

If a man's faith is unsteady, if he does not know the true law, if his peace of mind is troubled, his knowledge will never be perfect.

The Dhammapada, chapter 3

 ## Taoism Affirms the Power of Acquiring Knowledge and Wisdom

If only I had the tiniest grain of wisdom,
I should walk in the Great Way,
And my only fear would be to stray from it.

Tao Teh Ching, chapter 53

When a wise scholar hears the Tao,
He practices it diligently.

Tao Teh Ching, chapter 41

There is no calamity like not knowing what is enough.
There is no evil like covetousness.

Only he who knows what is enough will always have enough.
Tao Teh Ching, chapter 46

The Sage has no interests of his own,
But takes the interests of the people as his own.
Tao Teh Ching, chapter 49

Confucianism Affirms the Power of Acquiring Knowledge and Wisdom

The Master said, "Is it not pleasant to learn with a constant perseverance and application?"
Confucian Analects, book 1

The Master said, "If a man keeps cherishing his old knowledge, so as continually to be acquiring new, he may be a teacher of others."
Confucian Analects, book 2

The Master said, "Learn as if you could not reach your object, and were always fearing also lest you should lose it."
Confucian Analects, book 8

Chapter 33

Effort, Discipline, and Persistence

EVERY RELIGION HAS ADHERENTS who strive to learn and apply its teachings. These students are known as "disciples," for much self-discipline is required. They understand that with discipline comes freedom, and they apply themselves with persistence in absorbing all aspects of their particular religion along with the inner promptings of their heart.

What this principle of self-control is really about is mastery. For it is our divine destiny to become masters of ourselves and co-creators with God of our world. True freedom, joy, and fulfillment are the result of applying effort and self-discipline to become loving masters.

Effort and persistence can be a great joy, for they yield the desired result. When applied, progress on one's spiritual path can be swift. What initially requires great effort and concentration gradually becomes automatic and a permanent habit. Self-mastery and control become automatic with practice and no longer require effort. Then we are free to focus on the next level of attainment.

Abstinence from negative habits is essential to this process. Whether it's too much food, TV, sex, alcohol — in your innermost being it is clear what is good for you. Negative habits are a block to spiritual growth, and your Higher Self will guide you. Removing bad habits is an essential part of freedom.

Negative habits are an attempt to fill the emptiness inside. When the positive habits presented in this book are not practiced, the soul feels a tremendous lack. Without the correct spiritual knowledge, negative habits are embraced more readily.

A good way to get rid of negative habits is first of all to establish better substitutes to replace them. For example, having an apple instead of ice cream, or reading a good book instead of watching a not-so-good TV show. It's also important, in the spirit of persistence, to never give up, and not engage in self-condemnation if you temporarily slip back into a bad habit. Simply resolve to try again and do better the next day. After all, we need to understand, accept, forgive, and love ourselves as much as we do others.

Determination to stay your charted course comes from maintaining your perfect vision, staying connected to the energetic enthusiasm of divine passion, and building upon the necessary knowledge and divine wisdom. When these essential responsibilities are in place, the possibility of failure no longer exists. Despite the inevitable challenges to your spiritual path, applying these principles with perseverance will result in success.

 ## Christianity Affirms the Importance of Effort, Discipline, and Persistence

[God] Who will render to every man according to his deeds:
To them who by patient continuance in well doing seek for glory and honour and immortality, eternal life:
But unto them that are contentious, and do not obey the truth, but obey unrighteousness,
Tribulation and anguish, upon every soul of man that doeth evil, of the Jew first, and also of the Gentile;
But glory, honour, and peace, to every man that worketh good.
Romans 2:6-10

*And let us not be weary in well doing: for in due season we shall
reap, if we faint not.*

Galatians 6:9

*For the good that I would I do not: but the evil which I would not,
that I do.*
*Now if I do that I would not, it is no more I that do it, but sin that
dwelleth in me.*
*I find then a law, that, when I would do good, evil is present with
me.*
For I delight in the law of God after the inward man:
*But I see another law in my members, warring against the law of
my mind, and bringing me into captivity to the law of sin which is
in my members.*
*O wretched man that I am! Who shall deliver me from the body of
this death?*
*I thank God through Jesus Christ our Lord. So then with the mind I
myself serve the law of God; but with the flesh the law of sin.*

Romans 7:19-25

This refers to the struggle of the Real/Higher Self and the lower
nature.

*And he that sent me is with me: the Father hath not left me alone;
for I do always those things that please him....*
If ye continue in my word, then are ye my disciples indeed;
And ye shall know the truth, and the truth shall make you free.

John 8:29, 31-32

*Confirming the souls of the disciples, and exhorting them to con-
tinue in the faith, and that we must through much tribulation enter
into the kingdom of God.*

Acts 14:22

And you, that were sometime alienated and enemies in your mind by wicked works, yet now hath he reconciled

In the body of his flesh through death, to present you holy and unblameable and unreproveable in his sight:

If ye continue in the faith grounded and settled, and be not moved away from the hope of the gospel, which ye have heard, and which was preached to every creature which is under heaven; whereof I Paul am made a minister;

To whom God would make known what is the riches of the glory of this mystery among the Gentiles; which is Christ in you, the hope of glory:

Whom we preach, warning every man, and teaching every man in all wisdom; that we may present every man perfect in Christ Jesus: Whereunto I also labour, striving according to his working, which worketh in me mightily.

Colossians 1:21-24, 27-29

This quotation refers not only to the necessary striving we must endure, but also the Christ that dwells within us, "the hope of glory."

For I am now ready to be offered, and the time of my departure is at hand.

I have fought a good fight, I have finished my course, I have kept the faith:

2 Timothy 4:6-7

Strive to enter in at the strait gate: for many, I say unto you, will seek to enter in, and shall not be able.

Luke 13:24

We glory in tribulations also: knowing that tribulation worketh patience;
And patience, experience; and experience, hope:
And hope maketh not ashamed; because the love of God is shed abroad in our hearts by the Holy Ghost which is given unto us.
Romans 5:3-5

 ## Islam Affirms the Importance of Effort, Discipline, and Persistence

O man, thou must strive a hard striving (to attain) to thy Lord, until thou meet Him.
Qur'an 84:6

Do men think that they will be left alone on saying, We believe, and will not be tried?
And indeed We tried those before them, so Allah will certainly know those who are true and He will know the liars.
Or do they who work evil think that they will escape Us? Evil is it that they judge!
Whoever hopes to meet with Allah, the term of Allah is then surely coming. And He is the Hearing, the Knowing.
And whoever strive hard, strives for himself....
And those who believe and do good, We shall certainly do away with their afflictions and reward them for the best of what they did.
Qur'an 29:2-7

Verily God forgives my people the evil promptings which arise within their hearts as long as they do not speak about them and did not act upon them.
Hadith of Muslim

And certainly We shall try you, till We know those among you who strive hard, and the steadfast, and manifest your news.
Qur'an 47:31

Do you think that you will enter the Garden while Allah has not yet known those from among you who strive hard (nor) known the steadfast?
Qur'an 3:142

You should believe in Allah and His Messenger, and strive hard in Allah's way with your wealth and your lives. That is better for you, did you but know!
Qur'an 61:11

The most excellent jihad is that for the conquest of self.
Hadith

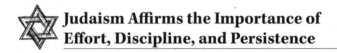 ## Judaism Affirms the Importance of Effort, Discipline, and Persistence

He whose ear heeds the discipline of life
Lodges among the wise.
He who spurns discipline hates himself;
He who heeds reproof gains understanding.
(Tanakh) Proverbs 15:31-32

My son, heed and take in my words,
And you will have many years of life.
I instruct you in the way of wisdom;
I guide you in straight courses.
You will walk without breaking stride;
When you run, you will not stumble.

Hold fast to discipline; do not let go;
Keep it; it is your life.
Do not enter on the path of the wicked;
Do not walk on the way of evil men.
    (Tanakh) Proverbs 4:10-14

The plans of the diligent make only for gain;
All rash haste makes only for loss.
    (Tanakh) Proverbs 21:5

My son, do not forget my teaching,
But let your mind retain my commandments;
For they will bestow on you length of days,
Years of life and well-being.
Let fidelity and steadfastness not leave you;
Bind them about your throat,
Write them on the tablet of your mind,
And you will find favor and approbation
In the eyes of God and man.
    (Tanakh) Proverbs 3:1-4

ॐ Hinduism Affirms the Importance of Effort, Discipline, and Persistence

Lord Shri Krishna said:
He who acts because it is his duty, not thinking of the consequences,
is really spiritual and a true ascetic; and not he who merely observes
rituals or who shuns all action.
O Arjuna! Renunciation is in fact what is called Right Action. No one
can become spiritual who has not renounced all desire.
For the sage who seeks the heights of spiritual meditation, practice is
the only method, and when he has attained them, he must maintain

himself there by continual self-control.
When a man renounces even the thought of initiating action, when he is not interested in sense objects or any results which may flow from his acts, then in truth he understands spirituality.
Let him seek liberation by the help of his highest Self, and let him never disgrace his own Self. For that Self is his only friend; yet it may also be his enemy.
To him who has conquered his lower nature by Its help, the Self is a friend, but to him who has not done so, It is an enemy.
The Bhagavad Gita, chapter 6

Though he be ever so tired by repeated failure, let him begin his operations again and again; for fortune greatly favors the man who perseveres in his undertakings.
Laws of Manu 9.300

(He who is) Always contented, self-centered, self-controlled, resolute, with mind and reason dedicated to Me, such a devotee of Mine is My beloved.
The Bhagavad Gita, chapter 12

Prosperity forsakes those who always dream of fate and favors those who persevere.
Matsya Purana 221.2

The student of spirituality, who earnestly strives, and whose sins are absolved, attains perfection and reaches the Supreme.
The Bhagavad Gita, chapter 6

When the mind, completely controlled, is centred in the Self, and free from all earthly desires, then is the man truly spiritual.
The wise man who has conquered his mind and is absorbed in the Self is as a lamp which does not flicker, since it stands sheltered from every wind.

There, where the whole nature is seen in the light of the Self, where the man abides within his Self and is satisfied, there, its functions restrained by its union with the Divine, the mind finds rest....

This inner severance from the affliction of misery is spirituality. It should be practised with determination and with a heart which refuses to be depressed.

Renouncing every desire which imagination can conceive, controlling the senses at every point by the power of the mind;

Little by little, by the help of his reason controlled by fortitude, let him attain peace; and fixing his mind on the Self, let him not think of any other thing.

When the volatile and wavering mind would wander, let him restrain it and bring it again to its allegiance to the Self.

The Bhagavad Gita, chapter 6

Under the sway of strong impulse, the man who is devoid of self-control willfully commits deeds that he knows to be fraught with future misery. But the man of discrimination, even though moved by desires, at once becomes conscious of the evil that is in them, and does not yield to their influence but remains unattached.

Srimad Bhagavatam 11.7

The saints with great effort find Him within themselves; but not the unintelligent, who in spite of every effort cannot control their minds.

The Bhagavad Gita, chapter 15

Through the spirit of renunciation thou shalt come to Me and be free.

The Bhagavad Gita, chapter 9

There is a point we can reach that transcends the sense of struggle and effort. Once we reach a level of achieving all our personal goals, one can enter the realm of selflessness, where every noble and worthwhile goal is for the benefit of others. Then one merges with Spirit, with mind at peace in Divine Love and bliss.

 ## Buddhism Affirms the Importance of Effort, Discipline, and Persistence

In the body restraint is good, good is restraint in speech, in thought restraint is good, good is restraint in all things. A Bhikshu, restrained in all things, is freed from all pain.
He who controls his hand, he who controls his feet, he who controls his speech, he who is well controlled, he who delights inwardly, who is collected, who is solitary and content, him they call Bhikshu.
    The Dhammapada, 361-362

The Blessed One addressed them and said: "Seeking the way, ye must exert yourselves and strive with diligence. It is not enough to have seen me walk as I have commanded you; free yourselves from the tangled net of sorrow. Walk in the path with steadfast aim.
    Buddha, The Gospel: Entering Into Nirvana

If you wish to find the true way,
Right action will lead you to it directly;
But if you do not strive for Buddhahood
You will grope in the dark and never find it.
    Sutra of Hui Neng 2

If an earnest person has roused himself, if he is not forgetful, if his deeds are pure, if he acts with consideration, if he restrains himself, and lives according to law — then his glory will increase.
By rousing himself, by earnestness, by restraint and control, the

wise man may make for himself an island which no flood can overwhelm.

Fools follow after vanity, men of evil wisdom. The wise man keeps earnestness as his best jewel.

Follow not after vanity, nor after the enjoyment of love [sense pleasures] and lust! He who is earnest and meditative, obtains ample joy.

The Dhammapada, 24-27

 ## Taoism Affirms the Importance of Effort, Discipline, and Persistence

He who knows men is clever;
He who knows himself has insight.
He who conquers men has force;
He who conquers himself is truly strong.
He who knows when he has got enough is rich,
And he who adheres assiduously to the path of Tao is a man of steady purpose.

Tao Teh Ching, chapter 33

He who thinks everything easy will end by finding everything difficult.
Therefore, the Sage, who regards everything as difficult,
Meets with no difficulties in the end.

Tao Teh Ching, chapter 63

Why did the ancients prize the Tao?
Is it not because by virtue of it he who seeks finds,
And the guilty are forgiven?
That is why it is such a treasure to the world.

Tao Teh Ching, chapter 62

 ## Confucianism Affirms the Importance of Effort, Discipline, and Persistence

The Master, by orderly method, skillfully leads men on. He enlarged my mind with learning, and taught me the restraints of propriety.
Confucian Analects, book 9

Yen Yuan asked about perfect virtue. The Master said, "To subdue one's self and return to propriety, is perfect virtue."
Confucian Analects, book 12

The Master said, "He who requires much from himself and little from others, will keep himself from being the object of resentment."
Confucian Analects, book 15

PART III

God's Code of Love and Life

GOD, THROUGH HIS PROPHETS, messengers, and saints, has given us the preceding thirty-three principles, each one located within the sacred texts of every world religion. This set of principles forms a Master Code of love that is a concise guide for growing ever closer to God through right living. Applying these principles consistently allows the flow of love to increase throughout our being and life experience. It also results in increased levels of peace, wisdom, success, joy, and countless other divine qualities.

This section lists the most salient points about each principle for ease in remembering and applying them. This list comprises a system of divine principles to live a loving life.

The 11 Principles of Understanding (Chapters 1-11)

The first three principles of understanding express **the meaning and purpose of life:**

1. **Life, with God, is good.** Life is meant to be good, especially when we share it with God. Despite outward appearances of negativity and suffering in the world, remember that sharing your life with God creates goodness.

2. **Love creates joyous living.** Love is the ultimate goal of life. The consciousness of love must be increased on earth for an increase in the demonstration of love — despite all appearances and situations. Joy is the result of living with love in close harmony with God. So love as much as possible every moment, seeing and loving the God (Divine Self) within others. We are to love and be loved.

3. **We are responsible** for our choices, for all we create as well as what we were supposed to do but failed to do (acts of commission and omission). A record is kept of our every thought, word, and deed. **We have responsibilities:** to know and apply what God has told us He wants us to do, spelled out in the twenty-two principles of loving living in part II. They are essential to fully realize this joyous life process expressed in the first and second principles. A sense of duty to perform them resides within our hearts, as they are a natural part of our Higher, Divine Selves — a part of our divine nature.

Modern life is complex and full of stress — so it is sometimes easy to forget that life is supposed to be joyous. When "life, with God, is good, joyous, and full of love" is forgotten, the incentive is lost to apply principle 3: to fulfill our twenty-two essential responsibilities with love.

The next two principles of understanding express **who we really are:**

4. **We are God's children.** We are divine sons and daughters of God. Our loving Father/Mother God has given to us the great gift of life. We issued forth from God in perfection and purity. God's gift of free will has allowed us to make imperfect choices at times with their resulting consequences.

5. **We have unlimited divine potential.** We can internalize and become more of the divine, positive, and glorious aspects of God. We have the potential to live forever as part of an unlimited flow of divine love, wisdom, and power. We are a part of God.

Knowing who we really are is important for living the best life possible. These truths provide us with tremendous ongoing enthusiasm, energy, and motivation to live in accordance with God's requirements for achieving divine freedom. These thirty-three universal truths are part of what God has shared with us in all seven of the world religions.

It is important to create and feed your enthusiasm for life. Reminding yourself of your true identity within your Higher/Christ Self as a child of God, several times every day, will magnify the "joy flame" within your heart. Joy is the motor of life.

Next, there are the six principles of understanding that express **six aspects of God.** Remember, these also describe your Divine Self and your potential for greater transformation toward these divine qualities.

6. **Unity — There is only One God.** We are all part of the One God, to the degree that we transmute within us that which is not a part of God. Our Oneness makes it very natural to love one another — as different aspects of our Divine Self.

7. **The Creator — God is the creator of all good things.**
    Whenever we create something good, we are working with
    God — we *are* God in action, co-creating with the one divine
    power of goodness and love.

8. **Omnipotence — God is All-Powerful.** We are a part of
    the energy and divine light of God. We have the potential
    to master limitless divine power.

9. **Omniscience — God is All-Knowing.** We are a part of the
    all-knowing divine awareness and divine wisdom of God.
    When we choose an intimate relationship with God, we
    are blessed with tremendous awareness, knowledge, and
    wisdom.

10. **Omnipresence — God is Everywhere.** With God, we have
    the potential to be anywhere and everywhere.

11. **Forever — God is Eternal.** We are eternal with God, unless
    we purposely deny the divine reality of life.

God loves all of His creation. Those who believe in and accept
His love experience greater love, peace, and joy than those who
do not. The more loving we become the more divine and holy we
become.

In addition to the preceding qualities of God:
   God is goodness and love.
   God is the meaning and purpose of life.
   God is our Divine Father and Mother.
   God is beyond our total intellectual comprehension.

One purpose of this book is to show the logic of our common
divine purpose as given to us in all the religions. Whether we
realize it or not, we wish to grow in God's divine wisdom, divine
love, and peace. As we do, we will enjoy a greater inflow of divine
power.

Divine Love x Divine Wisdom = Divine Power. Divine Love combined with Divine Wisdom results in Divine Power.

The 22 Responsibilities for Loving Living (Chapters 12-33)

The inclusion in one's life of the twenty-two essential responsibilities, or disciplines, will result in continually higher levels of joyful living.

Our responsibilities relate to all the areas of loving life. Each one of these responsibilities can apply to any aspect of life. They relate especially, but not exclusively, to these categories:

LOVE GOD. These four essential responsibilities help us to keep God intimately close in our minds and hearts.

12. **Have faith and hope in God.** Envision the best. Trust in life's ultimate greatness and joy, despite worldly troubles. Know that God is with you, willing and able to help according to His greater wisdom.
13. **Give praise and gratitude to God, and for all divine blessings given to us.** Our blessings are greater than we realize. Giving thanks for them strengthens our belief in goodness and God, and paves the way for a greater flow of divine gifts to us, and through us to others.
14. **Pray and meditate to grow in your ability to speak and listen to God.** We have the ability to communicate with God and receive divine guidance, assistance, and energy. God can communicate in numerous ways — an inner voice or feeling, a sign, through someone else, or a new situation or realization.
15. **Be humble.** Know that whatever is done well, for the good, is done by God in you. Give God the glory for your good

deeds. Disregard the illusion of the ego succeeding without God, for it is God in you who "doeth the work."

LOVE YOUR DIVINE SELF (Love God within you). These six essential responsibilities enable us to transcend the challenges in this world that would hold us back from our divine evolution. These enable us to eliminate self-centeredness and focus on loving God, others, and our work.

16. **Love the God in you.** This is not love of the lower, error-prone human self with its many faults. It is not egotistical. It is love of the Higher Self—that perfect portion of God within.

17. **Maintain inner peace.** Peace is the essential doorway to our true spiritual nature. Until we are perfected, we can always find more room for greater inner peace, regardless of outside circumstances. Greater peace allows us to be more loving. We have the ability to maintain inner peace even in the midst of chaos.

18. **Always aim for perfection and purity.** Know that it is possible. God looks at the intent in our hearts more than our mistakes along the way.

19. **Practice moderation and balance** in all your affairs.

20. **Be vigilant.** We are continually exposed to temptations and tests. Remaining vigilant allows us to develop and safeguard our growing love.

21. **Maintain good health.** Take good care of your body. It is God's temple.

LOVE THE DIVINE SELF OF OTHERS (Love God within others). These eight essential responsibilities enable us to more easily love one another and transcend the sense of separation so often felt between people.

22. **Live by the Golden Rule.** Love each other as we love ourselves.

23. **Have patience.** It is another form of love. Have patience with others and follow through with worthwhile projects.

24. **Do no harm.** Be benign and peaceful to others. Defend the innocent. Stand for truth and justice.

25. **Be charitable and help others.**

26. **Speak lovingly and be kind.**

27. **Be forgiving and merciful.** We are forgiven as we forgive.

28. **Be honest and truthful.** Deceit and lies are always exposed. God cannot be fooled.

29. **Respect others and be non-judgmental** of their choices, unless their choices clearly harm the innocent.

LOVE WHAT YOU DO (Love God within your work). These four essential responsibilities help us to achieve success in every endeavor that is aligned with the will of God. God always guides us to that which results in the greatest good and joy, if we focus on divine attunement with Him.

30. **Create and maintain your perfect vision.** Your perfect vision is your Divine Plan or mission. View it often to focus your divine passion.

31. **Cultivate divine passion, zeal, and enthusiasm** for life and the perfect vision of your life's mission or Divine Plan.

32. **Acquire knowledge and wisdom.** Draw from it as needed to achieve a successful loving life and accomplish your goals.

33. **Apply effort, discipline, and persistence.** With discipline comes freedom. With vision, enthusiasm, knowledge, and discipline, we can set any noble goal we desire and achieve it.

Each of the responsibilities can be done with love and joy. These essential responsibilities are for loving living, and enable us to love as much as we can, every moment. Every principle contains love, which is all-pervading and present in all positive aspects of life.

Life is about love. Love is intimate. It is ultimately all. It contains wisdom and power, goodness, beauty, peace, and joy.

The ultimate code of life is, in the most concise word: Love.

As we deepen our spiritual practice, we will develop a complete attunement with universal love. As this happens, we become less aware of God and His many blessings being separate from us — and we move closer to total Oneness, our mystical union with God.

PART IV

Commentary

Personal Power and Consciousness Raising

LOVE × WISDOM = POWER. The thirty-three principles in this book are about increasing our wisdom and love. As a result, their application increases personal power. According to these universal truths, when living a life with God we become "noble conduits" for the use of divine energy. We become trusted to use that power wisely, with love. As we work with these principles, we transmute the blocks that in the past prevented us from attuning to and consciously using greater amounts of ever-flowing power and light.

Every day we can strive to enrich and raise our consciousness, which results in more closeness and oneness with God. As we focus, we work with the divine light and energy that fills our temple. We can make ourselves radiating suns of love, light, and perfection that can be directed to anyone or any place at will. We can become the Christ — the God Consciousness personified within us as our motivating principle. We can be filled with the Holy Spirit — the Divine Fire that can fill our body temple with God's Presence.

Consciously practicing these principles every day soon leads to applying them automatically by reprogramming the subconscious mind. Develop a *richness of consciousness* by working with every universal principle that God has inspired. Anyone can apply these principles. They are simple, logical, and powerfully beneficial when applied. They will change your life forever. You will have spiritual experiences, sooner or later, in one form or another.

There are wonderful and positive truths that can be repeated with belief and feeling to reprogram the subconscious mind. Refer to the following affirmation section for a good starting point.

Finally, brethren, whatsoever things are true, whatsoever things are honest, whatsoever thing are just, whatsoever things are pure, whatsoever things are lovely, whatsoever things are of good report; if there be any virtue, and if there be any praise, think on these things.
      Philippians 4:8

Keys to Happiness

Life is meant to be enjoyable. When you include God in your life, regardless of your name for Him, you are open to the many positive God-qualities of life: beauty, peace, love, joy, and understanding.

Joy is the motor of life. There is a simplicity and joy in these principles that God has inspired in every world religion. Their application yields the power and the freedom to express our uniqueness while part of the One — to grow and succeed in positive projects. It's natural to then be filled with a deep gratitude toward God, and to readily flow with His divine mercy, grace, love, wisdom, and power.

Remember that you are a son or daughter of God. The joy, peace, and other positive life experiences you want for your own children is far surpassed by what your Heavenly Father wants for you, His child. The suffering in the world is caused by our sense of separation from one another and from God, for, in truth, we are one huge family, unique in our individuality, yet one at the same time. The sense of separation, forgetting our true identity, and mankind's misuse of our God-given free will are the cause of our sufferings.

We are God's children, and we are co-creators with Him. Every moment we create something, whether we realize it or not. Every thought and feeling is also a creation. God's light pours through us, giving us life, energy and consciousness. With our gift of free will we continually re-program our subconscious mind. We continually qualify that Light in a positive or a negative way. Our subconscious determines what our next thoughts, feelings, and reactions will be, unless we use our free will to override them. Whenever we are not overriding our subconscious with our free will, we are allowing past programming to determine our reactions, perspective, thoughts, and feelings.

We have free will to reprogram our subconscious mind in a positive or negative way. For example, whenever we want to relax, do we want our subconscious to bring up negatives so we will think, feel, and perceive in a negative way? Focusing several times a day on positive reprogramming will yield significantly noticeable results in just a few days. With several weeks of persistent focus, you can rebuild your subconscious mind to create a better life.

Some people get stuck in the intellectual portion of their mind, thinking and analyzing their life situations with a negative perspective and faulty conclusions. This can create a living hell. Regularly disengage the intellect (meditation is an excellent technique for this) and for a while afterward simply be aware of the wonderful things you have in your life. When the consciousness is entirely filled with "left brain" intellectual activity, there is no room left for spiritual attunement, for the peaceful and inspirational joys of beauty, art, nature, love, and the spiritual realities. Intellectual activity is composed of words, which are symbols, and are a step away from reality. We are spiritual beings and crave far more from life than mere intellectualism.

Life can be wonderful, joyous, peaceful, and inspiring with God. Every one of us who acknowledges God within our heart and mind, and feels His Presence at least several times every day, can be blessed with Divine Light and freedom.

When we allow ourselves to be distracted by the things of this world and exclude the higher divine realities, not allowing God to intimately share our lives with us, then life is empty, dull, lonely, and meaningless.

What we choose to focus on determines our state of consciousness. We are free, every moment, to turn away from our human senses, and focus our attention on the One Source of perfection, peace, and happiness.

Helpful Affirmations

If you will make yourselves an Eternal Fountain of Divine Love, pouring it forth into every place your thought goes, you will become such a Magnet for All Good that you will have to call for help to dispense it. Peace and Calmness of Soul release a power which compels obedience of the outer mind. This must be claimed with authority.
Unveiled Mysteries, Godfre Ray King

It is possible to raise consciousness by reprogramming the mind with powerful positive affirmations. Here are just a few:

1. I AM an Eternal Fountain of Divine Love, pouring It forth into every place my thought goes. I AM a Magnet of all good, and as this Good comes into my world, I will call for help to dispense it.
2. I acknowledge and accept myself as a Temple of the Most High Living God.

3. I AM praising and adoring the Presence of God with me, and I AM continually outpouring a feeling of Peace and Divine Love to every person and every thing unconditionally. I AM the Magic Key of Love that unlocks the door and releases instantly this tremendous Inner God-Power. I AM all Peace and Love. I AM Divine Harmony, the One Great Law of Life.

4. I love, praise, and bless the Great God Self within others and myself (using the Divine Love, Wisdom, and Power of God).

5. I love unceasingly without limit, pouring out Blessings and Peace to all — for I see and know our Oneness.

6. Dear God, you are fantastic! Your wonderful Light infills me so!

7. I love God above all things and I love my neighbor as myself.

8. In the name of my Mighty I AM Presence and Holy Christ Self, I AM a Great Love Star.

9. I am the Light of the Holy of Holies.

JOY AND EMPOWERMENT CREED

I AM a Divine Son/Daughter of God.

I AM Spirit, temporarily inhabiting the flesh.

My True Being is that of my Divine Father and Mother — pure, divine, dazzling Light!

I continually co-create with God, using His Divine Light and Power. I am further empowered as I develop more mastery in Divine Love and Wisdom.

I radiate Divine Light.

I see and communicate with the Divinity of others in my world.

I understand, accept, forgive, and love all others.

Throughout the day, I remember my Divine Reality, because I temporarily live in a world filled with many situations and energies that would otherwise distract me.

Whenever I need to, I stop to let the Joy of Spiritual Light work around and through me. (The Meditation on Light in chapter 14).

My True Divine nature is identical with that of my Divine Loving Father and Mother, for we are One in our joyful, loving service to others.

I feel the Joyful flow of Divine Light flowing through me from its infinite source as I direct it to others.

I focus on maintaining my Inner Peace so that I may stay attuned.

To hasten progress toward your goals, invoke the following:

In the name of (your choice, for example:) God/Jesus Christ/ Allah/Buddha:
I claim Divine Wisdom now.
I claim Divine Abundance now.
I claim Divine and Perfect Health now.
I claim Divine Peace, Harmony, and Balance now.
I claim Divine Love now.
...and, I AM grateful!

Have Faith — It Is Your Power

Without faith, one is powerless. A lack of faith often blocks the successful completion of a project that started out well. Have faith and confidence in the perfection of God acting within you and your world.

In Communion with Others of Faith, You Have Even More Power

Never doubt that a small group of thoughtful, committed citizens can change the world; indeed, it's the only thing that ever has.
   Margaret Mead, anthropologist

   Jesus said:

If two of you shall agree on earth as touching any thing that they shall ask, it shall be done for them of my Father which is in heaven.
For where two or three are gathered together in my name, there am I in the midst of them.
   Matthew 18:19-20

The Union of Religions

The blessed union between the faiths of the world does not lie in the exoteric side, where forms are different and ceremonies are varied, and each suits the idiosyncrasies of its people, and speaks to God in its own tongue. The union of religions lies in the spiritual truth, lies in the philosophic ideas, and lies above all in the mysticism whereby man knows himself as God, and seeks to return to Him whence he came.
Try to understand it [the difference of religions] and you will love it; then let us learn to love and not to hate; let us learn to understand

and not to criticize; let us love our own faith above all, but respect the belief of our neighbors. Muhammad, Christ, Zarathushtra, Moses, the Rishis, and the Bodhisattvas stand in one mighty Lodge, Guardians of humanity and of nations; they know no difference between each other, and we, the humblest of their followers, their children, let us catch one gleam of the all-embracing love. Only by love can they come to us: Muhammad cannot come to his own, as he is longing to do, until they throw away their bigotry, their narrowness and love all men as he loves them all; he is yours, O Muslims, but he is ours as well; we claim every Prophet that God has given to men; we love them all: we revere them all; we bow ever before them all in lowliest reverence. May the God of all nations grant that we, his children, shall no longer struggle in his name, whether we call him Mahadeva, Vishnu, Allah, Ahuramazda, Jehovah or Father — whatever name our baby lips may lisp, there is one God, there is none other, and we all worship Him.

Seven Great Religions, Annie Besant

Although the author of the above quotation (written in 1901) used Muslims as an example, every religion has a number of adherents who have exhibited bigotry and narrowness at one time or another.

We Need to Get Back to Basics

All great religious movements tend to shed the complexities, the extravagances, the rigid philosophical, theological, and moral aspects of institutionalized religion. These religious movements are a reaction to entrenched interests. People, feeling a need for simplification and meaning for their lives, eagerly receive the insights and compelling magnitude of ... the message they know in their innermost being is correct and relevant.

Religions of the World, Ronald J. Wilkins

In this first quarter of the 21st century we need to get back to the simple and natural concepts that we can find in all true religions, for they hold the key to spiritual progress and brotherhood among men.

Peace Is Essential – Now!

Together, we can create a more peaceful, undivided society. Every one of us is part of One Great Divine Being — although we each have our individual aspects, we will always be part of our One Divine Family. We need to go forward holding peace as a common vision. Together, we can create better solutions to problems such as renewable energy sources and cleaning up pollution. We can vastly improve our food distribution system, availability of pure drinking water, sanitation, and housing. We can unite in our prayers, focusing on the trouble spots on earth.

Let us raise our vision to that of a new Golden Age, despite the world's current problems. Let us all think positively and be proactive. Let us visualize our world without its severe problems. Let's believe in an end to war and an end to lack of the basic human needs. Let us put an end to ecological irresponsibility. The world can only be conquered or tamed by love, divine creativity, and mutual respect.

There is hope. Mankind needs hope in the form of a new foundation of agreement and a greater awareness of all we have in common. Hope requires mankind to know and practice these universal principles. We need to remember our Oneness and the all-powerful values we share in common. These values form our philosophy and contribute to a logical order of things, showing life to be magnificent beyond what man can fully conceive.

Embracing the thirty-three principles, we can build our universal foundation. We can help everyone transcend their differences, anger, and intolerance. These essential principles promote love, unity, and win-win projects for the benefit of all. What can be found commonly held within the world's sacred texts can be universally embraced.

The Problem

The problems of mankind are the result of a mixture of two causes. The first cause is ignorance of who we really are and the unlimited potential of every person. This includes a disbelief in mankind's potential to put an end to discord and unite in achieving a joyful, peaceful, and fulfilling society of love. What we currently have instead are beliefs in a very limited and unreal "reality" of strife, competition and limitation.

The second cause of mankind's problems is the lower nature of humanity, often fed by fear, which includes such things as greed, lust for power, and revenge. These negatives will gradually fade away when life's divine truths are fully embraced.

We Cannot Allow Lower Priorities to Take All Our Time

Simple, positive and peaceful principles of life exist from which no one should be distracted. They can be taught at the earliest possible age. Certain truths are so important that they need to be ingrained in the forefront of our consciousness and "habitualized" so that we can have the most successful, joyful, and fulfilling life.

In today's complex world, we receive incredible amounts of information, and experience many transactions and situations with others. Many have allowed this to take up all their available time. As a result, the truths presented here can easily be forgotten. This leads to unnecessary suffering in life.

Government

Every government should act in the very best and most loving way to its citizens. Government should enact and enforce laws that nurture the growth of love, harmony, and brotherhood. It should encourage the universal concepts found within the world religions, including the Golden Rule. It should rule with justice and protect its citizens, achieve harmony with other nations, and seek a "win-win" solution to every international situation. Every nation should do its best to help other nations in time of need or natural disaster. And finally, governments should acknowledge our One God, and be open to suggestions from spiritual leaders.

Separation of church and state makes sense when several religions within a nation compete with one another. No one religion should unfairly be placed above the others. That is no excuse, however, for any government to fail to acknowledge God and apply the universal spiritual principles found in all world religions.

Prayer in school can certainly be allowed and encouraged. Every student can be given some time to say their own prayers daily. Every child and every adult should always have freedom to live their life intimately with God. A priority must be placed upon freedom to practice any religion as well as freedom to not do so. Religious intolerance must never be allowed or encouraged by any governing body. Every individual's spiritual beliefs are sacred to them.

Effort

Life requires exertion so we can grow and enjoy the fruits of our labor. Fulfillment and understanding are not just handed to us. Our efforts, when fueled by the fire of divine passion, bring us success, and ultimately, joy.

Life has meaning when we set goals and strive to achieve them. Eventually we may progress to a point that transcends goal setting and striving. Staying attuned to spirit, the Higher Self — enables us to be divinely guided one step at a time.

The "Bad" Times in Life

This book is designed to express the positive aspects of life — its meaning and purpose, who we and God are, and the essential practices that will result in a positive life. Keeping those in mind will make the inevitable tests and trials of life much easier to pass.

There will still be death, illness, and suffering, but their impact can be significantly lessened. It will help to know how temporary any negatives are — for all is ultimately forgiven, all negative impact of bad occurrences removed, and we are reunited with all we love. The suffering we endure on earth is small when compared to our eternal spiritual life.

God's Wisdom for You

What God Really Wants You to Know is unique to your unique needs. Although this volume contains over eight hundred quotations from the sacred texts of the world's religions, and identifies the thirty-three universal principles they share, the greatest divine wisdom for each of us is what we find in our personal communion with God.

We are each unique aspects of God, even as we are One within God's Divine Family.

Prayers and meditations, as well as reading the sacred texts of the world's religions, both in this manuscript and others, will yield the most incredible spiritual insights and experiences.

Wisdom to each of us is somewhat unique depending on what we still have to learn. If we already know a certain teaching or universal truth thoroughly, its wisdom may be relatively unappreciated compared to our neighbor who has never considered that same truth.

So *What God Really Wants You to Know* is really what God will guide you to discover as you read and choose to apply this and other spiritual works. Commune directly with God in your heart and mind. Then the greater joys of life will be revealed.

Jesus Said: What Is That To Thee? Follow Thou Me!

Many people have been persecuted, some killed (as Jesus was) for claiming to be divine. Indeed, it can sound egotistical or even demented to those who haven't had true spiritual experiences. Their limited belief systems simply won't allow such "blasphemy."

Many people have difficulty forgiving themselves and others. These unfortunate souls have difficulty believing in their potential divinity. They simply cannot understand, accept, and forgive their past errors. Their inferior self-image cannot allow them to consider the truth of their (or anyone else's) unlimited potential.

Hopefully, civilization will come to the point where it stops crucifying individuals who have succeeded in realizing the truth of their inherent divinity. If we have the courage to develop and declare our spirituality, we can show by example how to let go of the tendency to judge those who are closely attuned with spirit. The degree of any individual's attunement with spirit is made clear over time.

We may risk opening ourselves to worldly difficulty when we openly declare our divinity.

For a good work we stone thee not; but for blasphemy; and because that thou, being a man, makest thyself God.
Jesus answered them, Is it not written in your law, I said, Ye are gods?

If he called them gods, unto whom the word of God came, and the
scripture cannot be broken;
Say ye of him, whom the Father hath sanctified, and sent into the
world, Thou blasphemest; because I said, I am the Son of God?
    John 10:33-36

God made us perfect. The mistakes we have made from our misuse of free will can be wiped clean. They do not define who we are.

Beware of Idolatry

Many believe that idolatry is simply the worship of false gods. In fact, idolatry can take many forms.

Without including God in our life, without sharing our life with God in an intimate way, we are prone to various forms of idolatry. Many things can displace God as the subject of our focus. Money, sex, violence, music, sports, body building, television, or anything can displace God as our primary focus.

Some people get caught up in idolizing a movie star or a less-than-noble character played by that actor. They wind up focusing on the appearance or behavior of that individual (smoking or drinking, as an example.) What can sometimes occur is an acceptance of a belief such as "Since they do these things, it is okay for me to do them. It is 'cool' to do them." Emulating less-than-noble behaviors will create a significant blockage in our pursuit of perfection.

Ye Are Loving Gods

The following quotation, from the book *Ye Are Gods* by Annalee Skarin, is a magnificent expression of how life filled with love can be.

With an understanding of this great and perfect gift of love one learns the power of using his mind, his heart, and soul as one, to send it forth. Controlling one's thoughts is no longer a struggling burden of trying to eliminate the undesirable thoughts, but becomes a practice of keeping the perfect thoughts of love always there. When one is learning to play some masterpiece he often makes a slip — and then he plays that one measure repeatedly until he has perfected it. So it is in the exercise of perfecting the melody of divine, Christ-like love. If for a moment the thoughts have strayed into discord and confusion, it is easy to stand quietly for a few minutes, and intensifying the vibrations of love, send them forth as a power of light to the very ends of the earth, scattering the darkness completely. Soon the melody will become a perfect glory and there will be no tones of discord, for one will find himself a great master of the most marvelous harmony of all existence. Love is the melody that will vibrate across the entire universe, in perfect tune with it. It will play a symphony on the stars. Love is the light that will reach into the very darkest corners of human hearts — and those hearts and minds of mankind can sometimes be much darker than the forgotten corners of earth. Love is as necessary in the life of every individual as is sunlight, food or drink. Lives grow warped and ugly without it.

Pour out love and watch a hungry, starving world respond. Pour it out as light, while you work, as you walk along the streets, and as you stand in throngs, or sit in quiet churches — send it out as light from every little cell and fiber of your being — a "pure love, unfeigned" — a love that is felt in every little tissue of the heart. Give love like this and your highway of life will become a highway of divine light, and you will know that you walk with God.

This great love automatically rises above all ego, all pride, all self-ishness, all discord, fear and confusion. It is perfection that steps beyond the weaknesses without even having to give them a thought. They are left behind. It is this love that blends with the holy desires of heaven and opens wide the portals to the storehouse of eternal knowledge, and all weaknesses, darkness and ignorance are dissolved as the morning sun melts the hoar-frost.

Then one knows that in exalting his neighbor he exalts himself. In forgiving his neighbor he has received the power to be forgiven. He will know that in the beginning, he was with God even "The Spirit of Truth;" as surely will he know this as he knows that love is a reality, more beautiful than many forests and great wealth. Love is the glorified string of pearls that belongs to every individual who desires to possess it. It is the greatest gift. As one wears this precious gift he will know also that his brother too is "The Spirit of Truth"—and he will understand that through his great, tender compassionate love he can help restore that vision to his brother. Perhaps not in words—but love plants it own glory. Then he will know that he and his brother, under the divine light and love can again become ONE—the glory of the Almighty.

Ye Are Gods, Annalee Skarin

God is great, and to Him alone belongs all glory. Those who know Him in their life become masters of life and dwell in eternal happiness.

Final Words

THANK YOU FOR INVESTING YOUR TIME reading about these universal and divine principles. Applying these principles will benefit you and those in your world. Share these truths with friends, family, and others whenever the spirit moves you. They are all based on love, and love is the great healer.

The differences and conflicts between the world's religions pale in comparison to the powerful and comprehensive core of spiritual truth that these religions hold in common.

It is my sincere wish that this book has contributed to enabling you to have a greater sense of the true meaning of life and your spiritual identity. May we work together to firmly establish divine principles of love and peace on earth. May we build upon the universal truths that God has given His children to create and maintain a new Golden Age of peace, love, and joy and put an end to all the suffering caused by ignorance, false beliefs, and greed. Let God and His many blessings be with you.

Book Orders

IF YOU BELIEVE IN THE POSITIVE BENEFITS that applying these principles will bring to others, consider spreading the word.

You may order multiple copies of *What God Really Wants You to Know* at a discount for distribution to family and friends as gifts for any occasion.

Help bring Heaven to Earth one person at a time by sharing these spiritual truths.

Most people want to help "save the world." You've already taken the first step by reading the principles that God gave to His children when He gave us the world religions.

Order online at www.whatgodreallywants.com

God's Code of Love and Life
(abbreviated version)

THIS IS A CONCISE OUTLINE of God's Code of Love and Life. It is a further reduction of the principles that are listed in Part III. This compressed version is helpful as a handy and easy-to-remember life guide. It is based on 33 principles common to the sacred texts of the world religions.

The 11 Universal Principles of Understanding

The meaning and purpose of life is:

1. **Life, *with God,* is good,** and filled with Love. Life is meant to be good, despite all appearances of negativity and suffering.

2. **Love creates joyous living.** Life with God, goodness, and love is joyous. We are to love and be loved. Love the God (Divine Self) within others. Joy is the result.

3. **We are responsible for what we do and don't do. We have responsibilities to fulfill as our part of this joyous life process.** A record is kept of our every thought, word, and deed. The list of 22 essential responsibilities for loving living follows this section. Our responsibilities are part of our divine nature. A sense of our duty to perform them resides within our hearts, as they are a natural part of our Higher, Divine Selves.

It is vital to live life knowing **who we really are:**

4. **We are Divine Children of God — Sons and Daughters of God.** We issued forth from God in perfection and purity.
5. **Our destiny is God. We have unlimited divine potential.** We can become more and more of the divine, positive, glorious aspects of God.

Each one of us can more fully incorporate the **many divine aspects of God**, including:

6. **Unity — There is One God.** We are a part of God, to the degree that we transmute all within that is not a part of God.
7. **The Creator — God is the creator of all good things.** Whenever we create something good, we are co-creating with God.
8. **Omnipotence — God is All-Powerful.** We are a part of the energy and divine Light of God. Through conscious cooperation with God, we have unlimited potential to increase our personal power.
9. **Omniscience — God is All-Knowing.** We are a part of the all-knowing divine awareness and divine wisdom of God. With God, we have tremendous awareness and wisdom potential.
10. **Omnipresence — God is Everywhere.** With God, we have the potential to be anywhere and everywhere, too.
11. **Forever — God is Eternal.** With God, we are eternal.

God is also the loving creator of all goodness in life, and has aspects that transcend our intellectual comprehension.

$$\text{Divine Love} \times \text{Divine Wisdom} = \text{Divine Power}$$

22 Responsibilities for Loving Living

We need to love as much as we can, every moment. That means to love God, love our divine self and other's divine selves, and love what we do. Although they are each listed in only one specific area of life below, each responsibility/discipline applies to all four areas of life. Here are the twenty-two essential responsibilities given to us by God that help us live up to our potential of an eternal, divine life.

Love God. These four essential responsibilities help us to keep God intimately close in our minds and hearts.

12. **Have faith and hope in God** and in all good outcomes. Lean on Him.
13. **Give praise and gratitude to God** for all of life's blessings.
14. **Pray and meditate** to grow in ability to speak and listen to God.
15. **Be humble.** Know that whatever is done for the good, is done by God in you.

Love Your Divine Self (Love God within you). These six essential responsibilities enable us to transcend the challenges in this world that would hold us back from our divine evolution. These enable us to eliminate self-centeredness and focus on loving God, others, and our work.

16. **Love the God in you.** Love your Divine/Pure/Higher Self.
17. **Maintain inner peace.** Be non-attached to outer circumstances. Peace is the essential doorway to our true divine spiritual nature.

18. **Always aim for perfection and purity.** Know it is possible. God looks at the intent in our hearts more than our mistakes.
19. **Live with moderation and balance** in all things of this world.
20. **Be vigilant.** There are continual temptations and tests.
21. **Maintain good health.** Your body is God's temple.

Love The Divine Self of Others (Love God within others). These eight essential responsibilities enable us to more easily love one another and transcend the sense of separation so often felt between people.

22. **Live by the Golden Rule.**
23. **Have patience.** It is another form of love. Have patience with others and follow through with worthwhile projects.
24. **Do no harm.** Be kind to all. Defend the innocent.
25. **Be charitable and help others.**
26. **Speak lovingly and be kind.**
27. **Be forgiving and merciful.** We are forgiven as we forgive.
28. **Be honest and truthful.**
29. **Respect others and be non-judgmental** of their choices, unless their choices clearly harm the innocent.

Love What You Do (Love God within your work). These four essential responsibilities help us to achieve success in every endeavor that is aligned with the will of God. God always guides us to that which results in the greatest good and joy, if we focus on divine attunement with Him.

30. **Create and maintain your perfect vision.** Let your Divine Plan feed your divine passion.
31. **Have divine passion, zeal, and enthusiasm** for life and your perfect vision (Divine Plan).
32. **Acquire knowledge and wisdom.** Draw from it to accomplish your goals.
33. **Apply effort, discipline, and persistence.** With discipline comes freedom.

With vision, enthusiasm, knowledge, and discipline, we can set any noble goal we desire and achieve it. All twenty-two of these essential responsibilities are for loving living, and enable us to love as much as we can, every moment. Love contains wisdom and power, goodness, beauty, peace, and joy.

APPENDIX B

"Sonship" in Islam

Even though the Qur'an contains numerous statements, as seen in chapter 4, affirming that we are children of God, it also contains statements that appear to express a different view. It is helpful to look objectively at these other statements because they reduce the clarity of our divine inheritance.

Wonderful Originator of the heavens and the earth! How could He have a son when He has no consort? And He created everything, and He is the Knower of all things.
  Qur'an 6:101

And the Jews and the Christians say: We are the sons of Allah and His beloved ones. Say: Why does He then chastise you for your sins? Nay you are mortals from among those who he has created. He forgives whom He pleases and chastises whom He pleases.
  Qur'an 5:18

What the Qur'an is doing here is denying that God would show favoritism, because this would oppose the principle that we are all created equal. At the time the Qur'an was written it may have been felt that the principle of equality needed to be upheld and that other religion's claims to superiority should be denied.

If Allah desired to take a son to Himself, He could have chosen those He pleased out of those whom He has created — Glory be to Him! He is Allah, the One, the Subduer (of all).

Qur'an 39:4

Yet the Qur'an does state that Jesus was a prophet, among many:

And this was Our argument which We gave to Abraham against his people. We exalt in degrees whom We please. Surely thy Lord is Wise, Knowing.
And We gave him Isaac and Jacob. Each did We guide; and Noah did We guide before, and of his descendants, David and Solomon and Job and Joseph and Moses and Aaron. And thus do We reward those who do good (to others):
And Zacharias and John and Jesus and Elias; each one (of them) was of the righteous,
And Ishmael and Elisha and Jonah and Lot; and each one (of them) We made to excel the people;
And some of their fathers and their descendants and their brethren. And We chose them and guided them to the right way.
This is Allah's guidance wherewith He guides whom He pleases of His servants.

Qur'an 6:83-88

It is possible to be created both equal, yet unique. Over time, however, those who strive with greater effort for perfection and achieve it would indeed please God. We were all created equal, but since then our level of attainment is due to our effort.

The reasons that the Qur'an contains certain statements like this should be viewed within the context of one of the chief concerns at the time it was written: that Jesus Christ, whom the Qur'an acknowledges as a prophet, was being worshiped as God because he was viewed by many Christians as being the only son of God.

It is possible that the Qur'an expressed this view for at least two reasons:

1. God, through Muhammad, wanted to affirm that all forms of idolatry are wrong, and that we are to worship only God and not Jesus.
2. God, through Muhammad, wanted to affirm that we were all created equal. If Jesus is the *only* Son of God, then the rest of us are not his children — only Jesus.

It is probable that the statements within the Qur'an denying that humans are the sons of God were referring to the lower self of man rather than the perfect, Divine Self. This would offer a valid explanation. Though God is within us and we have divine potential, if we use our free will to deny God we will not ultimately succeed in life.

It helps immensely to view Jesus as a soul who was more evolved, more perfected than his brethren, who came to show us the way back to God. Jesus demonstrated the ideal of including God in all his thoughts, words, and deeds, to the point that often when he spoke, God spoke through him. At those times, Jesus was fully attuned with God. As a result, what the followers of Jesus heard was God speaking directly to them. It is easy to see how many would tend to deify Jesus, to worship him instead of God. Jesus uttered God's words due to his attainment. He was a living example of God's love in action.

It is also possible to see the important distinction between loving Jesus because of his great love for us, his teachings, and the example he set, and worshipping him in place of God. This distinction, brought to us through Muhammad in the Qur'an, alerts us to the danger of idolatry, which results in ignoring God.

Bibliography and Source Notes

THERE ARE MANY SACRED TEXTS linked with every world religion. Although this book is not a substitute for the sacred texts, it does contain some of the best quotations from a selection of the more traditional texts from each religion (and a few not so traditional). Consider additional reading in these and other inspiring spiritual works.

Christian Sources

The Holy Bible (KJB), King James version (Philadelphia, PA: The National Bible Press, 1973)

Islam Sources

The Holy Qur'an (QUR'AN), translation by Maulana Muhammad Ali (Dublin, OH: Ahmadiyya Anjuman Isha'at Islam Lahore Inc., 2002)

Traditions of the Prophet, compiled by Javad Nurbakhsh (NY: Khaniqahi-Nimatullahi Publications, 1981)

Sayings of Muhammad translation by Ghazi Ahmad (Lahore, Pakistan: Sh. Muhammad Ashraf, 1968)

Nahjul Balagha of Hazrat Ali, translation by Syed Mohammed Askari Jafery (Pathergatti, India: Seerat-Uz-Zahra Committee, 1965)

A Manual of Hadith, translation by Maulana Muhammad Ali (Lahore, Pakistan: The Ahmadiyya Anjuman Ishaat Islam, 1944)

The Alchemy of Happiness, by Al Ghazzali, translation by Claud Field (London: J. Murray, 1909)

The Moslem World (Hartford, CT: Hartford Seminary Foundation, 1939)

Muhammad and the Islamic Tradition, translation from French by J. M. Watt (Westport, CT: Greenwood Press, 1974)

Sahih Muslim, translation by Abdul Hamid Siddiqi, 4 Volumes (New Delhi: Kitab Bhavan, 1977)

Judaism Sources

The Jewish Study Bible (JSB), Tanakh translation (NY: Oxford University Press, Inc., 2004). Excerpts reprinted from *Tanakh: The Holy Scriptures,* ©1985, published by The Jewish Publication Society with the permission of the publisher.

Treasury of Jewish Quotations, edited by Joseph L. Baron (Northvale, NJ: Jason Aronson, 1985)

The Babylonian Talmud, translation by I. Epstein (NY: Soncino Press, 1948)

Sayings of the Jewish Fathers (Pirqe Aboth), translation by Charles Taylor, 1897 (as quoted from www.sacred-texts.com)

The Living Talmud: The Wisdom of the Fathers, translation by Judah Goldin (NY: New American Library, 1957)

Hinduism Sources

The Bhagavad Gita (BG) translation by Shri Purohit Swami (NY: Vintage Books Edition, 1977 by Random House). Translation first published in 1935 by Faber and Faber Ltd, London.

The Bhagavad Gita (Easwaran), edited by Eknath Easwaran (Petaluma, CA: Nilgiri Press, 1985)

The Bhagavadgita: A New Translation (Bolle), edited by Kees W. Bolle (Berkeley, CA: University of California Press, 1979)

The Song of God: Bhagavad-Gita (Prab), translation by Swami Prabhavananda and Christopher Isherwood (Hollywood, CA:

Vedanta Press, 1944, 1972)

The Sayings of Sri Ramakrishna, compiled by Swami Abhedananda (NY: The Vedanta Society, 1903)

The Mahabharata, translation by Kisari Mohan Ganguli (1893–96) as quoted from www.sacred-texts.com

Songs of Kabir, translation by Rabindranath Tagore (NY: The Macmillan Co., 1915)

The Upanishads, Part II, translation by F. Max Muller, Vol. 15 of *The Sacred Books of the East* (Oxford: Clarendon Press, 1884)

The Vishnu Purana, translation by H. H. Wilson (London: John Murray, Publisher, 1840)

Srimad Bhagavatam: The Wisdom of God, edited by Swami Prabhavananda (Hollywood, CA: Vedanta Press, 1943)

The Upanishads (Easwaran), translation by Eknath Easwaran, founder of the Blue Mountain Center of Meditation, ©1987; reprinted by permission of Nilgiri Press, PO Box 256,Tomales, CA 94971, www.easwaran.org

The Upanishads (Nikhilananda), translation by Swami Nikhilananda, 4 Volumes (NY: Ramakrishna-Vivekananda Center of New York, ©1949, 1952, 1956, 1959 by Swami Nikhilananda)

The Spiritual Heritage of India, edited by Swami Prabhavananda (Hollywood, CA: Vedanta Press, 1963)

Mantramanjari: The Vedic Experience, edited by Raimundo Panikkar (Berkeley, CA: University of California Press, 1977)

The Rig Veda, translation by Ralph T. H. Griffith, 1896 (as quoted from www.sacred-texts.com)

The Srimad Devi Bhagawatam, translation by Swami Vijnanananda, 1921–22 (as quoted from www.sacred-texts.com)

Sourcebook in Indian Philosophy, edited by S. Radhakrishnan and C. A. Moore (Princeton, NJ: Princeton University Press, 1957)

The Laws of Manu, translation by George Buhler, Volume 25 of *Sacred Books of the East*

The Garuda Purana, edited by Manmatha Natha Dutt (Calcutta: Society for the Resuscitation of Indian Literature, 1908)

The Crest-Jewel of Wisdom, by Sankaracharya, translation and commentaries by Charles Johnston, 1946 (as quoted from www. sacred-texts.com)

The Ramayan of Valmiki, translation by Ralph T. H. Griffith (London: Trubner & Co. 1870–1874)

The Matsya Puranam, translation by A Taluqdar of Oudh, Sacred Books of the Hindus, edited by B. D. Basu (NY: AMS Press, 1974)

Buddhism Sources

The Dhammapada: The Sayings of the Buddha (Byrom), translation by Thomas Byrom (Boston, MA: Shambhala Publications, Inc., 1976). Alfred A. Knopf, Inc. copyright holder.

The Dhammapada (Muller), translation by F. Max Muller, Vol. 10 of *The Sacred Books of the East* (Oxford: Clarendon Press, 1881)

The Dhammapada (Thera), translation by Narada Maha Thera (Colombo, Sri Lanka: Vajirarama, 1972)

The Dhammapada (Radhakrishnan), edited by Sarvepalli Radhakrishnan (Madras: Oxford University Press, 1950)

The Diamond Sutra & The Sutra of Hui Neng, translation by A. F. Price and Wong Mou-lam (Boston: Shambhala Publications, Inc., 1990). Used by arrangement with Shambhala Publications, Ltd. Boston, MA www.shambhala.com

Buddha, the Gospel, by Paul Carus, (Chicago, IL: The Open Court Publishing Co., 1894)

Foundations of Buddhism, by Helena Roerich (NY, Agni Yoga Society, 1971)

The Sutta-Nipata, translation by H. Saddhatissa (London: Curzon Press, 1985)

A Buddhist Bible, by Dwight Goddard (Thetford, VT: Dwight Goddard, 1932)

Buddhism in Translations, by Henry Clarke Warren, Volume III of the *Harvard Oriental Series* (Boston, MA: Harvard University Press, 1896)

The Mahaparinirvana Sutra, translation by Kosho Yamamoto, 3 vols. (Ube City: Karinbunko, 1973–1975)

Scripture of the Lotus Blossom of the Fine Dharma, translation by Leon Hurvitz (NY: Columbia University Press, 1976)

The Lotus of the Wonderful Law, translation by W.E. Soothill (Oxford: Oxford University Press, 1930)

The Flower Ornament Scripture: A Translation of the Avatamsaka Sutra, translation by Thomas Cleary (Boston, MA: Shambhala Publications, 1984–1987)

The Two Buddhist Books in Mahayana translation by Upasika Chihmann [P. C. Lee], (Hong Kong: Rumford, 1936)

Saddharma-Pundarika, translation by H. Kern; Vol. 21 of *The Sacred Books of the East* (Oxford: Clarendon Press, 1884)

The Teachings of the Compassionate Buddha, edited by E. A. Burtt (NY: Penguin Books, 1955)

Buddhist Texts Through the Ages, edited by Edward Conze (NY: Philosophical Library, 1954)

Gradual Sayings, translation by F.L. Woodward and E.M. Hare, 5 Volumes (London: Bali Text Society, 1951–65)

The Laws of Manu, translation by Georg Buhler, Volume 25 of *The Sacred Books of the East* (Oxford: Clarendon Press, 1884)

The Buddhism of Tibet containing *The Precious Garland* by Nagarjuna and the Seventh Dalai Lama (India: Motilal Banarsidass, 1987)

The Udana, translation by Major General G. M. Strong, C. B. (London: Luzac & Co., 1902)

A General Explanation of the Buddha Speaks: The Sutra in Forty-Two Sections, by Hsuan-hua, translation by Bhikshuni Heng Chih (San Francisco, CA: Buddhist Text Translation Society, 1977)

Taoism Sources

The Tao Teh Ching (TAO), from *Tao Teh Ching* translated by John C.
H. Wu, ©1961 by St. John's University Press, New York. Reprinted
by arrangement with Shambhala Publications, Inc., Boston, MA
www.shambhala.com

Tao, the Great Luminant: Essays from the Huai Nan Tzu, by Evan S.
Morgan (Shanghai, 1933)

Laotzu's Tao and Wu Wei, by Dwight Goddard and Henri Borel
(Thetford, VT: Dwight Goddard, 1939)

The Book of Lieh-Tzu, introduction and notes by Lionel Giles, 1912 (as
quoted from www.sacred-texts.com)

Taoist Texts, by Frederic Henry Balfour (London and Shanghai, 1884)

T'ai-Shang Kan-Ying P'ien, translation by Teitaro Suzuki and Dr. Paul
Carus (LaSalle, IL: The Open Court Publishing Co., 1906)

Yin Chih Wen, translation by Teitaro Suzuki and Dr. Paul Carus
(LaSalle, IL: The Open Court Publishing Co., 1906)

Confucianism Sources

The Confucian Analects (AN), translation by James Legge, 1893 (as
quoted from www.sacred-texts.com)

The Doctrine of the Mean (MEAN), translation by James Legge, 1893
(as quoted from www.sacred-texts.com) NOTE: Because this work
only comprises a few pages and is not broken up into sections, no
specific locations within this work are cited.

I Ching: The Book of Change, translation by John Blofeld (London:
George Allen & Unwin, 1965)

Li Ki (The Book of Rites) translation by James Legge, Volume 27–28 of
The Sacred Books of the East (Oxford: Clarendon Press, 1885)

The Chinese Classics, translation by James Legge (Oxford: Oxford
University Press, 1895)

Multi-Religion/New Age Sources

The Essential Unity of All Religions, by Bhagavan Das (Wheaton, IL., Theosophical Publishing House, 1932, 1939, 1966, 1969, 1973)

Unveiled Mysteries, by Godfre Ray King (Chicago, IL: Saint Germain Press, Inc., 1982)

Oneness, by Jeffrey Moses (NY: Ballantine Publishing Group, 1989, 2002)

World Scripture, edited by Andrew Wilson (St. Paul, MN: Paragon House, 1991)

Ye Are Gods, by Annalee Skarin (DeVorss Publications, 9780875167183, www.devorss.com)

Climb the Highest Mountain, by Mark and Elizabeth Clare Prophet (Livingston, MT, Summit University Press, 1972, 1977, 1986)

Sacred Books of the East, edited by Max Muller (Oxford: Clarendon Press, 1879–1910)

The World's Religions, by Huston Smith (NY: Harper Collins Publishers, 1991)

The Portable World Bible edited by Robert Ballou (NY: Viking Press, 1944)

Seven Great Religions, by Annie Besant (Wheaton, IL: The Theosophical Publishing House, 1966)

Miscellaneous Sources

Webster's Ninth New Collegiate Dictionary, Frederick C. Mish, Editor (Springfield, MA: Merriam-Webster Inc., 1984)

Source Notes

Introduction

The Sayings of Sri Ramakrishna, as quoted in *The World's Religions,* p. 74

The Upanishads, as quoted in *The Essential Unity of All Religions,* p. 542

Chapter 1 – Life, With God, Is Good

Christianity: KJB: Romans 14:19; John 15:10–11; Galatians 5:22–23;
Matthew 7:9–12; John 14:2

Islam: QUR'AN: 4:40; 53:31; 6:160; 4:123–125; 16:30–31

Judaism: JSB: Genesis 1:3–4; 1:27–28, 31; Proverbs 3:13–18;
Ecclesiastes 3:12–13

Hinduism: *The Mahabharata,* Book 6, Section 29 (Chapter 5 of the
Bhagavad Gita)

BG: Chapters 14, 18

The Mahabharata, Book 14, Section 19

BG: Chapter 9

Buddhism: *The Dhammapada (Muller),* Chapter 15

The Majjhima-Nikaya, as quoted in *Foundations of Buddhism,* p. 83

Buddha, the Gospel: Anathapindika, the Man of Wealth

Gautama Buddha, as quoted in *Foundations of Buddhism,* p. 33

Taoism: TAO: Chapters 79, 27

Confucianism: MEAN (x2)

I Ching, 58, from *I Ching: The Book of Change*

Chapter 2 – Love Creates Joyous Living

Unveiled Mysteries, p. 235

Christianity: KJB: Matthew 22:37–40; Ephesians 3:14–19; 1 Corinthians 13:1–10, 13

Islam: QUR'AN 2:165; 5:93

Hadith of Suhrawardi as quoted in *Traditions of the Prophet* QUR'AN 3:159

Hadith as quoted in *Traditions of the Prophet*

Judaism: JSB: Leviticus 19:17–18; Deuteronomy 6:5–7; Proverbs 8:17, 21

Hinduism: *Svetasvatara Upanishad 5.4* as quoted in *Oneness* p. 188

The Bhagavad Gita (Easwaran), Chapters 12, 6

Songs of Kabir, Chapter 17 (II.61)

Buddhism: *Majjhima-Nikaya* as quoted in *Foundations of Buddhism* pgs 92–93

The Dhammapada as quoted in *Oneness,* p. 11

The Sutta-Nipata 149 Metta Sutta.

Foundations of Buddhism, p. 93

Taoism: TAO: Chapters 34, 10, 13

Confucianism: AN: Books 6, 12

Ye Are Gods, p. 176. Reprinted from *Ye Are Gods* by Annalee Skarin, DeVorss Publications, 9780875167183, www.devorss.com

Chapter 3 – We Have Responsibilities

Christianity: KJB: Galatians 6:7; 1 John 1:9; Matthew 5:16; 16:27; Revelation 14:13

Islam: QUR'AN: 17:13–15; 82:10–12; 99:1–8; 41:46

Judaism: JSB: Proverbs 24:12; Ezekiel 18:20–21; Psalms 62:12–13; Proverbs 28:6

Hinduism: *The Laws of Manu 4:240* as quoted in *Sacred Books of the East,* Volume 25

BG: Chapters 16, 7

The Mahabharata, Book 6, Section 38 (Chapter 14 of the Bhagavad Gita)

Buddhism: *The Dhammapada (Thera),* 116–118

The Milindapanha 65. as quoted in *Buddhism in Translations* pp. 214–215

The Samyutta-Nikaya 42 as quoted in *Buddhism in Translations* p. 228

Taoism: TAO: Chapters 51, 54

Confucianism: AN: Book 4
MEAN

AN: Book 15

Chapter 4 – Our Divinity

KJB: John 1:12–13

Christianity: KJB: Genesis 1:26–27; Romans 8:14, 16, 17; 1 Corinthians 3:16; Matthew 6:9; Hebrews 12:5–9; Mark 10:18; John 14:12; Mark 11:22–24

Climb the Highest Mountain, pgs. 153–154

KJB: John 10:30–38; Matthew 23:9–10; Romans 8:14–17; John 14:20; 14:23

Islam: QUR'AN: 32:8–9; 32:8–9 footnote.

Hadith of Baihaqi as quoted in *Sayings of Muhammad*

Hadith as quoted in *Oneness* p. 192

Hadith as quoted in *Traditions of the Prophet*

QUR'AN: 40:64, 67; 75:36–39; 15:28–30; 95:4–6; 50:16; 57:4; 35:38

Judaism: JSB: Deuteronomy 14:1; Isaiah 66:13; Malachi 2:10; Genesis 1:27; Malachi 1:6

Hinduism: BG: Chapter 13

The Katha Upanishad, II, 6, from Volume 15 *The Sacred Books of the East.*

BG: Chapter 9

The Bhagavad Gita (Bolle), Chapter 6, from *The Bhagavadgita: A New Translation*

Khandogya Upanishad III, 14 from Volume 1, *The Sacred Books of the East*

Brihadaranyaka Upanishad I, 4 from Volume 15, *The Sacred Books of the East*

BG: Chapter 13

Brihadaranyaka Upanishad, IV, 3–4 from Volume 15, *The Sacred Books of the East*

Buddhism: *Mahaparinirvana Sutra 220* from *The Mahaparinirvana Sutras*

Lotus Sutra 3 from *Scripture of the Lotus Blossom of the Fine Dharma*

Mahaparinirvana Sutra 214 from *The Mahaparinirvana Sutras*

Lankavatara Sutra, Chapter 4, from *A Buddhist Bible*

Lotus Sutra 3 from *The Lotus of the Wonderful Law*

Sutra of Hui Neng 1 from *The Diamond Sutra & The Sutra of Hui Neng*

Taoism: TAO: Chapter 4

Kwang Tze, 5 as quoted in *Oneness* p. 193

TAO: Chapter 6

Confucianism: MEAN

AN: Book 7

Chapter 5 - Our Destiny

KJB: Hebrews 11:6; 2 Corinthians 3:18; 1 John 3:1–2

Christianity: KJB: John 17:20–23, 26; 3:13; Luke 17:20–21; Galatians 4:19; Philippians 2:5–6; John 5:19–20; Philippians 1:19–20; John 14:1–6; 14:7–9; 14:10–14; Matthew 16:27; Philippians 4:13

Islam: QUR'AN: 89:27–28; 87:14–15; 84:6; 29:1–7

Khalifa Ali as quoted in *Oneness* p. 169

Hadith of Suhrawardi as quoted in *Traditions of the Prophet*

Al-Hallaj as quoted in *The World's Religions* p. 262

Judaism: JSB: Leviticus 11:44–45; Jeremiah 31:33–34

KJB: Psalms 107:8–9

JSB: 1 Samuel 10:6

(Talmud) Aboda Zara 20b as quoted in *Treasury of Jewish Quotations*

Hinduism: BG: Chapter 9

Katha Upanishad II, 5 from Vol. 15 *The Sacred Books of the East*

BG: Chapter 10

Vedanta Sutras I, 3, 19 from Vol. 34 *The Sacred Books of the East*

BG: Chapter 9

Buddhism: *The Dhammapada (Muller)* Chapter 25

The Garland Sutra 20 from *The Flower Ornament Scripture: A Translation of the Avatamsaka Sutra*

Sutra of Hui Neng 2 from *The Diamond Sutra & The Sutra of Hui Neng*

The Dhammapada (Byrom), Chapter 12

Lankavatara Sutra, Chapter 11, from *A Buddhist Bible*

The Dhammapada (Byrom), Chapter 25

The Dhammapada (Muller), Chapter 26

Taoism: TAO: Chapters 5, 21

Confucianism: MEAN: (x3)

Chapter 6 – Unity: There Is Only One God

Christianity: KJB: Ephesians 4:4–6; Mark 12:29, 32; 1 John 4:16; 1
    Corinthians 8:4–6; Romans 3:29–30

Islam: QUR'AN: 2:163; 16:22; 22:34

Judaism: JSB: Deuteronomy 6:4; Isaiah 45:5–6; Deuteronomy 10:17

Hinduism: *The Sayings of Sri Ramakrishna*

   Svetasvatara Upanishad, VI, from *The Upanishads, Part II*

   Brihabaranyaka Upanishad I, 4 from *The Upanishads, Part II*

   BG: Chapter 10

Buddhism: *Lankavatara Sutra,* Chapter 4 from *A Buddhist Bible*

   Gautama Buddha as quoted from *The World's Religions* p. 114

Taoism: TAO: Chapters 39; 32; 56

Confucianism: AN: Books 4, 15

Chapter 7 – The Creator: God Is the Creator of all Good Things

Christianity: KJB: Isaiah 65:17–18; Revelation 4:11; Philippians 4:8;
    Galatians 5:22–23; 2 Peter 1:5–8

Islam: QUR'AN: 13:16; 6:1; 14:32–34; 31:20

   Hadith as quoted in *Oneness* p. 165

Judaism: JSB: Genesis 1:27–28, 31; Psalms 19:2; Isaiah 43:7; Psalms
    145:8–12

Hinduism: BG: Chapter 10 (x2)

   The Vishnu Purana, Book I, Chapter 2

   BG: Chapter 16

Buddhism: *Buddha, the Gospel:* The Two Brahmans, The Three
    Characteristics and the Uncreated

   The Dhammapada (Thera) 151

The Gandavyuha Sutra from *The Two Buddhist Books in Mahayana*

The Mahaparinirvana Sutra 259

Taoism: TAO: Chapters 1, 4

Confucianism: AN: Book 17

    MEAN: (x2)

Chapter 8 – Omnipotence: God Is Energy/Light/Sacred Fire

Christianity: KJB: Revelation 19:6; John 1:1–9; 8:12; Matthew 28:18; Mark 10:27

Islam: QUR'AN: 2:20; 66:8; 24:35

Judaism: KJB: 2 Samuel 22:33

    JSB: Ezekiel 1:26–28; Exodus 15:18

Hinduism: *Katha Upanishad II, 5* from *The Upanishads, Part II*

Svatasvatara Upanishad, VI from *The Upanishads, Part II*

    BG: Chapters 15, 11

Buddhism: *Garland Sutra 2, 10* from *The Flower Ornament Scripture: A Translation of the Avatamsaka Sutra*

Taoism: TAO: Chapters 34, 25

Confucianism: MEAN (x2)

Chapter 9 – Omniscience: God Is All-Knowing and Wise

Christianity: KJB: Romans 11:33–36; John 16:30; James 1:5; Hebrews 4:12–13

Islam: QUR'AN: 14:38; 31:34; 24:35

Judaism: JSB: Psalms 139:1–6; Jeremiah 10:12

    KJB: 2 Samuel 14:20

Hinduism: BG: Chapter 13

Svetasvatara Upanishad, VI from *The Upanishads, Part II*

Sankaracharya's Atma Bodha as quoted in *The Portable World Bible,* p. 77

Buddhism: *Saddharma-Pundarika,* Chapter 5

The Surangama Sutra as quoted in *The Teachings of the Compassionate Buddha*

Taoism: TAO: Chapters 16, 10, 23

Confucianism: AN: Book 14

    MEAN

Chapter 10 – Omnipresence: God Is Everywhere

Christianity: KJB: Acts 17:24–28; Isaiah 57:15

Islam: QUR'AN: 4:126; 57:3–4

Judaism: JSB: Psalms 139:7–18; Proverbs 15:3

Hinduism: BG: Chapters 13, 9, 11

Buddhism: *Garland Sutra 37* from *The Flower Ornament Scripture: A Translation of the Avatamsaka Sutra*

Buddha, the Gospel: Conclusion

Taoism: TAO: Chapter 25

The Huai Nan Tzu, The Cosmic Spirit, from *Tao, The Great Luminant: Essays from the Huai Nan Tzu*

Confucianism: MEAN (x2)

Chapter 11 – Forever: God Is Eternal

Christianity: KJB: Romans 1:20; 1 John 5:10–12

Islam: QUR'AN: 3:2; 55:27

Judaism: JSB: Isaiah 57:15; Psalms 102:25–29

Hinduism: *Svetasvatara Upanishad, VI* from *The Upanishads, Part II*

BG: Chapter 10

Buddhism: *The Dhammapada (Muller),* On Earnestness, Flowers
   The Mahaparinirvana, 220 from *The Mahaparinirvana Sutra*

Taoism; TAO: Chapters 4, 14

   Confucianism: MEAN (x2)

Part II

KJB: Luke 11:9–10

Chapter 12 – Faith & Hope

Christianity: KJB: Hebrews 11:1, 3, 6; Mark 9:23; Matthew 14:25–31

Islam: QUR'AN: 2:256–257; 10:9–10; 58:22; 19:96

Judaism: JSB: Psalms 125:1; 31:22–25

Hinduism: *Bhagavad Gita,* Chapter 4, as quoted in *The Portable World Bible,* p. 64

   BG: Chapter 9

   Katha Upanishad II, 6 from *The Upanishads, Part II*

Buddhism: *Buddha, the Gospel:* Walking on Water

   Sutta Nipata 1146 from *Buddhist Texts Through the Ages*

Taoism: *Laotzu's Tao and Wu Wei,* Chapter 23

   TAO: Chapter 17

Confucianism: *Li Ki (The Book of Rites),* Part II, Book 45; Part II, Book 22

Chapter 13 – Praise & Gratitude

Christianity: KJB: Luke 17:11–19; 1 Thessalonians 5:18; 1 Timothy 4:4–5; Revelation 4:2, 6, 8–11

Islam: QUR'AN: 1:1–3; 39:7; 40:61, 64

Judaism: JSB: Psalms 100:1–5; 1 Chronicles 16:8–34

Hinduism: BG: Chapter 9 (x2)

Buddhism: *The Dhammapada (Byrom)*, Chapter 25

    Anguttara Nikaya, i.61 from *Gradual Sayings*

Taoism: TAO: Chapters 51, 32

Confucianism: AN: Book 16

    MEAN

Chapter 14 – Prayer and Meditation

Unveiled Mysteries, pp. 11–12

Christianity: KJB: Matthew 6:5–13; 7:7–11; 1 Timothy 4:15

Islam: QUR'AN: 29:45; 2:186; 40:60

Judaism: JSB: Isaiah 38:1–8; 2 Chronicles 6:29–33; Psalms 19:15

Hinduism: BG: Chapters 8, 9

    Svatasvatara Upanishad 2.3 as quoted in *Oneness,* p. 203

Buddhism: *Dhammapada (Thera) 282*

    Garland Sutra 11 from *The Flower Ornament Scripture: A Translation of the Avatamsaka Sutra*

Taoism: TAO: Chapters 43, 3

Confucianism: AN: Books 7, 17

Chapter 15 – Humility

KJB: Proverbs 16:18; John 15:4–5

Christianity: KJB: Matthew 18:1–4; 23:8–9; James 4:6; 1 Peter 5:5–6; Colossians 3:12–13

Islam: QUR'AN: 25:63; 2:45–46; 7:55; 7:205–206

Judaism: JSB: Proverbs 15:33

KJB: Micah 6:8

JSB: Job 22:26–29; Proverbs 16:18–19

Hinduism: *The Bhagavad Gita (Prab)*, Chapter 13, from *The Song of God: Bhagavad-Gita*

The Laws of Manu 2.162

Srimad Bhagavatam 11.4

Buddhism: *The Sutta Nipata* 205–206

The Dhammapada (Thera), 63

The Precious Garland, 406–412, from *The Buddhism of Tibet*

Taoism: TAO: Chapters 30, 39, 66

Confucianism: AN: Books 5, 13

Chapter 16 – Loving The God In You

Christianity: KJB: Ephesians 3:14–19; 1 John 4:12–13, 16; Ephesians 5:28–30; John 15:4–12; Luke 17:21

Islam: QUR'AN: 13:27–28

Forty Hadith of an-Nawawi 38 as quoted in *World Scripture*, p. 152

Hadith of Suhrawardi from *Traditions of the Prophet*

QUR'AN: 50:16

Nahjul Balagha, Sermon 54 from *Nahjul Balagha of Hazrat Ali*

Judaism: JSB: Leviticus 19:17–18; Deuteronomy 6:5; Isaiah 26:8–9; 57:15

KJB: Exodus 3:13–14

Hinduism: *The Bhagavad Gita (Easwaran)*, Chapter 8

Mundaka Upanishad 2.2:1–2 from *The Upanishads (Easwaran)*

Isha Upanishad 15–16 from *The Upanishads (Nikhilananda)*

BG: Chapter 6

Svetasvatara Upanishad 1:11–12 from *The Spiritual Heritage of India*

Svetasvatara Upanishad 1:11–12 from *The Upanishads, Part II*

Buddhism: *The Dhammapada (Byrom)*, Chapter 12

The Dhammapada (Thera), 166

Lotus Sutra 10, from *The Lotus of the Wonderful Law*

The Mahaparinirvana Sutra, 259

The Dhammapada (Thera), 160

Taoism: TAO: Chapter 72

Wu Wei, Chapter 1, as quoted in *Laotzu's Tao and Wu Wei*

Confucianism: MEAN

AN: Book 20

Mencius, Chapter 21, from Volume 2 of *The Chinese Classics*

Chapter 17 – Inner Peace

KJB: Psalms 46:10

Christianity: KJB: John 20:19, 21, 26; Philippians 4:7; Luke 2:13–14; Romans 14:17–19; Matthew 5:9; James 3:17–18; 1 Peter 3:10–11

Islam: QUR'AN: 6:126–127; 10:9–10; 49:10; 10:25; 2:248; 48:4

Judaism: JSB: Isaiah 32:17–18; Proverbs 3:13–17; Psalms 119:165; Isaiah 57:1–2

Hinduism: *The Bhagavad Gita (Easwaran)*, Chapter 2

The Bhagavad Gita (Prab), Chapter 18

Atharva Veda, 19.9.14 from *Mantramanjari: The Vedic Experience*

Buddhism: *The Dhammapada (Thera)*, 82; 201

The Sutta Nipata, 919–920

Taoism: TAO: Chapters 16, 31, 45

Confucianism: AN: Books 7, 9

Chapter 18 – Perfection & Purity

Christianity: KJB: Matthew 5:44; John 17:21–23; Luke 6:40; Ephesians 4:11–13

Islam: QUR'AN: 87:14–15; 91:1–9; 91:1–9 (note by translator Maulana Muhammad Ali)

Judaism: JSB: Psalms 24:3–5

    KJB: Deuteronomy 18:13; Genesis 17:1; 1 Kings 8:61; 2 Chronicles 16:9; Psalms 37:37

Hinduism: *Svetasvatara Upanishad,* 3:12, from *The Upanishads (Nikhilananda)*

    BG: Chapters 14; 8

    Katha Upanishad, 1.2:20–21, from *The Spiritual Heritage of India*

    Mundaka Upanishad, 3.1.5, from *The Upanishads (Nikhilananda)*

Buddhism: *The Sutta-Nipata,* Part III, from *The Sacred Books of the East,* Volume 10, Part 2

    The Dhammapada (Muller), Chapter 1

    The Dhammapada (Thera), 183

    The Dhammapada (Muller), Chapter 18

Taoism: TAO: Chapters 10, 28

Confucianism: *Li Ki (The Book of Rites),* Part II, Book 28

    AN: Books 7, 12

Chapter 19 – Moderation

Christianity: KJB: Philippians 4:5; 1 Corinthians 9:25; 2 Peter 1:5–7; Titus 1:7–8

Islam: QUR'AN: 7:31

    Hadith, as quoted from *Oneness,* p. 106

Judaism: JSB: Psalms 10:3; Proverbs 23:19–21; 30:7–9

Hinduism: BG: Chapter 6

Srimad Bhagavatam 11:7 from *Srimad Bhagavatam: The Wisdom of God*

The Mahabharata, Book 5, Section 33

Buddhism: *Buddha, the Gospel:* The Sermon at Benares

The Dhammapada (Muller), Chapters 25, 19

Taoism: *The Book of Lieh-Tzu,* Book II

TAO: Chapters 29, 44

Confucianism: AN: Book 11

Mencius, Chapter 16, from Volume 2 of *The Chinese Classics*

Chapter 20 – Vigilance

Christianity: KJB: 1 Peter 5:8–10; 1 Thessalonians 5:5–6; 2 Corinthians 10:1–5

Islam: QUR'AN: 11:93

Hadith, as quoted in *Oneness,* p. 178

QUR'AN: 17:41

Hadith, as quoted in *Oneness,* p. 97

Judaism: JSB: Proverbs 15:26, 28; 4:23–27; Psalms 130:5–6; Proverbs 21:2–3

Hinduism: BG: Chapter 18; 6

Katha Upanishad 2.3.11 from *The Upanishads (Nikhilananda)*

Buddhism: *The Dhammapada (Muller),* Chapter 3

The Dhammapada, as quoted from *Foundations of Buddhism,* p. 53

The Dhammapada (Muller), Chapter 22

Taoism: TAO: Chapters 65, 33

Confucianism: AN: Books 14, 15

MEAN

Chapter 21 – Health Maintenance

Christianity: KJB: James 2:14–16; Ephesians 5:28–30; Romans 12:1; Philippians 1:20; 1 Corinthians 6:19–20; 3:16–17; Matthew 6:22–23

Islam: QUR'AN 2:196

The Alchemy of Happiness, Chapter 3

QUR'AN: 5:6

Judaism: JSB: Leviticus 11:45–47

KJB: Isaish 58:5–10; Proverbs 4:20–27

The Babylonian Talmud, Taanit, llb

Hinduism: BG: Chapter 17

The Rig Veda, Book 1, Hymn XXIII

Buddhism: *Buddha, The Gospel:* The Sermon at Benares, The Jealousy of Devadatta

The Millindapanha, 90 from *Buddhism in Translations*

Taoism: TAO: Chapters 71, 12

Confucianism: AN: Book 10

Shu King, Part IV, Book 8, from Volume 3 of *The Sacred Books of the East*

Chapter 22 – The Golden Rule

Christianity: KJB: Matthew 7:12; Luke 6:31; Matthew 7:36–40

Islam: *Forty Hadith of an-Nawawi,* 13 from *The Moslem World* 29, no. 2

QUR'AN: 2:112

Hadith of Muslim, from *Sayings of Muhammad*

QUR'AN: 4:36

Judaism: JSB: Leviticus 19:18

Talmud, Shabbat 31a, from *The Babylonian Talmud*

Hinduism: *The Mahabharata,* Anusasana Parva 113.8, from *The Dhammapada (Radhakrishnan)* (listed under Buddhism)

The Hitopadesa, as quoted in *The Portable World Bible,* p. 79

Brihadaranyaka Upanishad, IV, 5 from *The Upanishads, Part II*

Buddhism: *The Udana,* Chapter 5

The Sutta Nipata, 705

Taoism: *The Su Shu,* Part III, from *Taoist Texts*

TAO: Chapter 81

Confucianism: AN: Books 15, 12

MEAN

Chapter 23 – Patience

Christianity: KJB: James 1:2–4; Luke 21:19; Revelation 14:12; James 5:7–11

Islam: QUR'AN: 40:55; 2:153; 103:2–3; 16:126–127

Judaism: JSB: Lamentations 3:25–28; Psalms 37:1–7; Ecclesiastes 7:8–9

Hinduism: *The Srimad Devi Bhagawatam,* Book 5, Chapter 4

The Mahabharata, Book 12, Section CLXII

Buddhism: *Lankavatara Sutra,* Chapter 9, from *A Buddhist Bible*

The Sutta Nipata, Part II, from Volume 10 of *The Sacred Books of the East*

The Dhammapada (Muller), Chapter 14

Taoism: TAO: Chapter 64

T'ai-Shang Kan-Ying P'ien, The Spirit of the Hearth

Confucianism: AN: Books 15, 9, 13

Chapter 24 – Harmlessness

Christianity: KJB: Matthew 10:16; Philippians 2:13–15; 1 Peter
3:12–14; Matthew 26:51–52

Islam: *Hadith,* as quoted in *Oneness,* p. 23

QUR'AN: 4:93; 5:32; 2:203–206

Judaism: JSB: Proverbs 3:29–30; Leviticus 24:17–22

Hinduism: *Mahabharata,* Shanti Parva 262.5–6, from *Sourcebook in
Indian Philosophy*

The Laws of Manu 2:161

BG: Chapter 12

Buddhism: *The Dhammapada* as quoted in *Oneness,* p. 22

The Dhammapada (Muller), Chapter 10

The Sutta Nipata 705

Taoism: TAO: Chapters 31, 42

Confucianism: AN: Book 12

Li Ki (The Book of Rites), Part I, Book 7

Chapter 25 – Charity and Helping Others

Christianity: KJB: 1 Peter 4:8–10; Galatians 6:1–2; Philippians 2:4;
Matthew 20:25–27; 5:42–44; LUKE 6:38

Islam: QUR'AN: 2:177; 30:38–39; 70:19–25; 57:18

Hadith of Bukhari, as quoted in *World Scripture,* p. 688

Hadith of Bukhari 3.763

Judaism: JSB: Psalms 112:4–9; Proverbs 19:17

Hinduism: *Rig Veda* Book 10, Hymn CXVII

BG: Chapters 3; 16

Rig Veda 1.125.5, from *Mantramanjari: The Vedic Experience*

Buddhism: *The Dhammapada (Thera)* 177

Sutra of Forty-two Sections 10, from *A General Explanation of the
Buddha Speaks: The Sutra in Forty-two Sections*
Sutta-Pitaka, as quoted in *Oneness,* p. 138
Taoism: TAO: Chapters 77, 81
Confucianism: AN: Books 7, 6, 17

Chapter 26 – Loving Speech and Kindness

Christianity: 1 Peter 3:8–12; Ephesians 4:31–32; 1 Timothy 5:1–2;
Colossians 4:6
Islam: QUR'AN: 2:262–264; 4:86; 2:83; 107:1–7; 4:148–149; 25:11–12,
14–15
Hadith of Baihaqi from *Sayings of Muhammad*
Hadith of Bukhari from *Muhammad and the Islamic Tradition*
Judaism: KJB: Proverbs 31:26, 28
JSB: Proverbs 18:19–21
Sayings of the Jewish Fathers (Pirqe Aboth) 1.2
Hinduism: *The Bhagavad Gita,* Chapter 7, as quoted in *Oneness,* p. 132
BG: Chapter 12
Buddhism: *The Dhammapada (Thera)* 368, 376
The Dhammapada (Muller) 133–134
Taoism: TAO: Chapters 8, 49
Confucianism: AN: Books 13, 14, 5

Chapter 27 – Forgiveness and Mercy

Christianity: KJB: Matthew 6:12–15; Luke 6:35–36; Matthew 5:43–48;
Mark 11:25–26; Matthew 18:23–35
Islam: QUR'AN: 7:199; 42:36–40, 43; 64:14
Hadith of Baihaqi from *Sayings of Muhammad*
Judaism: JSB: Jeremiah 31:34; Isaiah 1:18–20; 55:6–7

KJB: Micah 7:18–19

Hinduism: *The Mahabharata,* Book 3, Section XXIX

   BG: Chapter 9

Buddhism: *Buddha, The Gospel:* The Re-establishment of Concord; The Patient Elephant

Taoism: TAO: Chapters 63, 67

Confucianism: MEAN

   AN: Book 12

   Li Ki (The Book of Rites), Part I, Book 7

Chapter 28 – Honesty and Truthfulness

Christianity: John 8:31–32; 2 Corinthians 13:7–8; Philippians 4:8; Hebrews 13:18;1 Timothy 2:1–2; 1 John 1:8–10

Islam: QUR'AN: 17:35; 83:10–15; 39:3; 39:32–34; 16:116; 14:24–27; 61:2–3

   Hadith of Muslim from *Sahih Muslim*

Judaism: JSB: Exodus 20:13; Zechariah 8:16–17

   KJB: Proverbs 3:3–4

   JSB: Proverbs 12:18–22

Hinduism: *Narada Dharma Sutra* 1.210, from *Sacred Books of the East,* Volume 33

   Mundaka Upanishad 3.1.4–6, from *The Upanishads, Part II*

   Taittiriyaka Upanishad I, 11, from *The Upanishads, Part II*

Buddhism: *The Dhammapada (Muller),* Chapters 19, 22, 13

Taoism: *The Book of Recompenses* from *Taoist Texts*

   T'ai-Shang Kan-Ying P'ien, A Description of Evil-Doers

Confucianism: AN: Books 2, 15

Chapter 29 – Respect for and Non-Judgment of Others

Christianity: KJB: Romans 14:10–13; James 4:11–12; Matthew 7:1–5; Romans 2:1–3; Luke 6:37

Islam: QUR'AN: 3:84; 10:109; 4:58; 16:90

  Hadith from *Traditions of the Prophet*

Judaism: *Mishnah,* Abot 2.5, from *The Living Talmud: The Wisdom of the Fathers*

  JSB: Jeremiah 22:3; Deuteronomy 1:9–17; Leviticus 19:15–17

Hinduism: BG: Chapter 4

  Shrimad Bhagavatam 4.4.19, as quoted in *Oneness,* p. 43

  The Garuda Purana 112

Buddhism: *Buddha, the Gospel:* The Patient Elephant

  The Dhammapada (Thera), 252–253

  The Sutra of Hui Neng 2, from *The Diamond Sutra & The Sutra of Hui Neng*

Taoism: *Yin Chih Wen*

  The Book of Recompenses from *Taoist Texts*

  TAO: Chapter 47

Confucianism: AN: Books 12, 7

(From Introduction to Section IV):

Islam: *Hadith,* from *The Sacred Books and Early Literature of the East,* Volume VI, edited byCharles F. Home (New York: Parke, Austin, & Lipscomb, 1917)

Chapter 30 – Your Perfect Vision

Christianity: KJB: Ephesians 4:1, 3–8, 11–14, 5:17; 2 Timothy 1:7–9

Islam: QUR'AN: 2:148; 5:15–16

Judaism: KJB: Proverbs 29:18

    JSB: Joel 3:1

Hinduism: BG: Chapter 3

    The Crest-Jewel of Wisdom, Free Even in Life

    Srimad Bhagavatam 11.2, from *Srimad Bhagavatam: The Wisdom of God*

Buddhism: The Dhammapada (Byrom) Chapters 12; 22

Taoism: *Huai Nan Tzu:* Life and Soul; Response of Matter to the Cosmic Spirit; The Cosmic Spirit; Endeavour and Duty; all four quotations from *Tao, The Great Luminant: Essays from the Huai Nan Tzu*

Confucianism: AN: Books 19; 12

Chapter 31 – Divine Passion, Zeal and Enthusiasm

Christianity: KJB: Colossians 3:23; Titus 2:11–14; Galatians 4:18; Revelation 3:15–19; 1 Peter 1:22; 1 Corinthians 14:8

Islam: QUR'AN: 3:113–114; 5:48; 92:14–21; 4:114

Judaism: JSB: Ecclesiastes 9:10; Isaiah 59:17

Hinduism: *The Ramayana,* Book IV, Canto I from *The Ramayan of Valmiki*

    Chandogya Upanishad 7.22 from *Mantramanjari: The Vedic Experience*

Buddhism: *The Dhammapada (Muller)* 313; 282

    The Questions of King Milinda Book VII, Chapter 2.18, from Volume 36 *The Sacred Books of the East*

Taoism: *T'ai-Shang Kan-Ying P'ien,* The Spirit of the Hearth

    Huai Nan Tzu, Endeavour and Duty, from *Tao, The Great Luminant*

Confucianism: MEAN (x2)

    AN: Book 7

Chapter 32 – Knowledge and Wisdom

Christianity: KJB: James 1:5–7; 2 Peter 1:1–8; Luke 11:52; Philippians 1:9–11; 1 Thessalonians 4:9–12

Islam: QUR'AN: 2:269

Hadith as quoted from *Oneness,* p. 155

QUR'AN: 58:11; 5:83

Hadith of Baihaqi from *Sayings of Muhammad*

Judaism: JSB: Genesis 2:15–17; 3:4–5, 22; Proverbs 24:3–5; Ecclesiastes 7:19–20; Proverbs 28:1–2; 4:5–8; 16:16

Hinduism: BG: Chapters 10, 7, 4

Buddhism: *The Sutta Nipata* 261

The Dhammapada (Muller) Chapters 25, 18, 3

Taoism: TAO: Chapters 53, 41, 46, 49

Confucianism: AN: Books 1, 2, 8

Chapters 33 – Effort, Discipline and Persistence

Christianity: KJB: Romans 2:6–10; Galatians 6:9; Romans 7:19–25; John 8:29, 31–32; Acts 14:22; Colossians 1:21–24, 27–29; 2 Timothy 4:6–7; Luke 13:24; Romans 5:3–5

Islam: QUR'AN: 84:6; 29:2–7

Hadith of Muslim from *Sahih Muslim*

QUR'AN: 47:31; 3:142; 61:11

Hadith, as quoted in *Oneness,* p. 97

Judaism: JSB: Proverbs 15:31–32; 4:10–14; 21:5; 3:1–4

Hinduism: BG: Chapter 6

The Laws of Manu 9.300

BG: Chapter 12

Matsya Purana 221.2 from *The Matsya Puranam*

BG: Chapters 6, 6

Srimad Bhagavatam 11.7 from *Srimad Bhagavatam: The Wisdom of God*

BG: Chapters 15, 9

Buddhism: *The Dhammapada (Muller)*, 361–362

Buddha, the Gospel: Entering Into Nirvana

The Sutra of Hui Neng 2, from *The Diamond Sutra & The Sutra of Hui Neng*

The Dhammapada (Muller), 24–27

Taoism: TAO: Chapters 33, 63, 62

Confucianism: AN: Books 9, 12, 15

Part IV: Commentary

KJB: Philippians 4:8

Unveiled Mysteries, pg. 208

Margaret Mead quote from www.quotationspage.com/quote/33522.html

KJB: Matthew 18:19–20

Seven Great Religions, pp. 230–231

KJB: John 10:33–36

Ye Are Gods, pp. 176–177. Reprinted from *Ye Are Gods* by Annalee Skarin, DeVorss Publications, 9780875167183, www.devorss.com.

Appendix B: "Sonship" in Islam

QUR'AN: 6:101; 5:18; 39:4; 6:83–88

Glossary

Abide (*v.*): To stay; to continue in a place; to have one's abode: to dwell; to sojourn.

Abraham (*n.*): A founding father in the Bible, Torah, and Qur'an whom Christian, Jewish and Islamic believers view as the patriarch of the Israelites, Arabs, and Edomite peoples.

Abrahamic (*adj.*): Pertaining to Abraham. "Abrahamic religions" refers to the three religions that incorporate the Old Testament, specifically Judaism, Christianity, and Islam.

Allah (*n.*): The name of the Supreme Being, in the religion of Islam.

Amends (*n. sing. & pl.*): Compensation for a loss or injury: recompense; reparation.

Analects (*n.*): Selected miscellaneous written passages.

Angel (*n.*): A spiritual, celestial being, superior to man in power and intelligence. In the Scriptures the angels appear as God's messengers.

Approbation (*n.*): Approval; commendation; praise.

Arhat (*n.*): One who has attained enlightenment, or realized Nirvana.

Arjuna (*n.*): A central figure in Hindu mythology. A master archer, Arjuna was averse to participating in the great battle between his family, the Pandavas, and their adversaries, the Kauravas. His charioteer, Lord Krishna, changed his mind in their dialogue about courage, duty, the soul, and the nature of life.

Ascetic (*n.*): A person who lives an austerely simple life in self-denial of the normal pleasures of life, often for the purpose of spiritual discipline. (*adj.*): Extremely rigid in self-denial and devotions; austere; severe.

Attune (*v.*): to bring into harmony; to adjust to the same frequency.

Austerities (*n.*): Extreme rigors or strictness; harsh disciplines; severities of life.

Beneficent (*adj.*): Doing or producing good; performing acts of kindness and charity.

Bhagavad Gita (*n.*): Revered as sacred by most Hindu traditions, it is a Sanskrit text that is part of the Mahabharata epic. It contains 700 verses written in a poetic form that is traditionally chanted. It means "the Song of the Divine One," and contains a conversation between Arjuna and his chariot driver Krishna, just before the start of a huge battle. Krishna addresses Arjuna's concerns about duty, morals, and the loss of life that is about to occur. In it, Krishna is revealed as the Supreme Being. See Arjuna.

Bhikkhu (*n.*): A fully ordained male Buddhist monastic. One who practices a disciplined, meditative, and simple lifestyle which can result in attaining Nirvana.

Bhikshu (*n.*): See Bhikkhu.

Bible (*n.*): The book which is made up of the writings accepted by Christians as of divine origin and authority, whether such writings be in the original language, or translated; the Scripture of the Old and New Testaments. Also, a book containing the sacred writings of any religion; as, the Qur'an may be called the Islamic Bible.

Bliss (*n.*): Gladness; the highest degree of happiness; blessedness; exalted felicity; heavenly joy.

Brahma (*n.*): The creative force of Brahman (God). The One First Cause. Also, one of the triad of Hindu gods consisting of Brahma the Creator, Vishnu the Preserver, and Shiva the Transformer/Destroyer.

Brahman (*n.*): God. Also, a person of the highest or sacerdotal (priest) caste among the Hindus.

Bramana (*n.*): An ascetic.

Buddha (*n.*): A religious teacher of the Buddhists, esp. Siddhartha Gautama, the founder of Buddhism. The title of an incarnation of self-abnegation, virtue, and wisdom.

Buddhism (*n.*): The religion based upon the doctrine originally taught by Siddhartha Gautama, recognized by Buddhists as the Supreme Buddha, "the awakened or enlightened," in the sixth century B.C., and adopted as a religion by the greater part of the inhabitants of Central and Eastern Asia and the Indian Islands.

Christ (*n.*): The Anointed; an appellation given to Jesus, the Savior. It is synonymous with the Hebrew word "Messiah." The Universal Christ is the universal consciousness of God that went forth as the Word, the Logos that God used to fire the pattern of His Divine Identity in His sons and daughters and to write His laws in their inward parts. Each individualization of the Universal Christ is unique, because each individual was ordained by God to reflect in all of its glory a particular facet of the Universal Christ. Also, simply "God in man."

Christianity (*n.*): The religion of Christians; the system of doctrines and precepts taught by Christ.

Conceit (*n.*): An undeserved high idea of one's self; vanity.

Confucianism (*n.*): The system of doctrines and precepts taught by Confucius and his disciples, with an emphasis on political morality.

Confucius (*n.*): Living 500 years before Christ, he was a respected social philosopher, whose work has influenced China, Korea, Japan, and Vietnam. His teachings focused on morality, justice, sincerity, and relationships.

Conscience (*n.*): The faculty, power, or inward principle which decides as to the character of one's own actions, purposes, and affections, warning against and condemning that which is wrong, and approving and prompting that which is right; the moral faculty passing judgment on one's self; the moral sense.

Consciousness (*n.*): The state of being conscious; knowledge of one's own existence, condition, sensations, mental operations, acts, etc. Awareness of one's thoughts, feelings, and senses.

Contemplation (*n.*): The act of the mind in considering with attention; continued attention of the mind to a particular subject; meditation; musing; study. The act of looking at all sides or perspectives of something.

Contrite (*adj.*): Deeply sorrowful for sin because it is displeasing to God; humbly and thoroughly penitent.

Covenant (*n.*): The promises of God as revealed in the Scriptures, conditioned on certain terms on the part of man, as obedience, repentance, faith, etc.

Death (*v.*): The cessation of all vital phenomena without capability of resuscitation, either in animals or plants. An end to physical embodiment, not an end to life.

Dhamma (*n.*): see Dharma.

Dhammapada (*n.*): A Buddhist book of 423 verses in 26 categories, containing quotations from Gautama Buddha mostly on morals and ethics.

Dharma (*n.*): In Buddhism, the Teachings of the Buddha. Also, the fundamental principles of existence, both universal and individual. Universal law. The order in life and nature. It literally means "that which upholds or supports." Also, an individual's duty. The proper way of living.

Disciple (*n.*): One who receives instruction from another; a scholar; a learner; especially, a follower who has learned to believe in the truth of the doctrine of his teacher; an adherent in doctrine; as, the disciples of Plato; the disciples of our Savior.

Divine Self (*n.*): See Higher Self.

Earnest (*adj.*): Serious, ardent in the pursuit of an object; eager to obtain or do, zealous with sincerity; with hearty endeavor; heartfelt; fervent. Used in a good sense; as, earnest prayers.

Edify (*v.*): To instruct and improve, especially in moral and religious knowledge; to teach.

Effulgent (*adj.*): Diffusing a flood of light; shining; luminous; beaming; bright; splendid.

Ego (*n.*): Your awareness of your own identity, as distinct from others or the world. Also, egotism, conceit; an exaggerated sense of self-importance.

Empathize (*v.*): To be aware of, understand, and vicariously experience the thoughts, experience, and feelings of another.

Eulogy (*n.*): A speech or writing in commendation of the character or services of a person, often given for the recently deceased at their funeral.

Faith (*n.*): That which is believed on any subject, whether in science, politics, or religion; especially a system of religious belief of any kind.

Gentile (*n.*): A person from a non-Jewish nation or of a non-Jewish faith.

God (*n.*): The Supreme Being; the eternal and infinite Spirit, the Creator, and the Sovereign of the universe.

Godhead (*n.*): The Deity; God; the Supreme Being. Divine nature or essence.

Gotama Siddhartha (*n.*): see Buddha. A variation of the spelling of Gautama Siddhartha.

Grace (*n.*): The divine favor toward man; the mercy of God, as distinguished from His justice; also, any benefits His mercy imparts; divine love or pardon; a state of acceptance with God; enjoyment of the divine favor. Privilege conferred.

Hadith (*n.*): Originally, oral teachings containing the words and deeds of Muhammad, written down during the eighth and ninth century. Most Muslims view Hadith as containing important supplements to and clarifications of the Qur'an, and providing an important description of the Muslim way of life.

Heaven (*n.*): The abode of bliss; the place or state of the blessed after death. A place of supreme happiness, joy, and tranquility.

Higher Self: Associated with the individual's eternal and divine being; the Divine Self; the Christ Self. As opposed to the lower self associated with ego and imperfection. A term used by several belief systems, which can have various meanings depending on which group uses the term.

Hinduism (*n.*): An ancient religion, it contains a mix of beliefs and traditions, and has no single founder. It includes a vast number of teachings including the Vedas, the Upanishads, the Puranas, and the Mahabharata. It is mostly practiced in India, Nepal, and other southeast Asian countries.

Holy (*adj.*): Divine. Spiritually whole or sound; of unimpaired innocence and virtue; free from sinful affections; pure in heart; godly; acceptable to God; hallowed; sacred.

Humility (*n.*): The state or quality of being humble; freedom from pride and arrogance; a modest estimate of one's own worth; humbleness.

Iniquity (*n.*): Absence of, or deviation from, just dealing; want of rectitude or uprightness; gross injustice; unrighteousness; wickedness; as, the iniquity of bribery; the iniquity of an unjust judge.

Islam (*n.*): Based on the teachings of Muhammad, a seventh century Arab. Islam literally means "submission," as in a complete surrender to God. A practitioner of Islam is known as a Muslim—one who submits to God. It is the second largest religion after Christianity. Muslims believe that God revealed the Qur'an to Muhammad. The Qur'an along with the Hadith, which contains the words and deeds of Muhammad, are the fundamental sources of Islam.

Jesus Christ (*n.*): The central figure of Christianity. A Galilean Jew who was a teacher and healer. A true master, Jesus attained full attunement with God. Among his teachings are instructions on being totally forgiving, totally loving, and that there is no limit to what we can attain with God.

Joy (*n.*): The emotion excited by the acquisition or expectation of good; pleasurable feelings or emotions caused by success, good fortune, and the like; gladness, exhilaration of spirits; delight.

Judaism (*n.*): The religious doctrines and rites of the Jews as enjoined in the laws of Moses.

Karma (*n.*): One's acts considered as fixing one's lot in the future existence. The doctrine of fate as the inflexible result of cause and effect; the theory of inevitable consequence for one's actions.

Krishna (*n.*): The divine Lord expressing the teachings within *The Bhagavad Gita*. The most popular of the Hindu divinities, usually held to be the eighth incarnation of the god Vishnu.

Koran.(*n.*): See "Qur'an."

Light (*n.*): A word of many meanings. When capitalized, it can mean energy; power. It can also mean wisdom, illumination, Christ consciousness.

Logos (*n.*): The divine Word; Christ.

Longsuffering (*n.*): Bearing injuries or provocation for a long time; patient; not easily provoked.

Lord (*n.*): The Supreme Being; Almighty God; The Savior; Jesus Christ; one who has power and authority; a master; a ruler.

Love (*n.*): Due gratitude and reverence to God. Affection; kind feeling; friendship; strong liking or desire; fondness; good will; tenderness; as, the love of brothers and sisters.

Lower self: The unreal self; the human self. The carnal self; the body of desires; an illusion which will pass away. That which breeds everything that harms. The cause of the difference between man and nature. As opposed to the true, real, Christ self which is God in manifestation.

Mara (*n.*): The principal or ruling evil spirit. A female demon who torments people.

Master (*n.*): One who has achieved total mastery of life. A sacred conduit for wisdom; a helper to those who seek self-realization. One who has attained great skill in the use or application of anything. In addition, one who is not necessarily in physical embodiment.

Matter (*n.*): That of which the physical universe and all existent bodies are composed. Substance. As opposed to the non-material world of spirit.

Mean man: Not a noble man. A man of low character.

Mecca (*n.*): An Islamic holy city in Saudi Arabia's Makkah province. Revered by Muslims for being the location of the Masjid al-Haram, the holiest site of Islam. All able-bodied Muslims who can afford it are supposed to visit Mecca at least once in their life.

Meditation (*n.*): The process of engaging in a repetitious or singular activity in the mind to disengage it from its usual thought patterns and to give the mind a rest. This allows the opening of the mind to receive spiritual revelation.

Meekness (*n.*): The quality or state of being meek, mild of temper, not easily provoked, patient under injuries, not vain, not resentful.

Mind (*n.*): The power that conceives, judges, or reasons. Also, the entire spiritual nature.

Muhammad (*n.*): (Mohammed) 570-632, founded the religion of Islam. Muslims consider him to be the last prophet/messenger of God, restoring the original monotheism of Adam, Abraham and other prophets.

Muslim (*n.*): An adherent of the religion of Islam. It literally means "one who submits to God."

Mystic (*n.*): A person who experiences direct intercourse with the divine Spirit, acquiring a knowledge of God and of spiritual things unattainable by the intellect.

Mystical (*adj.*): Pertaining to direct intercourse with Spirit and the acquisition of spiritual blessings that transcend the intellect.

NDE (*n.*): Near death experience. Many who die and are brought back to life remember wonderful experiences, filled with light and a feeling of love. Often they don't want to return to embodiment. Many of those who experience an NDE change their life for the better, and lose their fear of death.

New Testament (*n.*): The final portion of the Christian Bible, written after the Old Testament. The literal translation from the Greek is "The New Covenant." Its original writing occurred between AD 45 and AD 140.

Nibbana (*n.*): See Nirvana.

Nirvana (*n.*): The highest, enduring, transcendental happiness and calmness that flows from enlightenment. Emancipation of the soul from the evils of wordly existence, as by absorption into the divine.

Non-attachment (*n.*): Not to cherish any desire for or aversion to any particular thing or idea. In Buddhism, it is the characteristic of mind-essence.

Ode (*n.*): A short poetical composition to be set to music or sung; a lyric poem; esp., a poem characterized by sustained noble sentiment and appropriate dignity of style.

Old Testament (*n.*): The first section of the Christian Bible, which also consists of the New Testament. Its contents vary to a degree by Christian denomination. It is nearly identical with the Hebrew Bible.

Omni (*comb. form*): A combining form denoting all, universally, every, everywhere; as in omnipotent, all-powerful.

Omnipotence (*n.*): The state of being omnipotent; almighty power; hence, one who is omnipotent; the Deity.

Omnipresence (*n.*): Present in all places at the same time; present universally or without bounds; ubiquitous; as, the omnipresent Jehovah.

Omniscience (*n.*): The quality or state of having universal knowledge, knowing all things, being infinitely knowing or wise; as, the omniscient God.

Pious (*adj.*): Of or pertaining to piety; reverential; dutiful; religious; devout; godly.

Power (*n.*): Ability to act, regarded as latent or inherent; the faculty of doing or performing something; capacity for action or performance;

capability of producing an effect, whether physical or moral; potency; might; as, a man of great power. Strength; force.

Prayer (*v.*): The act of addressing supplication to God; the offering of adoration, confession, supplication, and thanksgiving to the Supreme Being; as, public prayer; secret prayer.

Pride (*n.*): The quality or state of being proud; inordinate self-esteem; an unreasonable conceit of one's own superiority in talents, beauty, wealth, rank, etc., which manifests itself in lofty airs, distance, reserve, and often in contempt of others.

Prodigal (*adj.*): Given to extravagant expenditure; expending money or other things without necessity; recklessly or viciously profuse; lavish; wasteful; not frugal or economical; as, a prodigal man; the prodigal son; prodigal giving; prodigal expenses.

Propriety (*n.*): The quality or state of being proper; suitableness to an acknowledged or correct standard or rule; consonance with established principles, rules, or custom; appropriateness; as, propriety of behavior, language, manners, etc.

Purlieus (*n.*): The outer portion of any place; an adjacent district; environs; neighborhood.

Qur'an (*n.*): Also known as the Koran, it is the most important religious text of Islam. It is considered by Muslims to contain divine direction for mankind, and contains the revelations given by Allah (God) to Muhammad over a period of 23 years. It contains 114 chapters of varying lengths, known as "suras."

Righteousness (*n.*): The quality or state of being righteous; holiness; purity; uprightness; rectitude.

Sacred (*adj.*): Holy; consecrated; not profane or common. Designated or exalted by a divine sanction; possessing the highest title to obedience, honor, reverence, or veneration; entitled to extreme reverence; venerable.

Self (*n.*): The "True Self," or the "Observing Self," consciousness; pure awareness. It can also mean the ego, or superficial self; the personality.

Shaddai (*n.*): The name used for God by Abraham, Isaac, and Jacob, according to Exodus 6:2, 3.

Sheol (*n.*): The place of departed spirits; Hades.

Shiva (*n.*): One of the three primary aspects of God in the Trimurti system of Hinduism, where Brahma is creator, Vishnu is maintainer or preserver, and Shiva is transformer or destroyer.

Shramana (*n.*): A wandering, ascetic monk. In Sanskrit, "one who strives." One who meditates and does certain acts of austerity or mortification.

Spirit (*n.*): Life, or living substance, considered independently of corporeal existence; an intelligence conceived of apart from any physical organization or embodiment; vital essence, force, or energy, as distinct from matter. The intelligent, non-material and immortal part of man; the soul, in distinction from the body in which it resides.

Spiritual (*adj.*): Of or pertaining to the soul or its affections as influenced by the Spirit; controlled and inspired by the divine Spirit; proceeding from the Holy Spirit; pure; holy; divine; heavenly-minded; opposed to carnal.

Suchness (*n.*): Non-emptiness. The highest reality. Similar, but not identical to, soul and mind. A main concept in Buddhism and Hinduism.

Talmud (*n.*): The body of the Jewish civil and canonical law not comprised in the Pentateuch. The body of Jewish tradition comprising the Mishnah (the written record of oral instruction) and Gemara (commentary).

Tanakh (*n.*): An acronym that signifies the Hebrew Bible.

Tao (*n.*): A Chinese character often meaning "the Way." It can take on other meanings depending on its usage and other key words associated with it.

Taoism (*n.*): Religious and philosophical traditions and concepts of China, with an emphasis on unity, and nature. Taoism can have different meanings for different groups, often having themes of naturalness, peace, detachment, flexibility, and unity.

Tathagata (*n.*): The Buddha mind-nature hidden within every being. The mind of clear and pure reflection. Sometimes Gautama Buddha used this term to refer to himself.

Temperance (*n.*): Habitual moderation in regard to the indulgence of the natural appetites and passions; restrained or moderate indulgence; moderation; as, temperance in eating and drinking. Patience, calmness.

Tenet (*n.*): Any opinion, principle, dogma, belief, or doctrine, which a person holds or maintains as true; as, the tenets of Plato or of Cicero.

Torah (*n.*): In the Jewish tradition, the five books of Moses: Genesis, Exodus, Leviticus, Numbers, and Deuteronomy.

Tranquility (*n.*): The quality or state of being tranquil, calm, quiet, undisturbed, peaceful.

Transcend (*v.*): To rise above; to surmount, as, lights in the heavens transcending the region of the clouds. To pass over; to go beyond; to exceed.

Transmute (*v.*): To change from one nature, form, or substance, into another; to transform.

Truth (*n.*): A true thing; a verified fact; a true statement or proposition; an established principle, fixed law, or the like; as, the great truth of morals. Righteousness; true religion. The real state of things; fact; verity; reality. Exact accordance with that which is, or has been, or shall be.

Vedas (*n.*): A large body of texts that are the oldest in Hinduism. "Veda" means knowledge or wisdom. Categorized into four classes: the Samhitas, Brahmanas, Aranyakas, and the Upanishads.

Virtue (*n.*): Moral excellence; integrity of character; purity of soul.

Vishnu (*n.*): A divinity of the modern Hindu trinity. He is regarded as the preserver, while Brahma is the creator, and Shiva the transfomer/destroyer of the creation.

Wisdom (*n.*): Insight; good sense. The quality of being wise: knowledge, and the capacity to make good use of it; knowledge of the best ends and the best means; discernment and judgment; discretion, sagacity. Being enlightened, learned.

Yoga (*n.*): Outside of India, yoga usually refers to the practice of postures for health purposes, or the practice of Hatha Yoga. In Hinduism, disciplines of meditation and asceticism which promote spiritual experience and divine insight.

Zeal (*n.*): Passionate ardor in the pursuit of one's goals; eagerness in favor of a person or cause; ardent and active interest; engagedness; enthusiasm; fervor.

Index

F

faith, 142-156 passim; and acquiring knowledge and wisdom, 316; and being children of God, 66-67; and divine passion, 308; and hope in God, 341, 365; and inner vision, 300-301; and maintaining good health, 226; and pleasing Him, 73; and the fruit of the spirit, 16; and the importance of inner peace, 195-196; and the importance of vigilance, 217; and virtue, 211; and wisdom, 321-322; continue in the, 327-328; dwell in your hearts by, 27-28, 182; fruit of the Spirit is, 103; is power, 351-352; is Yours, 43; of Abraham, 18; of Jesus, 57; one, 93-94; prayer and, 5; reality of, 297; the unity of the, 203; trying of your, 244; unsteady, 221; fasting, 227, 233

forgiveness: a kind word with, 264; and mercy, 269-270, 272, 275; asking for, 179, 201; for being wronged, 26-27; for our errors, 48; is a characteristic of beings, 96; teachings about, 60, 112; the God quality of, 52, 90, 106, 259; the virtue of, 247

fulfillment, 1, 6, 26, 57, 168, 188, 297, 298, 300, 308, 325, 373

fundamentalist Christians, 60

G

Gentile(s), 94, 256, 326, 328

God, 1-5; acting within you and your world, 351; and Divine Light and freedom, 348; and dominion in our world, 315; and helpful affirmations, 348-349; and idolatry, 358; and keys to happiness, 346-348; and knowing our true identity, 235; and loving ourselves, 179-180; and negative feelings, 287; and seeing the Good in others, 237; and The "Bad" Times in Life, 356; and The 11 Principles of Understanding, 338-340, 363-364; and The 22 Responsibilities for Loving Living, 341-344, 365-367; and the JOY AND EMPOWERMENT CREED, 349-350; and The

Union of Religions, 351-352; and universal truths, 361; and Wisdom for You, 356-357; children of, 369-371; Consciousness personified within us, 345-345; getting "high" with, 225; in General Prayer Guidelines, 161-162; General Meditation Guidelines, 162; inner peace and, 193; looks at our intent and results, 201-202; self-control and, 325; self-forgiveness and, 269; tests us, 202; *Ye Are Gods* (Annalee Skarin), 359-360. *See also* Bible; Creator

God in you, 90, 142, 342

Godhead, 31, 58, 135, 179, 301

Golden Age, 353, 361, 373

Golden Rule, 237-242 passim, 247, 343, 355

Gospel of Thomas, 56

Gospel of Mary, 56

government, 355

grace, 40, 48, 59, 83, 97, 146, 155, 162, 172, 187, 197, 201, 202, 217, 255, 264, 269, 300, 301, 308, 315, 316, 320, 346

gratitude, 60, 153, 158, 213, 341, 346, 365

H

Hadith, The: acquiring knowledge and wisdom in, 318; and affirming we are children of God, 61-62; and deriving pleasure and grief, 104; and doing good, 297; and importance of moderation, 212; and your conscience, 219; characteristics of a hypocrite in, 282; charity and helping others in, 258; effort, discipline, and persistence in, 329-330; faithful servant in, 29, 81, 184; forgiveness and mercy in, 273; harmlessness in, 250; loving speech and kindness in, 266; respect for others and non-judgment in, 290; the Golden Rule in, 238

happiness: and foods, 230; and positive self-image, 49; and the doubting self, 149; as children of God, 72; being free is, 21; Buddhist philosophy of, 22; eternal, 83, 96, 116, 137, 360; finding and

J

K